Cold Blood Nightmare

(The Nick McCarty Series)

by

Bernard Lee DeLeo

*****

PUBLISHED BY:

Bernard Lee DeLeo and RJ Parker Publishing Inc.

ISBN-13: 978-1987902426

ISBN-10: 1987902424

Cold Blooded VIII: Rule of Nightmare

Cover Illustration by: Colin Matthew Dougherty

*****

License Notes

This eBook is licensed for your personal enjoyment only. This eBook may not be resold or given away to other people. Please respect the author's work. This is a work of fiction. Any resemblance to real life persons, events, or places is purely coincidental.

*****

Nick McCarty's Unholy Trio and Dependents (Main Characters)

1. Nicholas McCarty – Delta Force – 6' – Nicknames: Terminator, Muerto, Dead Boy, Delta Dawn, Gomez

2. Rachel Hunter McCarty

3. Jean Hunter McCarty – Nickname: Danger Girl, Daughter of Darkness, Viper

4. Deke the Dog - Dekester

5. Gus Nason – Nicknames: Payaso

6. Tina Nason (Wife of Gus Nason) – Nicknames: T-Rex

7. Ebi Zarin/Johnny Groves – Nicknames: Johnny Five, El Kabong

8. Cala Kadir Groves (Wife of Johnny Groves) – Nicknames: Cala the Cleaner, Reaper

9. Jian Chen – ex-terrorist – recruited to help Nick's crew – Nickname: Dark Dragon

10. Sonny Salvatore – Nicknames: Cracker - Parents: Phil and Clarice Salvatore

11. Quinn McCarty – Nicknames: Kong

12. Justin Rivers – Nicknames: Jay, Predator – Parents: Dale and Beth

13. Neil Dickerson – Pacific Grove policeman – works with Nick's crew

14. Paul Gilbrech – Director of the CIA

15. Clyde Bacall – Assistant and driver for Paul Gilbrech -works with Nick's crew

16. Ben McCarty – Adopted son in future Nick and Jean bonus story – Nicknames: Benny

17. Sammy – McCarty family's dog in future Nick and Jean bonus story – Nicknames: Sammy the werewolf

18. Robyn MacEachern - Homeland Security/CIA liaison with Canada, coordinates operations on the border with Canada Border Services Agency.

19. Ken Carter – CIA agent – collaborates with Nick during special assignments.

John Harding's Monster Squad and Dependents (Main Characters)

1. John Harding – Force Recon Marine - 6'6", brown haired buzz cut, 250 pounds – Nicknames: Hard Case, Cheeseburger (Cheese for short), Recon, Dark Lord, DL

2. Lora Radcliff Harding – John's wife, 5'7", long auburn hair, 130 pounds

3. Alice Radcliff Harding – John's stepdaughter, long auburn hair, ten years old – Nicknames: Al, Beeper-Girl

4. Lucas Blake – Force Recon Marine - 5'8", Black, buzz cut, 155 pounds – Nicknames: Ahab – Wife: Sarah, Children: Casey (named after Casey Lambert) and Linda

5. Casey Lambert – Delta Force - Nicknames - Night-shot – Wife: Anna – Children: Lucas (named after Lucas Blake)

6. Tommy Sands – Nicknames - T, Snow White Sands

7. Devon Constantine – Nicknames – Dev, Wife: Maria, Stepkids: Luke, Kelly

8. Jesse Brown – Nicknames – Jess, Wife: Rochelle

9. Jafar Kensington – Nicknames - Achmed the Dead Terrorist

10. Samira Karim Kensington – Jafar's Wife - Nicknames – Sam - Children: Mia

11. Dennis Strobert – Marine - Nicknames - Denny, Spawn – Wife: Maria – Children: Brewster

12. Gus Denova – Cruella Deville minion – former Cartel enforcer

13. Silvio Ruelas – Cruella Deville minion – former Cartel enforcer

14. Quays Tannous – Cruella Deville minion – former Cartel enforcer

15. Clint Dostiene – Air Force SOCOM– Nicknames: Man from Nowhere – Wife: Lynn Montoya

16. Lynn Montoya Dostiene – Nicknames: Cruella Deville, Crusader Crue, Dr. Deville – Children: Clint Jr.

17. Laredo Sawyer – Nickname: Laredo – Wife Sybil Moore

18. Danessa Moore - Nickname: Dannie – Lynn Dostiene's live in assistant

19. Amara Nejem – Lynn Dostiene's live in assistant

20. Earl Taylor – Oakland Policeman

21. Enrique Rodriguez – Nickname 'Rique – Oakland Policeman

22. Jeff Furlong – Oakland Policeman

23. Alexi Fiialkov – Former Russian Mob – Shipping Magnate – Handles USB matches

24. Marla Tomlinson – Favorite Waitress at The Warehouse Bar – Fiialkov's Girlfriend

25. Claude Chardin – Former Terrorist and Assassin – works with John Harding's crew now.

26. Della Sparks – John Harding's neighbor – Children: Lebron, Jim, and Kara

27. Hollywood Bounty Hunters – Kensy (Buffster) Talon, Kevin Halliday (ex-felon), Les Tavor (ex-Hell's Angel), Jet Lemarkus (ex-gangbanger), Daniel Atkins, Jerry Sooner, Calvin Douglas, Sigfried Kandelus, Charlie Dubrinsky (Lawyer/Manager)

28. Tom Wilder – Commander of a Seal Team – works with John Harding's crew

29. Janie Labrie – FBI agent who works with John Harding's crew

30. Sam Reeves – Janie Labrie's partner – FBI agent who works with John Harding's crew

31. Chuck Bushholz – Force Recon Marine – Red Dragon Security – Lucas Blake's friend

32. Sal Sallaz – Force Recon Marine – Red Dragon Security – Lucas Blake's friend

33. Thom McGaffey – Force Recon Marine – Red Dragon Security – Dog: Lando – Governor of the new Isle of Hope

Table of Contents

Chapter One: Hardened Hearts

Two weeks into their mission, Nick watched comfortably from his sniper's nest. The Army Corps of Engineers, Seabees, and a private contracting firm, worked day and night after the first few days of deportations to Western Sahara, landing thousands of mobile cottages. Three solar powered water desalinization capsules, engineered at intervals to service the relocated Muslims' new city between Dakhla Attitude and El-Aaiun would supply water for all purposes. After the water producing stations came on line within the first week, irrigation, and sewage plants with piping to the furthest reaches inland, calculated to provide water for all conceivable uses, could be tapped for added building. Nick had insisted on a state of the art crematorium, noting from the beginning, loss of life would be inevitable.

Johnny, Gus, Jian, and Cala watched in rotating shifts. Nick protected their facilities from assault by angry deported refugees without mercy. They were housed for the time being in a tent encampment, where they were given nothing other than K-rations. Gus spotted three men edging along the water toward the first desalinization capsule. Nick shot the first one in the head, spraying his compatriots with brain and skull material. The silenced .50 caliber round made little noise from a thousand yards away. The other would be saboteurs ran back to the encampment.

"Slow learners," Gus said. "How many ways do you need to say, 'if you try and sabotage anything, you die'? They've had twenty-seven casualties. The work detail idea helps the contractors and keeps the encampment clean, as long as there are 'shoot to kill' orders. The 'either work or don't eat' rule reinforces what we're doing here."

"Johnny found the desalinization capsule installation modules. We need the damn things in California," Nick replied. "I'm not letting these assholes sabotage them. They will work great with irrigation too. These parasites will learn to grow food, do menial labor maintenance to improve their own communities, and create ways to become productive, or we will allow their brethren in the nearby cities to enslave them. I've met with the forces controlling El-Aaiun and Dakhla Attitude. They have armed contingents willing to make sure our new city works on its own, or they will be allowed to make it happen in any way they see fit. They weren't happy until I told them they would have no interference if the experiment failed."

"I believe our captives are getting the message they will have no contact with the outside world until they earn it," Jian said.

"John told them they will stay here for a month. Any of the parasites who hate it here will get a one-way ticket to Syria, Somalia, or wherever the hell else they came from, dumped and catalogued so they will never plague anyone else," Johnny added. "That is more than fair, considering the crimes they committed against a host nation who gave them everything. Uh oh, Muerto… here comes another band of mutants to see if we have slacked off. Talk about stupidity. They will do anything to sabotage survival here."

"No mercy this time," Nick said, listening to Johnny calling out parameters for the shots. Each time he squeezed the trigger, a saboteur died, even in full flight back the way they had come.

"It is good you insisted on a crematorium, Muerto." Cala watched with interest as she stayed close to her husband. "They care for nothing. They live to destroy, even when it will mean survival."

"They believe if they sabotage everything here, the bleeding-heart liberals and globalists will take them back, complete with millions in payoffs," Nick replied. "That ain't happenin'. England is jubilant. They've embraced anyone who had anything to do with this action. They police their streets happily, while enforcing the three-pronged edict of either leave, renounce Islam, or die. The citizens of the UK are not going back to the ridiculous refugee thuggery."

"The refugees and other Death Cult acolytes are close to their grace period for deciding what they want to do," Gus said.

"The mosques have already been confiscated for conversion to housing. The explosives and weapons gathered from the fake religious mosques have proven what everyone with a brain understood. The mosques were armories for war. Islamic mutants do not assimilate. They infiltrate and conquer from the inside. Not this time."

Nick's crew settled in for their turn at the nightly watch. Nick relaxed, thinking of the civilian contractors erecting the small portable cottages at breakneck speed. They incorporated ready to attach plumbing and electrical, although all were solar powered. In addition to the five hundred million dollars in projected costs, the contractors would get one hundred million in bonuses depending on completed housing work deadlines, with quality control double checked by the Army Corps of Engineers. The Seabees erected a string of modular pontoon docks joined to allow transfer of materials and supplies. Later, they would act as landings for fishing and trade. The largest work force ever assembled, using the deported refugees as manual laborers had erected ten thousand of the easily assembled cottages.

Alexi's container ship, the Roma, provided non-stop delivery of supplies and materials, all paid for so far from the vast fortunes confiscated on Cafrey Island. Jafar used the inroads given him by Mehdi Al-Kazar to wipe out the Al-Kazar family to the tune of twenty-five billion dollars. The confiscation caused a Saudi Arabia protest at the UN to which they received the short answer from the United States, whom they blamed for the Al-Kazar family's vast fortune disappearing – 'we don't know where it went and we don't care'.

Because no one could find anything other than a note and video of a very intense and smiling Mehdi saying he needed to get away, interest in the matter waned quickly. All financial earmarks of the money leaving the Al-Kazar coffers were transferred to newly created foundations, by Mehdi Al-Kazar personally, therefore leaving the Saudis with no leads other than the family's financial controller. The scattering of the huge fortunes gathered took Jafar, Clint, and Laredo day and night careful threading over a week's time. Nick took a deep breath, letting it out slowly. He planned for this experiment to either end in complete success or the enslavement of the UK's refugee terrorists.

Sweden, Norway, and even Belgium had already expressed interest in adding to the settlement. They requested intervention. Nick didn't want any part of it. A meeting was scheduled for the next morning with everyone in the area with any power. It would take place on the Roma. Nick glanced at his comrades, knowing their enthusiasm for helping brainwashed adults, acting like murderous children, was wearing thin. Their dependents flew to England, enjoying every luxury imaginable. They planned for a reunion within days.

The building phase was crucial. Nick encouraged everyone to look for a leader in the mutant group not hogtied to the 'Death Cult'. He and Johnny had entered the refugee tent city when policing cleanup proceedings to interview for candidates. Only their no hesitation killing of anyone approaching with violence made sure the tent city people remained respectful. They forced them to separate and recycle everything. Any resistance to the program and the perpetrator's tent was taken away for a week. Latrine duties were shared after establishing a hundred portable units with sink and toilet. The recycling of the water in the over two hundred and fifty gallon tanks each unit stored was done by solar powered pump, draining and recycling constantly. It cost five hundred thousand dollars to make the sanitary recycling, state of the art facility. Hygiene was maintained by rotating cleaners from the numbered tents. If inspection teams found dirty facilities, all tents were taken away from the negligent parties for a week. Nick grinned.

"This place may become obsolete in a month's time. These lazy bastards would rather be back in their home country shit-holes than here where they need to maintain a modicum of cleanliness."

"You have that right, Muerto." Cala made a disgusted facial contortion. "They have beautiful beaches, same climate they were used to, food and drink, and the promise of much more - yet they bitch and moan about everything because they are forced to maintain it. They are incurable parasites. This experiment sucks. The mutants prefer squalor."

12

"We made a commitment to the experiment, my love," Johnny reminded her. "Muerto and I have seen some leaders amongst the group, who may have been playing along with Islam so as not to get their heads taken. This bunch needs secular leaders who can build upon what we give them. Iran under the Shah was a paradise compared to what it is now under the mutants. Secular leaders know how to deal with their Islamic Sharia Law Mutants. They understand only violence and death. I learned early from my childhood the only exit from Islam was death. After years of brainwashing, we do indeed turn into mutants."

Johnny squeezed Cala's hand. "Thanks to Muerto, I was dragged from the dark side into the light. With Cala at my side, I will seek to save others."

Gus lowered his range finders. "So, you have seen some promising leaders?"

"Yes," Johnny answered. "They have pulled us aside when no one was looking, hoping we were not allowing another Sharia Law blasphemy. They do not want to ever return to Somalia. We also have one Syrian, who has been on a perform or die status with some in the encampment. He had wanted to accept the UK as his new home, but was reminded they were in the UK to establish the new Caliphate, sweeping over Europe, Canada, Australia, and the UK."

"One bright spot was they believe like the Russians did during the cold war that we have too many guns in the hands of American citizens to wage a civil war," Nick said. "They believe stockpiling weapons of mass destruction in America will be the only way to overcome us. Apparently, they don't give much credence to the snowflake enablers of Islam. I wish I could believe the same. John's run in with the Islamic airhead teacher and jihadi husband is the tip of the iceberg. Uh oh… oh my, check this one out."

Nick pointed at the guy dressed in full length robes, who had entered the death scene. He waved a white flag wildly above his head. "It looks like he wants to parley. Go find out what he wants, Johnny."

Johnny laughed. "Yeah, right. You are wondering if he has somehow smuggled something to attack us unsuspecting dolts with, and now want me to be the poor sap who finds out."

"He can't have anything very dangerous. They would have used it on you and me already," Nick reasoned. He stood. "You're good with the M107. Shoot him in the head if he makes a bad move. He looks like the guy from Syria named Khan, who doesn't want to go back. Maybe he figured to have a chat with us about the direction we might take."

"We'll be watching, Muerto," Gus said. "Let him talk from twenty feet away."

Nick smiled. "He doesn't have some cell-phone bomb, Gus. I hear you. I'm not getting stupid. If anything, a setup would only work with him drawing me close to be jumped. We all know how that would end. Relax. We'll be off point in a couple of hours. I know this Sand shit is wearing on us all. Let's get 'er done."

Nick walked down in the darkness toward the lone figure with his entire crew arming for long range shots with whatever they had. Gus readied the M2 machine gun camouflaged near their watcher's cottage with Jian near him for range and sighting. Cala stayed with Johnny, rangefinders in hand.

Nick waved at the man as he neared him, speaking to him in Arabic. "Hello, Khan. Did you think about our conversation?"

"I saw an opportunity to speak with you. These men you killed are the worst of our group. I am glad you did not allow any to live. I do not want to return to Syria or even the place of my birth in Turkey. I can tell from working on construction, this can be a home here without the Sharia Law scum. I joined with them that night because they threatened to kill my wife and daughter. I will do anything if you can bring my family here after the construction is finished."

"You have my word on it. Speak the address into my phone. I will have them brought here when we have order established."

Khan stated the address in London where his family was housed.

"Did you speak with the other men we pointed out to you?"

"Yes, Muerto. They want a life away from the 'Death Cult' as you called it. I recognized your friend. He is Ebi Zarin. I saw him in Syria once before the civil war. I can tell he has found peace."

"You are correct. Ebi Zarin is now John Groves." Nick smiled. "I nearly tortured him to death when we first met. He is like a brother now. Like you, he never wishes to be part of Islam's plague again. Will the Somalis follow you?"

"They asked me to approach you with such a pact. It will be dangerous, but I believe we can recruit a small army of like minds to rule this new city. I realize we cannot have weapons, but we will need enough dedicated men to establish order."

"How have we been doing in thinning out the worst of the worst?"

"Very well. Those three who tried now to follow the first attempt were three of the worst ones trying to sabotage everything in the encampment. The people watching tonight, encouraged me to meet with you. After two weeks here, they see this is not a game. They realize they will be shipped back to their country of origin whether they like it or not. Many, like me, are missing our families."

"We have identified everyone in the encampment. More will be arriving, including all relatives still in the UK. As we explained at the beginning, we are not here to make friends. We organized this encampment to save the UK. My team and I will meet you and the contingent of people you can trust after my briefing on board the tanker ship."

"I will prepare for it," Khan replied. "Eventually, we will need weapons, or we will be killed before we can establish the city."

"I realize your problem. You must realize ours. Right now, we can keep order, because we are the only ones with weapons. Remember how we made examples when those goons tried to sabotage our mobile toilet facilities with recycling station?"

Khan nodded. "You warned everyone to only go inside and out the same way. Anyone seen moving around the toilet stations, piping, or recycling station would be shot on sight. Everyone noted they are in full sight of your sniper nest, and still nearly ten idiots lost their lives because they tried to destroy the facilities."

"We know there are many who would rather war against everyone in the name of Islam and Sharia Law. That you had as many women shipped here because they participated in the London Arab Spring attempt, worried us. While we control this new city, there will be no female genital mutilation, stonings for breaking Sharia Law crap, beating women, or pedophilia. After we leave, I realize we cannot control the brain-dead mutants amongst your population. Any you point out to us will be shipped out immediately. Trouble makers will be killed on the spot, especially any who fight against you and your men. Did you locate the men who threatened your family?"

"They were killed the night of our Arab Spring attempt," Khan replied. "One was killed by the woman I have heard called Crue."

"Do you have any women tough enough to side with your policing efforts?"

"I will check. Perhaps that would be a great way to move in a secular direction."

"Two men coming up on your left, Nick," Gus said in his ear.

"There are two men approaching. If they are friends, all well and good. If they are not, I want to know now," Nick told Khan.

Khan spotted them coming over the sand dome. He took a deep breath, stepping back slightly. "They are Syrians, two organizers of the attempted London Arab Spring."

"Thanks," Nick replied. "Halt there."

One kept approaching, pointing at Khan. "Why are you here speaking with this man?"

Nick drew his Colt and shot him in the head. He then shot the other man before he could run, center mass, following both shots with one each in the head, just to make sure. "This is how we will establish you and your team, Khan."

"Ten more rushing you," Gus said.

"Handle it, Payaso. No survivors. Finish them off when Gus blasts them, Kabong."

"Understood."

Gus used Ma Deuce to cut down the ten sappers with expertly fired short bursts. Johnny shot each one with the M107 sniper rifle.

"It appears we have thinned out the bad guys." Nick handed Khan a satellite phone. "Take this with you so we can stay in contact. Go back to the encampment with the news. Establish communications with your picks for allies. Think about the woman angle. I will speak with you again tomorrow afternoon."

"I will explain the new direction. This has been a costly night for the radicals. They must have thought you were alone."

"My crew and I will clean this mess and take the bodies to their departure zone. Tell your other bad guys we use bullets dipped in pork grease. When we cremate this bunch, we will shove pork into them before cremation."

"I...I will tell them."

Nick grinned after turning to walk away. He knew Johnny would have the M107 pointed at their hoped for new friend. The amusement over his promise about disposal and bullets continued almost until he rejoined his friends.

"Oh, Muerto, you... nailed Khan but good with that edict," Johnny said.

"We're going to do it from now on, Kabong. We need fear. The ruse will work if it's not a threat, but a fact. All we need do is mix a very small amount in with our cleaning and oiling works. As to the act before cremating, I meant every word of it. The moment John gets here to relieve us, we will collect the bodies in the Humvee."

"Hell!" Gus turned to Johnny. "Muerto brought an ice chest along. I thought it was for a cold one after watch. You have pig's guts in it don't you, Muerto, you very bad man?"

Nick shrugged. "It seemed like the right thing to do. I'm sick of this crap. We may as well have some fun. We'll do a movie with us in our Unholy Trio masks, stuffing pig guts down the throat of the Kabuki dancers before they go into the fire. We'll show the movies tomorrow on a portable screen, along with video of me coating Ma Deuce .50 caliber slugs and MP5 ammo with a rag dipped in pork grease."

"We have full control," Jian said. "We protect everyone on the ground using our teams. This will break them. Your idea of recruiting women adds to the threat. Any jihadist killed by a woman never reaches paradise. We need to get Samira, Crue, and Cala involved in our meeting. They will be armed with MP5s, loaded with pig coated ammo. I like this idea. I miss Pacific Grove."

A shared groan of agreement rippled around the sniper's nest. Nick shrugged. "It is what it is. We'll see this through with a vengeance from now on. We take the gloves off from now on. This decree will force Khan's hand and reveal the fanatics."

　　　* * *

The smiles I saw while walking into the sniper's post brightened my less than enthused Monsters. We had reached the point already where we were ready to nuke the place from orbit. Lynn came along only because with Clint on the M107, she would go down and gut anyone who approached our facilities.

"Wow... you Muerto people look happy. Tell us how we can be happy with you." I drew chuckles from my crew of Lucas, Casey, Clint, and Lynn.

After Nick described the night's happenings, he recruited us full bore into the idea, especially Lynn.

"I'm bringing my knives to the meeting tomorrow, Muerto. I'm dipping them in pig's blood right in front of the audience. We need to quit pussy-footing around with these assholes. I bet these retards are so stupid, we could make up a mythical place where they are condemned for eternity if knifed by a woman with pig's bloodstained knife. We'll call the land 'Qaf' land of the Jinns, the Islamic demons."

We enjoyed Lynn's desecration of the mutants' dead for a few moments, imagining a Cruella Deville demonstration in front of the masses.

"I have pork to dip your knife in tonight, Crue." Nick fetched his cooler of pork guts. "After our watch, I doubt you'll have any candidates, but it would be hell on wheels if you did."

"Oh, hell yeah!" Lynn dipped her knife in the sealed container of chilled pork guts. "I may need to go into the encampment on a hunt. Are you with me, man from nowhere?"

"I have your six through eternity, babe," Clint answered.

I could see Nick's expression. He wanted to go on the hunt too. I gripped his shoulder. "Go have fun making movies to show. You bunch killed more than we'll see tonight. Get some rest when it's done."

"Thanks, brother, I got caught up in the Cruella Deville hunt for sure. I gave Khan a phone to hide and contact us with in an emergency. If you need to do something big inside the encampment, call Khan. It won't take him long to give you the mostly likely troublemakers' tent numbers. We'll discuss more tomorrow... or later in the day as it is now."

We watched Muerto lug his ice chest to the Humvee and ride down to gather bodies. Once they were all loaded, Nick waved at us and started toward the crematorium. "That was a great addition to the tool chest. Even if it doesn't work, I feel better already."

"I'm with you, Cheese. I hope to God I see something amiss in the encampment. I'll leave a real cute message behind for the awakening populace. Muerto always thinks of the grandest ideas."

"Muerto needs to charm the populace with more than pig guts though," Lucas replied. "It's a damn good start because I'm sick of the Sand already. Please don't bother with the rah/rah stuff. I know we signed on for the duration. These ass-wipes are sick. We spend our time here protecting their latrines and drinking water because they want to sabotage them for publicity. What's wrong with that picture?"

"Everything," I admitted. "Let's back Muerto full bore into this new threat to poor old peaceful Islam. We're hitting the encampment tonight with Lynn. Bring plenty of ammo. We need to soften these bastards up if they try to engulf us."

"You do understand we have at least twenty-five thousand mutants in the encampment, right?" Lucas had moved over in my face. "Think this through, Recon! I don't care how much ammo we bring, if the herd mentality ushers them into an attack, we will be overwhelmed."

"Not if we drive down there with the Humvee, Casey on Ma Deuce and you with the XM307. If they start trouble, we'll end it with massive casualties. Besides, all the firing will bring Muerto and his crew back in a flash. Then the battle gets serious."

"I'm in," Lucas replied, gripping my cheek. "I think you've been around Dead Boy too long this time."

"Maybe," I admitted. "I only know when we leave here, if we don't make an impression, these troglodytes will surely butcher each other. Another ten thousand housing units will be arriving this week, along with dependents from the UK. The English want to dump them in the ocean. That's how happy they are to be rid of this yoke around their neck. I'm not adverse to the pleas from

Norway, Sweden, Australia, and all of Europe with what we've done. We may be able to open it up to all if we establish something solid. Hey… what the hell do we have a crematorium for if we don't use it?"

My remark drew the intended ease of raw nerves. "I will get the Humvee into place and park it. That will draw attention from our sappers, Clint and Lynn. We won't do anything until they scope the encampment out. We know there will be groups plotting after the Muerto wakeup call. Nick left me a picture of Khan and his Somali guys' IDs. They're on your phones."

I turned to Crue. "You have what you want, Sis. We're allowing you and Clint to forage through an encampment of mostly true believers. We will be close by but not close enough if you are both overran at the beginning."

Lynn pinched my cheek. "Awwww… that's so sweet. Clint and I will move through the zombies until we find a cause. We know the retreat point will depend on you guys on the outskirts where you can protect your flanks. We'll get to you if we have word of something going down. We'll be on cam and audio. Kick back and watch how a couple of psychos tear into posers."

"We'll be watching," Lucas said. "Case will be on Ma Deuce and I'll be playing the bagpipes with the XM307. If there's trouble… you better duck, suckers."

"Give us twenty minutes on approach," Clint said. "Don't move the Humvee before then. We're all on the network. We won't say much other than a one-word acknowledgement. We need to hurry things along in these negotiations. The sappers attacking during Muerto's watch makes it clear that new idiots are replacing the old dead ones."

"I don't think we should wait for Muerto to hear of a battle," Lucas said. "Call him now. He and his crew are still at the crematorium. Instead of waiting until tomorrow, we can straighten this sapper crap tonight. I'm sure that Khan already spread the word Muerto gave him. Instead of letting them get all fired up about it overnight, we'll go in with two Humvees ready with M2 machine guns. It will give him a chance to contact the Khan guy before someone kills him. I know he gave you the number, but Khan knows Muerto."

"We're listening," Clint said on the network. "If the people know we're seriously backing a group to keep order tonight, we may be able to establish a plan before the big meeting on the Roma."

"I like it," I admitted. "I'll call Muerto back. We're going to catch hell no matter what we do anyway. If we can pull this off without mass casualties, we may be able to get some slack from our official sources tomorrow. I hate to say this, but getting involved in the UK's Moslem crap may be the dumbest move we've ever made."

Grudging agreement amongst our crew on duty ended with Clint's reminder. "We either do this here for the UK or we'll be fighting them off in the USA. Canada keeps importing more and more Moslem hordes. Mexico lets as many as can get over the border flow from the South. At least we'll know we made a stand. Lynn and I are on the outskirts of the encampment. Something's going on. Can you see from where you are, John?"

The rest of us stopped running our mouths and got the rangefinders out. I didn't like it. "We see it. They're having a big meeting with a lot of gesturing and shouting. Hold position. I'll call Muerto."

* * *

Nick and Johnny shoved the last pork grease anointed saboteur into the crematorium. "We sure made a ruckus tonight. I hope we didn't make it too hard on John and his crew."

"Meeting with Khan Eshieh was the right way to go," Gus replied.

"Maybe. I..." Nick's phone beeped. "Hey, John. Miss me already. No, didn't call me. I'll call him and we'll join you shortly. We will key back into the network."

Nick called Khan after telling his crew to rejoin the network. His contact answered in whispers amidst what sounded like a riot. "I have heard from our other team something bad is going on in the encampment."

"We...we gathered together when I returned. My Somali friends wanted to speak with others about a group capable of keeping order. I told them what you warned your forces will do from now on, and what happened to the ones killed tonight. They are upset. I believe they will kill us soon."

"Tell them to watch our demonstration. Explain we will bomb the encampment if they do not move to the portable road at the perimeter of the camp where we may all speak. We will have machine guns and grenade launchers."

"I will tell them."

"Keep the line open." Nick pulled his phone away for a moment. "Lucas, please put a few nice explosions in the sand near the encampment. We'll join you at the portable road perimeter, locked and loaded."

"Firing now," Lucas said. Using the XM307's electronic targeting from the Humvee turret, Lucas detonated three spaced shots of airburst 25mm grenades outside the perimeter. The expertly targeted shots tore the sand area to the edge of the encampment.

"Very nice, Pap," Lynn said. "That shook them up. I guess we'll wait here for you."

"Thank you," Khan said to Nick as he reengaged his contact. "They have backed away from us. I told them they must move to the perimeter or be blasted with the pork smeared rounds of explosives. They are scared but moving. I have a dozen men who will stand with me. They want nothing to do with Sharia Law. Two very brave women have joined us too. They spoke out against returning to the old ways."

"Good, we are on our way now," Nick said as Gus drove the Humvee with Johnny on the M2 machine gun and Jian at the mounted XM307. "Have your group come out in front of the crowd and tell them to stay back."

23

"We'll watch for them, Dead Boy," Clint said. "I have an idea along the lines of street challenges back home. They probably think they have a cutter somewhere in the crowd."

"Oh yeah! Damn… I wish Tommy were here," Lynn added, "but he doesn't speak Arabic anyhow. Most of these punks know English though."

"I like your idea, Clint," Nick said. "Isis assholes believe if killed by a woman in combat they go to hell. I'll negotiate for Lynn if that's okay with John."

"Fine by me, Nick. We have your six. If they try to swarm, hit the ground because we will open fire with the M2s at pointblank range."

"It's a good thing we finished with our remote sound system for just this kind of duty," Nick said.

The perimeter lighting cast shadows, but Nick could see the huge crowd were staying at a safe distance inside the perimeter. Khan led his chosen enforcement group nearer to the Humvees on the portable road laid in the sand. Nick got out with MP5 at the ready. He looked over each of the dozen men, and the two women, who did not wear the hijab. A mixture of Syrians, Somalis, and three Nick thought might be Libyans, all seemed steady.

"Listen closely to my words to the encampment. If I say anything you disagree with or will not enforce, rejoin the others. No harm will come to you. Is that clear?"

The group expressed agreement with Nick's words, nodding and murmuring in unison.

Gus handed Nick the wireless microphone. "I will make this simple. These men and women will enforce encampment law. It will not be religious law. Everything you know of Sharia Law ends now. How you worship in your own tent is fine. If you all want to go out in the sand together and pray five times a day, that is allowed. If anyone in the group wants out of the prayers, that will be allowed too. This will be a secular city."

Nick let that sink in as the people muttered. "These men and women will make sure no one is punished for living a non-religious or other religious life. The punishment for disobeying a lawful order by this group is death. When your dependents are shipped here, there will be no child marriages, no female genital mutilation, no wife beating, and no Imams preaching hate. That carries a death sentence. There will not be a dress code of any kind other than comfort. I will have the basic laws of the encampment made by tomorrow. Anyone wishing to return to Sharia Law will be shipped to their country of origin. Protect these men and women with your lives. If anything happens to them, we will decimate this encampment with pork smeared machine gun fire."

"We need our phones!"

Nick grinned. The cell-phone demands he expected would help him launch his Cruella Deville ploy. "No one gets a cell-phone other than our law enforcement group until the city becomes self-sufficient. The irrigation channels have already begun changing the land. Soon, as some other desert nations have done, you will be able to grow crops. The only way you could win a phone would be to challenge our most excellent knife fighter. Do you have a cutter?"

A murmur of excitement rumbled through the crowd. Five minutes later, a hawk-faced man stripped off his upper robe. Slender and whipcord taut, the six-footer flexed his hands and arms before gesturing at Nick. When he spoke, his scraggly beard seemed to poke from his face.

"I have prayed to Allah for the chance to kill one of you kafirs. He blessed me with this opportunity. Where is the dog you wish me to butcher?"

Lynn strode forward, her blonde hair tied back, excitement glistening over her features. She wore tan slacks, light weight tan hiking boots, sleeveless black silk shirt, and seemed to glide over the portable road to stand near Nick. "Clint said it's time."

"Yep," Nick answered. "This guy has been praying for a chance to kill a kafir."

25

"Ask him what kind of blade he wants."

Nick repeated the question in Arabic. The man waved him off. "I speak English. You want me to fight this blonde whore? Is this some kind of joke?"

"No joke," Lynn answered. "Kill me and you get a cell-phone. Tell us what kind of knife you like, Betty, and quit stroking yourself. This isn't a camel race. Put up or shut up."

Nick chuckled at the effect Lynn's derisive challenge engendered in the man. He literally stomped around, spewing curses and threats with fist clenched fury before finally facing Nick.

"Do you have a stiletto, kafir?"

Nick took his out and tossed it to the man, who caught it, judged weight and feel, and released the blade. He nodded in satisfaction. "Yes. This is a fine knife."

"I've seen Nick's tactical knife before," Lynn told him. "It's ten inches total in length. That's eight inches longer than your dick."

"I will slice you to pieces for that insult, slut. No more talk. Get your blade."

In a split second, Lynn's butterfly knife appeared as if by magic. She moved into position across from her opponent. "I have it right here, Betty. Let's do this before you chicken out."

The man showed concentration. Lynn's complete lack of concern unnerved him. He crouched into a knife fighting stance jutting toward Lynn with threatening feints. Lynn remained upright with knife at her side, one hand on her hip, and foot tapping impatiently.

"Oh, for God's sakes, Betty. Show me what you got. I'm not a goat. You don't need to romance me."

That was it for her opponent. With a stabbing motion remarkably fast, he tried an eviscerating stroke to Lynn's lower belly. The crowd screamed out for Lynn's death. At the last possible instant, Lynn twisted with blade slashing upward. Her opponent missed. She didn't. the Balisong's razor sharp blade sliced the nose from his face. He screamed, falling to his knees, Nick's knife tumbling to the ground as the nose-less man gripped his spurting opening. Lynn pirouetted around him, stabbing, slicing, and slashing finally across his eyes. Lynn then twirled in front of the blinded man, stabbing upward through his neck to the hilt. She kicked free of him before wiping away the blood on his clothing. Lynn retrieved Nick's knife. Dead silence followed her swaying walk to Nick's side.

Nick accepted his knife from Lynn before addressing the crowd again. "Anyone else want to try and win a phone?"

After a minute of continued silence, Nick shrugged. "I guess that concludes our business for tonight. Remember. Guard these people with your lives. I want everyone in their tents in fifteen minutes, so do whatever you need to and turn in."

Nick gestured for his proposed law enforcement group to remain. "We will bring vests with insignia tomorrow, identifying all of you as law enforcement personnel. Respect for each other is of the utmost importance. This group must lead by example. Be strict, fair, and adamant giving orders. No one will follow a leader who screams without reason. I will get the postings of rules to Khan tomorrow. He will be in charge of operations inside the camp. Anyone challenging him, challenges us. Thank you for taking on this responsibility. Hopefully, Khan will find many more willing to throw off the old ways. Goodnight."

After his chosen group walked away, Nick breathed in deeply while looking at the dead man. "That was a lesson they won't soon forget. Excellent lesson, Crue."

"Oh, Muerto… that was the best time I've had since we landed in this pit. I hope some more cell-phone addicts want to gamble on a phone. Maybe you should throw in a tablet too."

Nick chuckled. "I will. I'll go deposit Pinocchio in the fire of redemption."

Chapter Two: Rule of Law

I outlined our progress after last night's hoedown in the encampment. After Lynn's cell-phone contest, the evening passed without incident of any kind. If Khan could recruit a vetted force of determined secular police, we would have more chances to root out the bad ones disrupting the camp. It was impossible to say how many avid Sharia Law acolytes we had in the camp. The secular police would be our eyes and ears inside the camp. My audience, officials both military and civilian from America and the UK listened attentively to my list of successes. They seemed surprised at the problems. I brought Nick, Lucas, Casey, Clint, Lynn Johnny, Cala, and Jian to help me explain the mindset we faced. Jafar was ready to do his video on the encampment. He also had some surprises for our guests. Our former Muslims gave their talks first, explaining why we needed to proceed as we did with harsh and immediate judgements.

"We are facing a backlash in the UK over this stunt, Harding," a Labour Party official, named Liane Babbott stated after Cala explained the treatment of women in the encampment would not be under Sharia Law.

We did our research on the participants of the conference, her included. A round faced, dark skinned woman, with glasses and bangs nearly covering her eyes, reminded me of Mrs. Potato-Head from when I was a kid. Being an ogre with scars myself, I try to always look beyond a person's appearance. In Babbott's presence, I found it impossible. Jafar showed me many interviews with this woman. Her entitlement mentality, terrorist enabling, communist manifesto type comments triggered my barf reflex every time she opened her pie-hole.

"You and your team run the encampment like a gulag," Babbott continued. "We have reports of mass executions and horrid conditions."

"My associate, FBI Special Agent Jafar Kensington, will now show a video of encampment conditions. I have already explained the rules of the camp. Sabotage and confrontation is punishable by death. An option for dumping the Sharia Law, brainwashed zombies in the ocean when we arrived here, and let them wade to shore, was also considered. With our own money, we have begun an experimental secular city where the inhabitants can become productive, independent, and eventually establish trade."

I paused as Mrs. Potato-Head muttered something. "Our solar powered desalinization capsules have already worked miracles with the soil. They also have proven capable of not only providing water in abundance, but also will supply fresh water to the surrounding cities. This part of Western Sahara, long ago abandoned as uninhabitable, will soon be a modern-day Israel, producing crops the surrounding cities are eager to buy. First though, saboteurs and common Sharia Law thugs will be weeded out of the population. They can ask to be deported to their nation of origin. Many choose to stay and sabotage our efforts. They will be shot on sight if caught by our team or the secular police inside the encampment."

Jafar started his presentation, highlighting and explaining our fresh water and irrigation plans, finishing the sequence with details of our stat of the art waste recycling stations. Housing and plumbing, complete with an inside inspection of the mobile cottages, provided a broad view of what we had accomplished in weeks. He then showed the attempts to sabotage and terrorize the encampment, forays to destroy our water plants and waste treatment operation. Before Babbott could spew her familiar claptrap about jobs and human dignity, Jafar ran our video compilation of the one world order globalists, some of whom sat at our conference table now. The video showed Babbott and her friends causing nearly every terrorist act inside the UK with out of control importation of terrorists, releasing rapists and pillagers, and idiotically refusing to deport anyone, including known terrorists. It finished with the globalists allowing Isis fighters back into the UK after warring against UK troops. When Jafar finished, there was red-faced silence, except for Mrs. Potato-Head.

She leaped from her seat as much as her bulk allowed, screaming at me in a finger-pointing frenzy. "This is an outrage! Who leaked these videos? I want their names right now!"

"They are videos of you and your other traitorous accomplices selling out the UK at every opportunity. If I had my way, you would be put on trial for treason. I will reveal nothing to you, traitor. Sit down and keep your mouth shut or I will have my colleague FBI Special Agent Lynn Dostiene escort you to a locked room."

Lynn stood and waved at the flabbergasted Babbott. "You don't want that, sweetie. I tend to get physical with traitors, importing the enemies of civilization to terrorize their own citizens – all for the purpose of establishing some form of global nightmare. Now sit your fat-ass down!"

One look into Lynn's eyes and Babbott sat down, sobbing. "No crying in here, Babbott. Stifle yourself or get out!"

At Lynn's final warning, Babbott stood and walked out, watched by one of Alexi's crew from the Roma. No visitor was allowed the run of the ship, especially her. Lynn sat down and I continued.

"We'll be happy to talk plans and progress. We won't talk over rules of the encampment. We know Babbott was lying. The real citizens of the UK are going wild over our handling of this situation. They will be escorting a new wave of dependents and thugs to be deported soon. In other good news from the English, Scottish, and Irish Defense Leagues is that a majority of the Sharia Law acolytes have renounced Islam, and consented to be watched for any taquiyya nonsense of lying to the infidels. The globalists, like some of you slimy worms at the table, are very unhappy as is the traitorous BBC. I believe change is at hand. Please remember we were asked in to handle the Sharia Law Mutant problem. The Roma flies the United States flag. We have paid for this experiment. The only thing we ask is protection against the Islamo-Fascists who would like to blow us to kingdom come."

The representative from the State Department stood. "Thank you, Agent Harding. The State Department and

Department of Defense will continue to back this program. We appreciate your straight forward logic in dealing with this mess, brought on by nations dumping a known enemy of civilization in droves on their own citizens. We stand ready to return anyone unwilling to abide by the encampment laws to their country of origin. It is the least we can do. I have been ordered by the President to declare this new city-state under the protection of the American military. We will deal with outside forces attacking as Agent Harding and his team deal with saboteurs inside the encampment… with deadly force."

I waited for a moment while the UK representatives squirmed. "Thank you for your backing in this project, Sir. My associate, US Marshal and FBI/CIA consultant, Nick McCarty will handle the rest of this briefing."

"Thanks, John." Nick stood with a smile of greeting. "We all know the UK government is locked into a war between patriots and globalists. We side with the English, Scottish, and Irish patriots who do not want their nations turned into a cesspool of rampaging mutant troglodytes from the Sand. We also have a contingent of encampment inhabitants who want to make this experiment a success. They will lay down their lives to escape from Islam's clutches. I supplied them with vests designating their new station as secular police. Anyone assaulting them in any way will be killed. Globalists from the UK are not welcome here as we made plain with Babbott, yet the UK allowed three to attend our briefing. Please refrain in the future from sending any agents from the UK Labour Party. They are terrorist enabling communists, hell bent on destroying their own nation. We will-"

"How dare you! I'll see you in hell!"

The UK Labour Party lead representative, Gemy Borebyn, reached for a sidearm, pulling the weapon part way out as the same stiletto a cell-phone contestant tried to use the night before, entered Borebyn's right eye, puncturing it and his brain. Nick walked around the table and retrieved his knife, plucking it from Borebyn's eye-socket. He wiped it on Borebyn's clothing before returning to his seat amidst Monster Squad contingent.

"I see you are all shocked, as am I," Nick stated. "We are not an organization you fetch in to correct petty crimes. Your governments asked us in to solve a worldwide conspiracy against Western Civilization. We fear nothing. We deal with threats with death. The United States backs our plan, initiated by a call to arms from the UK government. I have not seen or heard any backtracking by the Prime Minister. She apparently has decided to stick her finger into the wind after the statement of approval for our action, to see which way the wind was blowing. My friends and I do not stick our fingers into any wind. We know the threat that Sharia Law Mutant infiltration amongst civilized nations poses, as the idiot globalists seek to betray their own citizens and establish a one world order fantasy. We have no clue as to why, other than they think for a second they will get a seat at the ruling table. My brethren and I stand fast. We know the threat and we know placating Islam leads to either death or enslavement. The encampment is our hope for isolating and initiating a restructure of a monstrous ideology. That ends our briefing... unless you would like us to remove Borebyn's body and continue."

The occupants, other than the United States contingent and remaining UK government group, representatives from the English/Scottish/Irish Defense League, and representatives from Canada, Australia, and all of Europe stayed in their seats. Nick's brutal killing of Borebyn cast an eerie magnetism to the scene. Some in attendance were in obvious horror at what had transpired, but made no move to leave or protest. Alexi Fiialkov's men removed Borebyn's body. The discussions about complete German surrender to the Islamic horde dumped on the German citizens went as expected. Germany was lost, except for a bloody civil war, illustrated by the two German representatives formally walking out. The representative from Sweden was the first to speak.

"Can you help us?"

Nick hesitated for a moment. He put his hands on the table in front of him, leaning toward the representative. "No. Your government and far too many of your people have turned a blind eye to the murderous mutants allowed inside your nation. We were given a foothold in the UK to defend and expand. Your nation's dimwitted population still greets these imbecilic marauders from the sixth century like the 'Little Sisters of the Poor'. They rape, pillage, and subjugate with Sharia Law no-go zones. Yet, your government does nothing."

Nick straightened, gesturing toward all. "The rest of you have done little else besides your citizens posting Sharia Law Mutants doing hideous things to innocent people on Facebook. We don't fight on Facebook. If you would like to join us in our experiment, begin deporting your mutants back where they came from no matter what the European Union orders. We helped the UK because they threw off the chains of the EU. We still have sycophants in the UK trying to sabotage our efforts. I can only imagine what would happen if we interceded in the rest of Europe. We would be hung out to dry. I'm sorry, but until your nations show some backbone, we will not transfer the monkey on your back onto ours. Yes, we know the dangers. For example, we back the Czech Republic, Poland and Hungary's stance against importing the mutants completely."

"What right do you have to label them as mutants?"

Nick grinned at the last UK Labour Party leader. "You are an idiot and a traitor. You were wise to keep your treasonous mouth shut. I label the Sharia Law acolytes as mutants because they refuse to assimilate into civilization. They do honor killings of their own children, beat their wives to death or stone them for the slightest offense. They do female genital mutilation and throw Gays off the rooftops of buildings. They rape, pillage, and murder in every nation they are allowed in. Pedophilia is so rampant amongst these degenerates, I would like to nuke their nations from orbit. Reformation is a joke! Forcing secular governments upon these hideous perversions of humanity is the only way."

"I will inform the Prime Minister and our followers that the Labour party will have nothing further to do with this travesty of human rights and your murderous ways."

"I'm happy to hear you say that," Nick replied. "Show this wanker what we have for him."

Jafar started a video. It showed the Labour Party official on Cafrey Rothstein's Isle of Darkness with a twelve-year-old girl. Gasps and muttering denouncements rippled around the table as the official, Calvin Morgan, watched in stunned shock. Jafar turned it off at Nick's signal.

"Go ahead and make a big stink about our encampment, Cal. We'll let the people see what kind of a sick, twisted little shit you really are."

Morgan stood abruptly, sending his chair crashing to the floor. "I want that video and every copy of it!"

"Sure." Nick gestured at him. "Come get it. You need to go through me first though. I don't like your chances. If you have a hideaway piece, like your buddy Borebyn, draw it. If you live, my friend John Harding will give you the video. Otherwise, you need to leave. Just looking at your pedophile face makes me nauseous."

"You have not heard the end of this from me!" Morgan turned to stomp out.

"One more thing before you leave," Nick said. "Resign the moment you get back to the UK or I will release the video everywhere."

Morgan's fists clenched but he continued walking out.

Nick sat down and I stood to end the briefing. "I wish we could help all of you. The key is to get the globalists out of your governments and end your affiliation with the EU. Then, give the migrant infiltrators the three choices as done in the UK by the Prime Minister: leave the country, renounce Islam and be monitored, or die. Your citizens are still strong enough with military assistance to win your nations back, but you need to harden your hearts. Our secular city here may take in refugees from other nations, but they can't expand right now without making their own way to independence. That concludes the briefing. The Roma will be leaving port for the UK tomorrow."

The State Department official joined Nick and I by the conference table. "I can honestly say I never attended a briefing like that one. May I make a suggestion? When you have another briefing, perhaps it would be good to disarm the attendees before allowing them to enter. Then, Marshal McCarty would not need to throw a knife through someone's eye-socket."

"I confess we assumed no one in the UK would have a weapon, or for that matter, any attendee at all," Nick replied. "The UK Labour Party resembles the liberal airheads we have in America in every detail: steal from the working populace to pay for entitlements in order to gain votes, label everyone who doesn't agree with you a racist, open the borders to allow more entitlement parasites in to vote, destroy the military with social experiments, and destroy the rule of law."

"Your point of view is as sharp as your knife, Marshal."

"Sorry, the Sand brings out the worst in me. We will make sure no one gets killed at the next briefing, right John?"

"Absolutely," I agreed. "We'll be moving the encampment into housing very soon after we thoroughly vet the ones we have. Our secular police will be compiling a list of refugees who would rather return to their place of origin."

Nick looked at his iPad. So far Khan has a hundred and twenty-nine people to be returned. Thirty-one of them are simply incorrigibles who will not obey our rules. The rest are Sharia Law advocates. We'll put them on planes from Dakhla Airport for their destinations. We won't know how many saboteurs are left. Khan knows that is a top priority."

"We have the DNA, fingerprint, and photo ID database of all living encampment members," I said. "It will be vital for the UK and all other nations to keep the trolls out of their countries once they leave here. The only reason we're not shooting them all in the head is they are obeying the rules for now."

"Thank you for the briefing. I like what I see. Goodbye for now."

The official left. Our Monster contingent began moving to the door. Alexi transported one of our UH-60 stealth helicopters. Laredo awaited us on the Roma's helipad. The first solar powered building was a combination Humvee garage, helicopter hanger, fueling/maintenance, and living quarters. We needed to be able to transport people to be deported easily without driving the Humvees everywhere. The living quarters were large cubicles. We had air conditioning, but tried to use only the fans. Luckily, we had plenty of sun, which kept the encampment and our refuge powered more than adequately.

Alexi met us at the door. "I'm glad I caught you. Word got out that you were overseas, John. Abu Dhabi wants to host a fight between you and Darius the Destroyer. That's a fifteen-hour flight. I talked to Eugene. He told me he didn't mind you fighting Darius first. He knows what we're doing here is important."

"It's a good thing Tommy's back at the encampment," Lynn said. "I know what he'd be saying. I'll fill in for him. Are you mental? You just fought the fight of your life to earn the UFC championship belt back. Now, you want to fight some ringer in his own hometown arena? You're not goin'. I'm not buying you another ticket to idiots' island. Dev ain't bringin' the Latin, and we ain't goin' to Yabba Dabba Do!"

By the time Lynn finished her Tommy impersonation, we enjoyed her Flintstone's sign off on Abu Dhabi with loud amusement, including Alexi.

"This new scheme, on top of Muerto stealing my eyeball throw, messes with the mental outlook I have for the rescue business." Lynn folded her arms as if miffed.

"Hey… I didn't catch a strange knife and fire it back through someone's eye socket," Nick reminded her. "Even I'm not real enthusiastic about trying that one."

"Well, ok then." Lynn sighed. "You sure added some spice to that briefing. I think Cheese better talk with Tommy, Alexi. With everything we've been doing, another fight this soon after the blast in Vegas, might just barbeque the burger."

"I saw Darius fight with Jess and Dev," Jafar said. "He is very impressive. Although many of his fights were in Abu Dhabi with MMA fighters from Europe and the Middle East, when he broke into the UFC, his five wins came against ranked opponents.

Darius has all the tools with three knockouts and two submissions."

"Talk it over with Tommy," Alexi said. "I'll handle discussions with Darius if you decide to fight."

"Abu Dhabi's outdoor arena is very nice," I said.

"We're going to be on mission for a while," Nick added. "We could make it a celebration type ending to a successful task, or a lot of dead terrorists, if you do decide to fight. I would only caution you that word will get out about our new secular city once the rejects get deported back to their own countries. Abu Dhabi is a Sharia Law country. It's a bad place to get taken."

"Nick's right," Clint agreed. "You did the Abu Dhabi fight scene once. Maybe if the venue was somewhere else, it would be something to think about. That place is a hotbed of Islamist gettogethers."

"We'll think it through, Alexi," I told him. "It would be risky to say the least, especially if they find out I was part of the assault force that ruined their UK Caliphate."

"I had not thought of it in that light, John. I will inform Darius's handlers the venue is out of the question. I will add that he is not the first in line to fight when you return home. I wonder if Eugene would like to fight him. Eugene holds ranking above him. The payday would help Eugene for certain. The UFC would certainly sanction a fight between 'The Rattler' and 'Darius the Destroyer.'"

"That sounds like a winner to me," I told him. "Eugene could use a good payday and I need to stay the hell out of Sharia Law nations unless I'm going on a bombing run. Jafar, Lucas, and Casey will be shipping aboard for your return. Samira has Mia in London now and the other dependents wanted to see England without Sharia Law Mutants. Casey and Lucas will be touring with their wives and kids. They'll be flying in the day after tomorrow."

"Excellent. The freshness and regal quality of England has returned," Alexi replied. "The streets are clean and absent the stench of fear. The EDL patrols without letup, following through on the tenets of what the Prime Minister declared. The mosques, with irritating speaker systems, have all been revamped as housing. The health care crisis, socialized medicine carries with it, has eased significantly since entitlements have been cut off completely from the refugees remaining. They either work and renounce Islam or they are put in quarantine at the largest of the mosques until they can be deported here."

"Do you have enough men to handle the next batch. I don't want any mistakes causing the Roma to be lost in a combat situation at sea."

"That will not be a problem, John. I have hired a team of SAS veterans to man our machine gun nests and keep order. They have no rules of engagement. Anyone protesting will be shot and tossed over the side. Any coordinated assault will be met with machine gun fire. The group being deported are being warned by the SAS team right now. Many have optioned to be fingerprinted, photographed, and DNA samplings taken so they may pay their own way to their native countries."

Nick grinned. "So, our idea they would self deport is actually working?"

"It is indeed," Alexi answered. "If they don't have the money, they are being allowed to wire their families for the fare. If they do not have family members with money, it means deporting them here to the encampment to work their way home. Your videos of encampment life, rules, and handling of saboteurs has been played for the group to be deported. That was when many found the money for going home on their own. No one from an Islamic state may visit England on business or tourism without paying for an EDL escort."

"Are the SAS trainers getting the populace trained fast enough to be doing all this with weapons," Clint asked.

"They work with the growing number of citizen soldiers every day, training them in proper weapons handling, firing, and tactical situations. There is no shortage of volunteers anywhere in the UK. The membership in the English, Scottish, and Irish Defense Leagues grows by the thousands each day. The UK citizens want the Islamists gone, period. The former Muslims renouncing Islam have been issued badges and special IDs so they may pass patrols without problems. They are watched by everyone. If they pull the 'offended' card, they are transferred to the deportation zones without being able to file a grievance of any kind."

"Thank God they're making it work back there," Lynn said. "It will make our job here much easier. I really want to see this through to the end where we can watch the city we've built in action."

"At some point, we're going home," Nick said. "Between fixing Cafrey Rothstein's Isle of Darkness, Muslim rehabilitation center building, and meeting with suicidal globalists, I'm nearing the limit of my social worker caring phase."

"Amen to that." Until we made some progress the night before, I considered turning the encampment over to whoever wanted it.

* * *

Two weeks passed with daily deportations, encouraged by Khan and his secular police team. The people who hated the encampment rules, work schedule, and no Sharia Law aspects refrained from sabotaging the project on pain of death. Khan's team convinced them to await deportation rather than causing problems for everyone in the encampment. Khan impressed Nick and me with the amount of trouble he avoided. Khan's people proved loyal to him. They worked tirelessly to ferret out encampment inhabitants with no will to work or embrace change. Nick and Cala alternated with me and Laredo to fly the deportees to the Dakhla Airport for their flights.

The construction crews, with motivated workers from the encampment, finished adding the ordered number of cottages. The technology involved in the rolled-out roads joining the communities performed solidly, making movement between everything in the city and the encampment smooth. Khan moved people dedicated to making the secular city state work into the cottages first, making sure they knew with the number of secular police now numbering a hundred and fifty, they would be inspecting all aspects of the new city. Recycling waste was a key factor. Learning the ropes of agriculture and irrigation, the encampment understood growing crops and fishing would become their source of income and trade with the cities around them. Contractors brought in to teach solar panel upkeep and maintenance on the agricultural equipment, waste treatment, and water desalinization capsules were guarded every minute.

Nick, Johnny, Jian, and Cala moved amongst the people freely without the previous stares of resentment. Muerto, in particular, was popular with Khan's growing secular force. Muerto taught the secular police force to operate using tactics from the old 'Road House' movie rules for bouncers – be nice until it was time not to be nice, then, use overwhelming force and a take no prisoners attitude. Deportees and dependents arrived, using the old spotless encampment tents and facilities. The leftover thugs sent from the UK learned quickly they would have the same choices as before: be sent home to their origins, obey the rules and work with vigor, or be executed.

With a third of the secular force being women, the changes in the men's attitudes evolved from the Sharia Law medieval misogyny to an outlook toward women more like the way it was in Iran before the Ayatollahs turned the world inside out. Khan led the secular force with full respect for its female members, making certain respect for each other would be earned and maintained. Patrolling became an integral part of making the city work. Everyone understood sabotage of facilities, homes, or community structures and equipment carried a death sentence. Nick and Gus took their turns in England with family, returning for the final phases of city building. They insisted the Monsters return home. We all met in our compound building.

Nick began the meeting. "Johnny and Cala have made many friends amongst our new secular city dwellers. Their story of how they came together, coupled with their skill sets, elevated them to rock star status. Jian trades stories and patrols with the secular police daily, always ready to turn a tense situation into one with humor. Khan, Gus, and I work with not only the police force, but the maintenance, irrigation, and farming crews. We're helping Khan to understand the duties of a leader. We've talked it over with Rachel and Tina. Our squad will stay on for the next couple of months. We'll make sure you get all the videos of progress. If we need instant help, I'll call right away."

I could tell from the faces of my crew there would not be any arguments on the side of staying. "The security factor bugs me, Nick. They will notice your reduced force. We've developed relationships with every one of the secular force. I believe in them too. They've handled being armed with stun-gun nightsticks and mace with a professional attitude. You've vetted them very well. The city grows daily. I'm worried you could be overrun once we're gone."

"Did you just insult me?"

Our standard comical reply drew the usual amusement.

"We know the risks. Gus and I spent a week with our family. Denny's keeping the supplies coming in until we get on our feet. He and Paul make sure we don't get thrown under the bus before we complete the mission. Khan knows all the signs when an undercurrent of hostility begins. He and I handled a situation two days before my vacation. Khan's people noted a group of thug arrivals surrounding another new arrival as if they were in the middle of a meeting. We investigated quietly, revealing a plot to begin forging another Sharia Law attempt towards fundamentalism with hate preaching Imam, Abdul Rence. I shot him in the head and we deported his nine followers. Our force noticed what they were supposed to and the other citizens helped."

"Muerto will keep us posted," Lynn agreed. "My minions have been holding down the fort at home but we need to get back. We're not much more than prison guards now."

Hearing the muttering agreement from my crew, I didn't need to draw this out. "I know you wouldn't take this on and endanger your crew without being sure of the risks. We'll ship back home with Alexi. He and Marla are getting married next month. I'll get another look at England when we take on containers meant for the USA. We've caused a stir in Europe. I believe the

41

European Union is finished. I think civil war will be the only way for some of the nations to oust their Islamic infiltrators."

"We can only do so much," Nick replied. "If they throw off the EU yoke, nationalism will return, and with it will come protection against Islam's scourge. Out irrigation system and fertilization has turned this desert into a much more promising place. We're on target to grow wheat, corn, avocados, kiwifruit, guavas, mangoes, and possibly even grapes. The rest of Western Sahara are watching closely. Once we begin making money from our crops and fishing, this place may become a rich city state. Khan knows allowing any unvetted Islamist in here can crush everything. We'll see you all back in the states soon. Now that we have docking facilities, supplies move in and out easier, and we'll be able to get a fishing industry moving along."

"I've been having a blast getting people interested in the fishing prospects," Gus added. "The trawler we acquired is ready for a fishing expedition. Now that our city dwellers know they can get a plane ticket home, there's less chance of sabotage. We've been pulling in some nice meals too from dockside. Khan will still need a couple of guards on the boat of course, but it is progress."

"Are you still set on a benevolent dictatorship," Clint asked.

"Absolutely. It may evolve into something more like the parliamentary system or even a republic. Right now, these people know their place in the community, their jobs, and what's expected of them under Khan. Keeping him alive is the main reason I'm staying on for a time. His family joined him the day Gus and I sailed for England with Alexi. Since the dependents reunited with many of the first deportees, we have much improved good will amongst a people with purpose. The women threw off the slave costumes with enthusiasm. Clothing donations from abroad, coupled with materials and equipment to start their own textile market, has drawn both men and women into yet another industry."

"You do realize the problems they face with all the social mores, right?"

"I do, Lynn. We're in deep discussions everyday now with Khan and his force. They know soon we will need something to replace Islamic tyranny. We have many of the construction crew quarters we can convert into cafés, restaurants, and bars if the city state would like to ease restrictions. Johnny, Jian and Cala have explained what it has been like to live without the crushing weight of Islam. They do not try and convert anyone. They merely suggest the possibility of a much more benevolent spiritual way of life without the yoke of militant Islam."

"You all have seen the difference in the faces of those who came here on the original voyage," Cala stated with some excitement. "For the first time in their lives a force protects them having nothing to do with fear mongering, beatings, and death. They understand if they work hard and obey simple social rules, no one preys on them like wolves, looking for the smallest excuse to destroy their lives. Johnny and I are going to begin the first café, where all are welcome. Muerto brought all the necessary equipment to get started. We will begin putting in our sound system for music and installing all the accouterments of a real restaurant."

Nick shrugged with comical emphasis. "Yes. Eventually, jails, bars, liquor, and all the sins of a regular city will become part and parcel to their city's development. We won't be around to prevent it. This whole experiment could explode into chaos. I have discussed with Khan the importance of he and his lieutenants maintaining the rules of the city at all cost. It will remain the prerogative of the population whether to descend once again into darkness by destroying what we've accomplished. Cala is right. If the people cannot worship quietly in their own way, and religious fanaticism reappears, all will be lost. I brought a piano back with me from England. I plan on entertaining in our new café, but we're a long way from that. We brought back big screen projection equipment with surround sound to be worked on. It's a process. Islam permits nothing. We hope to allow people to enjoy life as an alternative under a secular governing system."

"I hope it all works, Dead Boy," Clint said. "Knowing human nature the way we do, the chances of it working are pretty slim. They have all the ingredients: solar powered everything, beaches and ocean, developing work opportunities, and they do have citizens from all walks of life to teach others. I'm glad we're going. When they piss it all away, don't try to make things right. Get the gunship in the air and get the hell out of here. I want you back home entertaining in the 'Grove', or up in our neck of the woods, so Lynn and I can have more date nights like you treated us to in England."

Nick's facial features took on the grim caricature, his daughter labeled the 'Terminator'. "Believe this, Clint. Before I allow an experiment to hurt my crew, I will blow the shit out of this place and fly off into the sunset with all guns blazing."

Clint smiled. "That's what I wanted to hear."

"Thanks for the early out, brother," Dev said. "I said this before and didn't abide by it – I hate the Sand, and I ain't comin' back."

"We're keeping you here, Dev," Nick said. "We may need rain."

Dev jutted out his arm, palm toward Nick. "Talk to the hand."

* * *

Six weeks later, Nick played piano in their homemade nightspot. The building they revamped for their café and entertainment center could only accommodate five hundred people with dance floor, tables and chairs. Whether to pipe the music out to anyone nearby the large isolated building was voted on. The vast majority of the city's inhabitants voted to approve the broadcast music. Movies and sporting events were shown to the different zones inside the city state on a night by night basis. They incorporated six zones within the city. Every Sunday night, Nick entertained for all, plus playing at slow intervals in the café at any time.

As Nick finished his forty-five-minute music set, the packed café gave him a standing ovation. A groan went up from the people dancing. He waved his thanks. "I'll be back in half an hour."

Johnny turned on the jukebox music before he and Cala returned to the table, where Jian, Gus, and Nick sat. Khan Eshieh joined them with his wife, Sela. They had been dancing too.

"You have a real gift, my friend," Khan told Nick, toasting him with his glass of beer.

Everyone joined the toast. Nick smiled. "It is a pleasure entertaining instead of sitting in the dark with the M107. Your police force is doing an amazing job. I saw them talk down a group rumbling with each other in the stands after today's soccer match."

Khan sighed. "The sports field, thanks to the wonderful irrigation, gives everyone a chance to ah… what do you call it… blow off steam. They do get a little too competitive in these city zone tournaments. The baseball and basketball team tournaments lead to less bickering than soccer. We remind the audience to have fun rooting for their team and be happy for good plays, but it is a process. I am also glad you do not need to be in your sniper post. I like you better at the piano."

"As do I," Sela agreed. "You know so many songs. It is amazing."

"Music soothes the heart and mind," Johnny said. "Having the radio station with DJs playing requests, or doing some funny news reports from around the city, has a huge following now. The radio tower serves a dual purpose, allowing the DJs to keep watch on everything while having fun."

"We wish you all would stay longer," Sela replied.

"We'll be back for visits to see all the improvements and industry," Nick promised. "Remember, we can talk and trade videos on Facebook now, since we have satellite internet. Your idea to create a new Facebook page with all your citizens involved, posting updates, and advertising your City of Hope accomplishments was inspired, Khan."

"Everyone wants to send us things. A police department in Texas donated all our uniforms and utility belts," Khan added. "Best of all is the interest by hotel firms wanting to develop tourist trade. They loved our pictures of the beaches with snack bars and all the accouterments of places like Aruba that Gus helped us design."

"Not much designing needed. I remembered the fancy cabanas and bamboo furniture," Gus said. "Out here, we need shade. Then, it was a matter of piping water into our shower and restrooms at our snack-bar/café. Add some palm trees, thanks to our irrigation system, and we have a great beach front."

Khan's phone buzzed. "Yes, Iman?"

The smile fled Khan's face. "Muerto is here with his crew. I will tell him. Keep us informed. Go dark, Iman. You will be fine."

Khan stood. "It is Iman Kaar in the radio tower. Three boats are approaching the coastline. He can see many men in black on each boat with his night-vision range finders. They are heavily armed. Iman is afraid they will target the tower."

"Johnny, Cala, and I will go to the beach with the new XM307 and lots of ammo, unless you want to fly the stealth."

Nick grinned. "It's loaded. The Gatling guns, hydra rockets, and the hellfire missiles. Think of the Monster Squad getting the video of us doing a nighttime 'Ride of the Valkyries' assault on sea craft. I've only had half a beer and Cala hasn't had anything."

"Yes! We must go," Cala leaped to her feet. "Poor Iman will believe he is going to die at any second. Hurry."

Johnny and Gus enjoyed Cala's enthusiasm as they joined her. Nick turned to Khan as he stood too. "We'll handle this, my friend. Before Iman leaves the radio tower, tell him to have everyone go back to their cottages and go dark. Will you and Sela close the place for us?"

"Yes, Muerto… but don't you need us to confront these invaders?"

"I hope not. You have the key to the armory. If they get us, you will need to arm your people. They will either try to land quietly on the beach in rafts or simply dock the boats on our long pier. Spread your people with the MP5s along the beach and at the pier. They have been trained. Do not fire until they are either ashore, on the beach, or almost off the pier."

Khan clasped Nick's shoulder. "Do not get killed, my friend. You do not have to do this. We can fight for our land."

Nick grinned. "I know. I told Gus this long ago. I don't like being hunted, even when I deserve it. I've never asked for mercy, and I don't issue it in return… even if I'm begged to. My crew rides where I ride. Watch the 'Ride of the Valkyries' assault, Khan. You will hear our battle and see much fireworks."

"You are quite crazy, Muerto," Khan replied.

"So, I've been told. I have to go or Cala will drag me out by my ear."

* * *

Cala got in the pilot's seat with Johnny as her co-pilot. Jian inspected the helicopter's frame with his flashlight, running his hands over everything as Nick had taught him. Nick and Gus loaded the XM307 on board and attached it to its tripod mount near the door. Nick loaded and checked over his M107 sniper rifle while Cala and Johnny did pre-flight checks.

"We are lucky the stealth was ready for a flight to the Dakhla Airport," Cala said. She started the engines, preparing for lift off.

"It is never luck to be prepared," Nick stated. "Through skill and daring, while reading the minds of our enemies from far away, sensing danger, we are ready."

"Oh man… I think I just threw up in my mouth a little," Gus retorted to the amusement of his cohorts.

47

Cala lifted off. Each wore a communications helmet. Jian, Gus, and Nick had night-vision capability. Nick worked inside his harness at the hatch, swinging slightly to cover as much range as possible, while Gus and Jian readied the XM307.

"Muerto ready."

"Payaso ready."

"Kabong ready."

"Dark Dragon ready."

"Reaper on the fly!"

"Let's go dark and do a flyover recon, Cala. I want to get good movies of these boats so we can possibly identify them later."

"On it." Cala circled the UH-60 out over the pier, flying in a spherical pattern to take them far past the approaching boats. "They've stopped at a mile out, Muerto."

"Hold her steady. I see them." Nick put aside his range finders. Jian called out all the parameters while Nick readied himself in the harness with his M107. "They're going the motorized raft route. I need to give them something to think about without giving away our position."

Cala hummed with a smile on her face, zoning into the light firmness of touch needed, giving Nick a broad view of the target craft. Nick sighted in with his own self-hypnosis of concentration. Hitting anything from a harness aboard the Blackhawk Stealth in the dark on a floating target to a novice would seem a miracle. Nick smiled and squeezed the trigger with the same confidence he played piano. Nearly fifteen hundred yards away, his .50 caliber spent uranium slug passed through the boat's pilothouse shield, pulping the inside center mass of the man at the controls. Still grinning while shifting slightly, Nick repeated the impossible twice more. He executed the men in the other boats' pilothouses.

"Jesus, God in heaven!" Gus made the sign of the cross while Jian simply gaped open-mouthed at Nick, his rangefinders dangling. "Stake him, Jian. The demon terminator is loose. Take no pity. Stake him! No damn human being could make those fucking shots! Stake him!"

By then, everyone aboard, including Nick, enjoyed Gus's rant with loud amusement. Nick settled in again, hitting targets on the boats as they scurried around, and in the rafts being boarded by assault teams. He hit everything with absolute silence around him but for the sound of wind, ocean, and Blackhawk Stealth. The assault boats' crews, unable to pinpoint where the deadly fire from the heavens came from, pulled the rafts back aboard in panic mode. It did them no good. Nick took his time, blowing away any isolated target stopping for even a second. The boats' hulls offered no protection from the loads the M107 fired.

Nick leaned back with absolute certainty no one aboard the three boats would be a threat to the Blackhawk. "I believe it's time for the 'Ride', my friends. Johnny on the Gatling guns, with Gus and Jian working the XM307. It's a kill mission, kiddies. We salt the earth on this one."

"Yes!" Cala hit the switch for the sound system. The rumbling roar of terror filled the skies with sound, blanketing everything.

'Ride of the Valkyries' blasted into the night as Cala flew low and hard. Johnny stitched the boats across with Gatling guns blazing, nearly cutting them in half. Cala tight circled the Blackhawk for a broadside of 25mm grenade shots from the XM307, obliterating everything on the water. Cala laughed and shouted through run after run until nothing but toothpicks of the boats floated on the water. She turned the Blackhawk toward their hangar, doing a flyby with the 'Ride' cutting into the silence of night like a hatchet. Khan watched from the beach with a grin as his city's inhabitants ran for their homes in terror. He saw his secular police did not move from their positions. His phone vibrated. He smiled at the picture of Nick in full Muerto costume.

"I see you had much fun upon the waters, my friend."

"Light the fires, big daddy," Nick quipped from 'Independence Day'. "We're coming in for a landing and going straight for the bar. I plan on entertaining and drinking until the wee hours of the morning."

"I will have Iman know to announce it," Khan replied. "He has been on in speaker mode through your entire spectacle. I believe he thinks you are a Jinn. Sela and I will be there to dance through the night."

"We saw your troops held position. Excellent, my friend. They saw your courage hold and they could do no less. You proved to everyone your leadership is unequaled in the city. This was a bloody way to illustrate it, but I believe everything happens for a reason. I thank God we were still here when it happened. The only problem is determining where they came from. We could not take chances tonight. I would have liked to investigate this attack. We have already contacted the Navy about the assault. They are trying to isolate where the boats came from. We'll be going over the videos to hunt for clues also. We have videos from every angle during our attack."

"Is there not debris in the water, Muerto?"

"Ah... no... sorry, Khan... we don't leave debris after a 'Ride of the Valkyries' assault. It is called a 'salt the earth' mission."

"I see. You attack and blast everything to dust and salt the actual ground you have assaulted so nothing can grow."

"That is the definition of a 'salt the earth' mission. Our Navy will investigate origins. It's in their hands right now. We are returning for a moderated party night. I do not care who does it, but have someone take over the radio tower, with full knowledge there may be another attempt. I doubt there will be another attack. To be safe, I need you to pick a replacement for Iman, who will do the same excellent DJ job, playing music to soothe, and watching the horizon. We need to award Iman. Without his diligence, we would have been under assault in the city."

"He shall be honored for this," Khan replied. "I will see you all in the café."

"Yes... you will."

Chapter Three: Final Touches

"You have the XM307 on a tripod mount with Ma Deuce mounted at the bow," Nick said. "The MP5s you have are insurance only. Run the trawler back to our port until I contact you. I don't want the trawler stopped by the Moroccan military. I doubt they have patrol boats, but I don't want to take any kind of a chance. They claim this part of the Western Sahara. It's a hell of a good hideout for an Isis terrorist leader, like Dar Sultan, especially since half the world's searching for him."

"I'm interested in why the Navy didn't let us know they were intercepting the signals between Dar and his boats," Gus replied. "They only figured something was wrong when we annihilated them."

"You can't blame them for that. By the time they translated the cross chatter, we had already sent them all virgin hunting," Nick said. "I think they should have sent a drone over and blasted the shit out of him, but Denny told me Morocco might use a strike like that to attack our City of Hope when we're gone. He didn't like my counter suggestion of warning Morocco if they did anything like that, our Navy would erase Marrakesh from this dimension. Anyway, here we are. I'll get the prick."

"I should go with you." Johnny and Gus helped Nick lower the raft into the water. "I could watch the raft for you and be nearby if you need help."

"You don't speak French well enough, Kabong. I want you with Gus in case some entity tries to stop our boat. Don't let them. You know what to do. Shoot first, ask questions later, while you're sailing past the dead bodies. Denny isolated the blockhouse where the signal came from. He sent me an excellent marked satellite image. All those damn huts in Guerguerat look the same. I'd sure like to know how Dar gathered a strike force like he launched. Denny figured he had help from Syria. We sent a lot of those assholes back to Syria when we should have shot them in the back of the head."

"If that force had landed in secret, they could have wiped out all our facilities," Gus agreed. "Call us when you need us, Muerto. We're close enough to fly the gunship in and get you."

Nick shoved away from the trawler. "Just make sure you bring an extra raft in case I lose mine. The camo cover should keep it safe in that isolated stretch of beach I picked, but who knows. This reminds me that we need to get the hell away from the Sand."

"Amen to that, brother," Johnny called out.

* * *

Dar Sultan smashed a fist on the table. "I want to know what happened!"

His companion gestured calmingly. "French only. The Moroccan military would sell us out if they discover our true identities. These huts are too close together. We cannot trust the people of this town. The force arrived in position from Nouakchott after they dropped us off. It cost a fortune to have Mauritania cast a blind eye on our operation. Our benefactor in the Emirates will demand an accounting, but we have no way to learn the truth of what happened."

"We should have gone on the mission with our assault force. I was in contact with them to the last minute before they were to board the rafts for the beach. Our contacts in Syria told us most of the force stationed to protect the city left, leaving only a few behind. We do not even have rumors. We should fly into Dakhla Airport. They will have rumors of a battle."

"The force prided themselves on being elite and did not want us along. Our passports worked in Mauritania, but we may be captured in Dakhla Airport. We can get land transportation over the crossing. The military cares little about who crosses unless they are Westerners."

Dar nodded in agreement. "At least then we can learn what happened. I hate it here. The Afghan mountains would be preferable."

"It is not safe for us to go anywhere at this time. We were very nearly detained in Nouakchott. The bribe money is gone. Without sufficient funds, we must abide here. No one suspects us, but it is a small town, and people talk. Once over the border, if we learn the fate of our assault force, we should wire Amir Mohammed Kostler again for money. He knows our value, being so close to this vile city of blasphemers."

"They should have killed the small force left to guard them by now," Dar retorted. "You are right. Let us sleep and leave at first light for the border."

Something arched through the open window and rolled under the table.

"What was-"

The grenade's explosive force, contained by the solid stone walls, collapsed the roof onto the mangled bodies of Dar Sultan and his companion. Nick, dressed in simple, well-worn robes, moved quickly down the road. The five-kilometer trek to the ocean in the dark drew no one's attention. It resembled a lunar landscape because of all the sand mining done. Many of the dunes, bulldozed for the sand to make cement, created craters due to natural climate incidents such as storms and droughts. Nick found his camouflaged raft easily enough. He called Gus.

"That was fast."

"I heard what I needed to hear. I have enough water and food to get through a couple of days. I don't want you and Johnny to get caught up in some kind of dragnet on the water the military might initially set into place."

"Oh crap, Muerto... you used a grenade, didn't you?"

Silence.

"Okay... call us when you're ready," Gus said with Johnny, Jian, and Cala enjoying the exchange.

"Will do. El Muerto... away."

Nick settled in for the night under the camouflaged raft, against the sand crater's side, MP5 in hand. He smiled, imagining his friends' conversation after his call. No one runs out of their house to check on anything after an ET-MP grenade explosion. Amir Mohammed Kostler made his list tonight. He needed to call Paul soon. The information concerning the ease an assault force formed in Mauritania would need to be dealt with through other channels.

* * *

Johnny caught the rope thrown to him. He pulled the raft tight against the trawler. Nick threw his equipment bag to Gus and climbed aboard. They secured the raft.

"You smell like a carcass rotting in the desert," Gus complained. "We should throw you in the ocean for a few moments."

"They sent patrols out," Nick explained. "For two-days straight I needed to stay undercover. That's why I didn't call you guys until today. I'm damn glad I removed all trace of my footsteps because they were looking. I thought I would need to shoot one patrol. If not for the sand excavation companies are doing, I wouldn't have had a good enough place to lay low. Anyway, let's get going. I'll throw my clothes over the side and get cleaned when we get underway."

"Good... but until then, go stand on the fantail."

"That's hurtful, Gus."

* * *

"Uh oh." Johnny watched the fast approaching boat. "We have company. It looks like a patrol boat."

Nick grabbed his M107, checking in the direction Johnny indicated. "It's a patrol boat flying the Mauritanian flag. They shouldn't be this far up the coastline."

The sirens and lights came on. Gus increased speed. "We can't outrun them, Muerto. The wind kicks back toward them. Stay on the fantail. When they get a whiff of you, they'll reverse course."

"This is no time for insulting jokes. Besides, I'm clean, you prick," Nick retorted after both he and Johnny enjoyed Gus's quip. "I have an idea."

"This is not good, Payaso."

"Tell me about it. Every time I hear Muerto say 'I have an idea', it usually involves ET-MP grenades. That can't be it so please tell us all about your idea, Muerto. They're at one mile and closing."

"Johnny has the sound system going. We have our lucky XM307 on tripod, loaded for bear up top. I say we turn to and go dead in the water, dark and still. They'll slow their approach. I will blow away the bridge with M107 spent uranium slugs. Then we blast out our 'Jaws' theme while edging toward them, alternating a moment later with 'Ride of the Valkyries' to herald our assault. Johnny and I will fire the XM307 until nothings left of the patrol boat but a vapor trail, all on video to make Lucas's head explode in envy."

"Oh, Lord… hep me… hep me, Lord!"

"Calm down, Payaso. I vote for us to do it," Johnny said. "It is a vicious surprise move. Do not ruin it with your negativity."

"Fine! Say when!"

Nick and Johnny had already climbed to the top deck's camouflaged XM307 nest. Nick readied his M107. "Now! You have the music switch too, Payaso. I've already started the video recording. I will call out when it's time to move."

"Understood." Gus slowed immediately, using the boat's momentum and steering to face the oncoming craft, righting the wheel perfectly to point dead on their pursuer.

"Very nice, Payaso." Nick shot the gun crew at the bow of the boat, using short bursts to cut through the armor and men. His next bursts tore through the pilot house, ending their sirens, lights, and movement. "Approach with 'Jaws', Payaso!"

The trawler creeped forward, the haunting theme from the movie 'Jaws' blasting from the speakers with deep base thumping tumult.

Gus pumped a fist as he heard Nick and Johnny celebrating on the upper deck. He increased throttle. "Here we go!"

The 'Ride of the Valkyries' turned the night into a horror show for the patrol boat as 25mm airburst grenades rained hell on earth down upon the floating target. Gus slowed, staying well back from the flaming wreck. The patrol boat exploded in spectacular form. Gus maneuvered into a sweeping turn on their original course toward the 'City of Hope'.

"I sure hope the crew didn't call out a distress signal to the Mauritanian military authorities," Gus said when Johnny and Nick joined him in the pilot house.

"I'll call Paul and request the Navy seal off any approach by formal military from Mauritania. They can keep watch by satellite on the Mauritanian ports. I'm wondering if Morocco requested the patrol boat. Their little claimed piece of land between Mauritania and Western Sahara doesn't have a Navy. Of that you can be sure. We need to make sure we don't leave for home without our lucky XM307 as well as the UH-60."

"I withhold opinion until tied at the City of Hope pier concerning the word lucky," Gus stated.

"Oh ye of little faith. I'm going down below and write some more. I only have the final chapter to write in 'Hell Zone'. In the final chapter, Jed will lose his leg in a terrible accident aboard his boat and Diego formally begins calling his old friend 'Pegleg'."

"Not funny, Muerto!" Gus called out after Nick, as he descended below decks.

* * *

Khan and Sela danced as Nick continued his Sunday night piano man entertainment. Johnny and Cala swayed next to them with many others. Nick ended his set with the Temptations 'My Girl' to thunderous applause. He waved at everyone, signaling a break, which evoked the usual groans. Johnny turned on the jukebox selections. He and Cala brought cold beers back to the table for everyone.

"I wish we could convince you to stay longer, Muerto," Sela said. "This has been the happiest time of our lives."

"Our work here is done, Sela. We will keep in touch with friends made for a lifetime. I promise to visit once the hotel opens. My wife, Rachel, will love to meet you all, but she is spoiled. Roughing it to her is a five-star hotel without a balcony."

"She went through much during the time when they wanted to kill her and your daughter, Jean. After such a time, I am not surprised she takes no chances," Sela replied.

"Once everything works for the new City of Hope, I will fly your family to California for a visit," Nick promised. "We will all sit around on my balcony overlooking the foggy sea and I will play piano. We will all sit down on our chosen beach at Otter's Point and sip Irish coffees."

"Do you really think that possible, Muerto?"

Nick's countenance changed to a more solemn state. "I never say things lightly, my friend. You have made this experiment work, freeing tens of thousands from the 'Death Cult'. I will make your visit happen. I trust your lieutenants and so does the city. The community pressure on the new arrivals makes the transition phase much easier. Compared to what you and your original companions went through, this is like paradise. The thugs get shipped as always. You have an armory to defend this land. I trust you implicitly to never misuse it. The surrounding cities are your barriers to the Islamic curse. They are jealous of the success, but as

57

long as they are treated with special privilege in goods and services, they can be a great protective force around you."

Khan nodded in agreement. "Our meetings with the outside cities will go on as you have established. I must be political when interacting with them. It is a key to our survival as you have taught me."

"Know this," Nick said. "If you have a problem, call me immediately as you see it develop. I do not abandon my friends ever. We have powerful forces now behind us because we conquered a place once thought of as the 'Isle of Darkness'. It is now the 'Isle of Hope'. What we gathered there will hold our power in place for many years."

"I am jealous of how much good your violence has accomplished," Khan replied with hoped for amusement. "Perhaps someday we will be a beacon of hope for Muslims around the world to understand there is a brighter future without a medieval death cult involved."

"That, my friend, is what we all pray for."

"Muerto is right," Johnny said. "We all pray for your success here. Cala and I will never forget you. We look forward to the day you and Sela may visit us in Pacific Grove. We may leave Gus here with you. He is positively radiant without his wife, Tina, the Tyrannosaurus Rex."

"Very funny, Kabong." Gus raised his glass. "To good friends, good times, and a future without Islam."

The group clinked glasses solemnly in support of his toast.

* * *

"Oh my… this is heaven," Nick sipped his Irish coffee with everyone around him on chairs at Pacific Grove's Otter's Point beach. Deke, flopped across his feet, moved from his human, only if ordered to. The reunion between Deke and Nick surpassed human interaction.

Jean, Sonny, and Jay sat in chairs too, unwilling to leave their trainer for a moment. They missed Gus, Johnny, Cala, and Jian, but the most difficult absence had been that of Nick. The months had seemed like years, because they feared the worst at every moment. They watched Nick holding the sleeping Quinn against him while sipping his coffee as if it were a miracle.

"I am with child," Cala announced suddenly as Johnny grasped her hand.

Her revelation energized the close-knit group into celebration mode. It evoked tears of joy from her closest friends, Rachel and Tina, who moved to hug her in silent congratulations. Nick, Gus, and Jian gripped Johnny's hand in solemn comradery.

"The Reaper is with child. Oh, good God in heaven," Tina straightened to wave her arms to the heavens. "What forces will be called out to balance the cosmos."

"Sit down, T-Rex." Cala giggled. "You saw my solo 'Ride of the Valkyries' to protect the City of Hope. My son will be apprised he was within me when his mom blasted the crap out of the 'Death Cult' of Islam. He will be very proud."

"That was awesome, Cala!" Jean gripped her hand. "The Monster Squad called the moment dad returned. They've been playing the videos of your gunship attack, and the battle with Mauritania's patrol boat, over and over. They're making John wear his Muerto t-shirt."

"John told me Lucas never destroyed the Muerto pajamas I sent him," Nick added. "On the night they played the videos, Lucas wore the pajamas to Pain Central. By the time Lucas finished modeling, John thought he'd need to give Lynn oxygen."

"Tell us what John said about the Arab Emirates guy," Rachel said. "You took the phone in the other room after the pajama talk."

"I switched to a secure line. John believes the offer to fight Darius the Destroyer in the Emirates was meant to lure the Monster Squad into a trap. This Amir Mohammed Kostler owns Darius's contract. They wanted to get us shorthanded defending the city and strike in both places. The Facebook webpage for the City of Hope already generated a fatwa by multiple bearded trolls. The happy people without Sharia Law in the City of Hope have generated millions of likes from all over the world. The inhabitants, at Khan's advisement, refuse to talk religion. Their pictures of progress caused the Arab Middle East to demand they be taken off Facebook because their existence blasphemes Islam. I would not be surprised if the Islam ass-kisser who owns Facebook gives in to the Sharia Law Mutants. Johnny has solved that problem."

"I created a web page for them," Johnny said. "We advertise their successes and coming tourist attractions, including a port for cruise ships to dock. No one can block them unless they take away the internet. They have so many millions of hits on their site, thanks to advertising everywhere, that advertisers are lining up to pay for space. The 'City of Hope' has its own YouTube channel where they garner more advertising money through their nearly unlimited viral videos highlighting the agricultural, textile, and fishing industries. Khan made sure to show his citizen army reserve training, along with the nearly two hundred secular police who act as the City of Hope's military."

"The UK and American governments are so pleased with the result, they agreed to act as the patrol force along the coast to prevent any aggression. Both nations have a naval presence in that part of the Atlantic any way," Gus explained.

"The surrounding cities in Western Sierra are purchasing foodstuffs and clothing," Jian added. "We have heard they are talking about easing restrictions on their own people. I think John Harding has the plot against us figured out correctly. It was too much of a coincidence when Alexi Fiialkov received the Darius offer."

"What's the plan for Kostler?"

"Nothing for now, Rach," Nick answered. "He can't attack the City of Hope, nor can he get at the Monster Squad and us back here. He's too late to stop what's happening. He won't be the only Middle East potentate mad at us. Sharia Law helps them control the populace, just as the leading globalist rats all over the world want to do - keep the citizens prisoners of violent predators in their own nations. Each time a brainwashed mutant watches a City of Hope video, Islam loses some of its grip."

"Muerto's right," Cala agreed. "Those people in the City of Hope were much like the awful thugs still in Europe. When forced to live without Sharia Law fears, the difference was incredible to see. I never imagined it could work. I went along to be with Johnny and wipe them out when they tried to sabotage the city."

"We did need to do some of that too," Gus admitted. "It was a thin line until Khan stepped up and became a leader. Muerto trained him the entire time we were there. We knew if they send someone to kill him and he isn't ready, it would plunge the city into chaos. He now has a woman and man as lieutenants who are leaders in their own right. They would take over if something were to happen to Khan."

"All this seems more a threat with everything you say," Rachel pointed out. "The mutants don't reason. They revenge when your back is turned. I hope this ends the world building tour."

"I liked being a hero," Jian stated. "We did what was right."

"Shut up, Dragon Breath," Rachel ordered.

Jian's eyes widened, but he relaxed when the rest of his friends enjoyed Rachel's comment with loud hilarity, including Rachel. Jian nodded. "Good one, white eye. Have you been on a diet? You do not look a pound over one-forty."

"I'm not that easy, Chow Mein." Rachel chuckled with everyone else. "I have the Daughter of Darkness poking me day in and day out. Your noodles are soft if you think you can top her."

"We're not going back to the Sand," Nick stated. "It's one thing when you control a situation with deadly force. When the situation controls you, with a cast of players in the tens of thousands, the situation can get ugly real quick. They're armed and dangerous. We made sure Khan and his people could hold the city.

Once that trust is passed on, any visit in the future will be after hotels and resorts are there with everything working right."

"I am glad we talked John out of going into the Emirates," Johnny said. "You were right about that situation smelling bad, Muerto. I wonder if his friend, Eugene Cummings, went in his place. It may have been equally dangerous for 'The Rattler' to go. I'm sure Kostler knows Alexi handles both fighters."

"I believe Alexi's connections can keep Eugene safe," Nick replied. "Alexi is not someone to take lightly. His container ships help make the world run. The Roma is merely his favorite. Without him as an ally, we would not have been able to bring our UH-60 and lucky XM307 home."

"I want to go on a 'salt the earth' mission," Jean stated.

"Not me," Jay said, shaking his head. "Some of us need to be support personnel. That's me."

"What about you, Cracker?"

Sonny looked with grim determination at Jean. "I go where you go, Viper… always."

Nick clasped Rachel's hand, shaking his head with a smile. "I'm not taking the kids on 'kill missions'. When Jean's ready, trained, old enough, and has the passion for it, we won't be able to stop her no matter what we say. Sonny will make his own way."

"Yeah, Mom… calm down," Jean ordered.

"I see what you mean, Rachel," Jian said. He pointed warningly at Jean, who was gearing up for a smiling addition for Jian. "Do not disrespect your elders."

Nick leaned toward Jean, passing Quinn over to Rachel. "What he said, only double. Are we clear?"

"Yes, Sir," Jean answered in crisp, respectful tone.

* * *

Nick finished 'Hell Zone' with a satisfied flourish while typing 'The End'. He leaned back gazing at the darkening skies.

Jean and Sonny worked on their homework. Nick had promised to play piano for everyone after dinner. He smiled at the sense of excitement he had even playing for their small group. His phone buzzed. The Dark Lord in Muerto t-shirt appeared on his screen, drawing a laugh from Nick.

"Oh my… you've really gotten into the Muerto mood, huh John?"

Silence. Then scurrying around with Jafar yelping in the background amidst much amusement. Harding came back on the phone a few moments later. "Sorry, Nick. I had to rearrange the disrespectful attitude of my IT worker who decided to prank my caller ID."

Nick heard the loud cheering in the background, yelling encouragement to Samira. "It sounds like a party."

"Samira is trying to choke me out in defense of her husband, Jafar, the IT prankster stuffed upside down in our trash barrel. She'll give up in another few moments."

Nick heard an 'Arrrrrghhhh' of disappointed assault. Lynn called her off, having trouble speaking. "Tell Lucas, that was the best! I can't even explain the amount of chaos he caused here in his Muerto pajamas."

"Believe me, Muerto, he knows. I have a problem. Eugene fought Darius last night to a draw, even in the Emirates. It was an incredible match. After the match was the problem. Eugene disappeared. Alexi has every contact he knows decorating the streets with money to find him. Eugene's wife called me."

"Oh boy… I just finished promising I wasn't going back into the Sand. What do you need, brother?"

"It's a trap. Unfortunately, it's in the Emirates' territory. Our government has no interest without proof of foul play. Believe me, Denny and Paul are not happy with this obvious setup. Do you have anyone you trust in the territory."

"I did, but I used them on my last mission there. I relocated them forever with their families. I can make a call to him and see if anyone else he knows would like the same deal. I heard you made an approach through the desert with Claude Chardin's help so as not to be seen in the country while acing Ahmed Quadir. He took you by way of Saudi Arabia. I'm afraid that approach would be my death warrant and yours too after what we did to Cafrey's Isle of Darkness."

"Very true. You're well informed about past missions."

"I found out everything I could about your team after our first meeting," Nick replied. "If I might suggest something, it's possible Claude could help us track down the only one we know could be responsible for this: Amir Mohammed Kostler. Most of these kingpins have wives, lovers, sons, daughters, etc. If Claude located an offspring or loved one of Kostler's, perhaps living here in the states, going to school, or whatever, we snatch them and get Eugene back. Then we deal with Amir down the road at the first opportunity."

Nick listened to the chorus of agreement in the background. "It would be safer than our teams returning to the Sand for another excursion into 'Mission Impossible' territory."

"You're right as rain on that," John agreed. "It seems the Monsters like your idea a lot better. Claude owes you. If I namedrop you into the mix, he'll root out whatever he can. I'll call you back. If we can't find a hostage, I think I'll work on grabbing Kostler. The Rattler getting taken is on my head. I should have told Alexi to ignore the Middle East. If those assholes want a fight, they'll need to bring it to Las Vegas or one of the other UFC venues. Talk with you in a bit. Thanks for the input, Muerto."

"Don't you say it, boy!"

Nick chuckled at Lucas's warning. "Live up to the Legend!"

"That sounded bad," Jean remarked.

"Not really. One of our good guy acquaintances has been taken. John's looking into my idea of taking one of the bad guy kidnapper's loved ones. I should have taken the call out of the room. I'm invoking our secrecy clause, kids. There really isn't anything to talk about anyway until John investigates my problem solution."

"You won't go overseas again this soon, will you, Dad?"

"Not by choice, but some people I can't say no to," Nick replied. "John won't take this lightly. He knows the dangers of going into the Sandpit this soon after our intervention there, and this latest trap set for him in the United Arab Emirates."

"What will you do, Sir," Sonny asked.

Nick moved over to the piano. "I'll sing and play. Sand problems will all go away. Then, I can surely stay."

"Oh barf!" Jean made gagging noises while Sonny enjoyed the interchange with Deke giving out a short bark at Jean's playacting. "Please don't do that rhyme in front of anyone."

"You mean like, 'Once there lived Jean, who craved danger. She treated her dad like a stranger. He trained her not to be so hyper, but she still turned into a Viper. Her friend, Sonny, knew not what to do. He followed her lead without any clue. Throughout her life she got him in trouble, until finally their lives were in turmoil and rubble."

By the time Nick finished his rhyme, Jean was trying to strangle him with Deke tugging on her jeans, growling and nipping. Sonny knew better than to get in the middle of a McCarty family rumble. Rachel entered with a serving tray of veggies and dip.

"What the hell is going on up here? Sonny?"

"No comprende, Senora McCarty."

"Okay… break it up. We have guests coming over."

"Dad's doing rhymes. It was horrible!"

"I shall play piano tonight in honor of my finishing 'Hell Zone'." Nick stood to embrace Rachel. "You can sit next to me."

"Just so she doesn't sing," Jean inserted, trying to placate Deke.

"Very funny, Daughter of Darkness. I'll have you know my singing voice has brightened the day for many people."

"Maybe in Zombie-land. Deke can carry a tune better than you."

Rachel turned to Nick. "Do you have a rhyme for this disrespectful turd."

"Daughter of Darkness, still thy mouth, or I see all your electronics going South. Like buggy whips and hippie style, your iPhone and iPad will be in exile. Gone will be guns and knives, replaced by notepads, pens, and boring lives."

Rachel giggled. "What he said."

"You were in the Sand too long, Dad. It melted your brain."

"You need to fill your mouth with food before anymore tidbits of sarcastic, lifestyle changing crap spews forth," Rachel warned.

"C'mon, Sonny, let's eat before I get locked in a dungeon."

* * *

Nick finished the old 'Four Tops' song 'Reach Out' with Quinn in a swing next to him, gurgling along. Gus, Tina, Johnny, Cala, and Rachel teaching Jian how to dance, filled their huge balcony's makeshift dance floor. Even a very uneasy Sonny swayed with Jean, trying not to misstep, or do something that could get him killed. Nick enjoyed the hesitant Sonny the most as the kid looked at him during each move. As Nick sipped an iced Jim Beam, his phone buzzed with the back to normal Dark Lord on the screen.

"Hey, Dark Lord, what's the good word?"

"I hear laughter and the muttering of people who have been enjoying Muerto the Musician. I am pissed Lora and I aren't there with you."

"Easy, DL. I will come visit my new home in 'The Bay' very soon. You and the Monster Squad, along with the Snow

White Auxiliary are invited to hear the dulcet tones of Muerto anytime down here in the 'Grove', brother."

"Yep. We need to do much more of that and less world saving. You were spot on with suggesting Claude be read in on this. He knows Amir Mohammed Kostler personally. He stopped doing contracts for him a couple of years ago, because Kostler stiffed him on a million-dollar sanction for a Saudi oil executive's demise. Claude warned him, Amir would not be the only one in danger. Someone advised Amir to pay up and shut up. He did, but Claude refused the offers he's received since then from Kostler."

"Nice," Nick replied, seeing right where the conversation was heading. "During the time Claude thought he might get stiffed, he catalogued some relatives of our buddy, Kostler."

"Exactly, my brother, and guess where Amir's number one son goes to college."

"Oh... tell me it ain't so. Picture me with my hands making 'Great Kreskin' gestures of mind concentration. I...I see... the esteemed dreadnaught of higher education, perversity, treason, and snowflake creation laboratories at the California State University at Berkeley, sometimes known as CSU-Berzerkeley."

"Great Muerto Kreskin... you have so nailed it. Amir tried to hide everyone from sight. Claude found them all. He focused on the first son, who goes by the name of Barry Rowlings on the internet. He doesn't seek snowflake degrees. He's in his last post year of med-school and has already completed an internship. Jared Amir Kostler wants to be a surgeon."

"Outstanding, DL! You and the Monsters can collect the seed and get your buddy, Eugene, back safe and sound. Thanks for the update. I'm sure Rachel will be glad."

"Woe... I say woe!"

Nick laughed at John's reference to the 'Foghorn Leghorn' cartoon, complete with voice imitation. "Okay... what's my connection, Dark Lord. Make it vital or the next time I see you will be when I'm playing piano and singing at a chosen meeting spot."

"You number one assassins are kind of needy."

"That's us… or me… as you like it."

"You'll never guess… or yeah, you will… who he watches on YouTube multiple times."

"It must not be the Dark Lord, or this call would be an afterthought. Young Jared would be sharing cells with Mario Garcia, the former agent for violent events involving the MS-13 gangsters."

"We gave Mario a hundred-grand stake to go straight somewhere, along with a new identity. He's a Cruella Deville pet project. We all liked the weasel. You're right. If I was his hero, young Jared would be with me now. His hero is Muerto. We're not sure whether it's your scalpel skill or your absolute emotionless torture unto death of the targets. Jared has an obsession with you."

Nick's mind imagined and projected at breakneck speed. "I'm in, DL. Let's grab him. I won't insult you by asking whether he's under surveillance. I need to deal with this kid out of the shadows in my Muerto persona with Payaso and Kabong. I have plans."

"Please tell me those plans do not involve us in allowing Amir to go free. If they do, you will need to square that with Cruella Deville. She's beginning to dream of an Amir meeting."

Silence.

"Uh oh." John handed the phone over to Lynn Montoya Dostiene.

"Hello… Muerto."

Nick smiled at the slow expulsion of feeling in those two words. "I will explain the nuclear option to you one time, my beloved sister of violence. Please turn to your husband, Clint, and ask him what became of the last couple who thought they could threaten me with extinction. I'll wait."

Nick grinned as he heard Clint whispering rapidly in Lynn's ear. This interaction could go either way. He heard bits and pieces Clint tried to explain to Lynn.

"You do know Clint and I fear nothing right?"

"That's a lie, Sis. You fear for Clint Jr. I fear for Rachel, Jean, Quinn, Deke the dog, and everyone else in my care as the Terminator. To progress in this operation, you need to know I will allow Amir to live at this time, until I see in the soul of Jared. Our mission is to get Eugene Cummings alive, and back to his family. From that point, some options are open. Others are not."

"Did you torture Kate Fuller to death in front of Jean?"

"Jean was in a limousine, driven by Payaso. They sped away after I pulped Kate's paramour, Sam Jessop's head, and put a .50 caliber round through Kate's shoulder. She did not see what followed, although I realize rumor states differently. You can ask her."

"You had an affair with Kate."

"So… what's your point, Lynn? Kate was ready to kill me after our group action in Oakland, John called me into. I warned her and Sam to never come after me once that gig was over. They ignored my warning. You and Clint understand this as I do. I go full bore until I know everyone is safe or I have lost everything. Then, the closing round bell rings. Nothing in creation will be safe after that happens. No words, no promises, no begging, pleading, or monetary recompense ends until my heart stills."

"Kate was like me, wasn't she?"

"Nope. Kate didn't have your skills, your intelligence, or your loyalty. That fact cost her. Kate lost the rather narrow life she had carved out doing killings without feeling, purpose, or passion for what she believed in. She died of stupidity. Kate probably talked Sam into taking the hit on me from Frank Richert."

"This isn't a threat then, right?"

"Only if you make it so, Lynn. If I give my word to someone that another human being will not perish if they do as I say, that word carries weight. I will never kill you or Clint. We're family. If you take out Amir Mohammed Kostler, after I promise he won't be killed to his kid, I will never contact John's Monster Squad again. I will kill Jared to leave nothing and no one at my back. Then, we part ways."

Lynn chuckled. "That leaves it that if Amir doesn't go straight and narrow, he could meet with an accident, right?"

"Absolutely. I'd make that a stipulation when dealing with young Jared."

"What's the long view in this you have plans for?"

"Our new City of Hope needs doctors. I'd like to see where Jared's head is at. If he wants to heal people while observing how former Muslims live from the same background after throwing off Islam, the City of Hope can use him."

"Well hell… that's a damn good plan. Maybe I won't need to carve you up after all."

"Gee… thanks, Lynn, I appreciate that."

"You handled that nicely, Muerto." John took over the call again. "Jared lives off campus, which helps us immensely. I would like to do this snatch quickly and quietly in the night. We'll EMP the outside to make sure nothing gets recorded. It's a gamble using the electromagnetic pulse rifle. We would like to take a look at his electronics inside, but that can't be helped. You, Payaso, and Kabong will pluck him after a sleepy-time syringe shot, letting Jared see who is taking him. At Pain Central, you guys can explain the situation to him while I get Amir on the phone. Claude has both his email address and his private cell-phone number. Unfortunately, he uses an ancient phone without GPS, or we'd be wheels up, going to get him."

"I like the plan. When would you want to do this?"

"We would like to watch his every move for a couple of days, especially his night moves. Would Friday night be okay with you?"

"Sure, John. We'll fly up for the weekend. Has Amir contacted you in any way?"

"Not yet. We think he was waiting for us to fly into his trap inside the Emirates first. We figure he'll contact us through Alexi in the next day or so. We may even have his son by the time he contacts us. That would be very convenient and intense. By the way, Denny had the Ranger steamed down into our port. She's huge. We all wanted to see her since the improvements. Besides, Lucas is hot to take her out on a real cruise. It would be great to have Gus and Lucas piloting us somewhere with everyone on board."

"It would indeed," Nick agreed. "I'll tell the troops we're heading for 'The Bay' Friday after the kids get out of school. Jean and Sonny are here with us. As you heard, we were having a small celebration."

"Does Sonny ever go home?"

Nick glanced at Sonny's grim face. "Not much. His folks have some other plot in the works I'm hoping is just one of their usual schemes. I have their house bugged because those two are dangerous. Sonny and Jean handle the investigation. Sonny goes over the audio at the end of the day with Jean taking notes on anything questionable."

"Phil and Clarice are quite a pair. I bet it makes you think the stork delivered Sonny."

"Rachel believes he was stolen from the maternity ward," Nick answered. "California is due for another dry spell. Have Dev call down the rain."

Nick listened to his audience in Pain Central enjoying Nick's solution to California drought season.

Chapter Four: Home Fires

Nick's audience awaited word with intense anticipation. "No Sand. You probably heard we need to journey to 'The Bay' for the weekend. Cala can pilot with Johnny working co-pilot for practice. The UH-60 will get us there in no time. We'll visit the 7D Experience and kill some zombies. I love our house there."

"You're avoiding the elephant in the room," Rachel said. "I know you have a mission to help the Dark Lord with the cartoons, but what was the discussion with Crue? I heard you mention Kate and Sam."

"Lynn had other ideas for Amir Mohammed Kostler. I needed to make it plain if I promise his kid the dad lives if Eugene Cummings isn't hurt, then I don't want him getting the Dr. Deville exploding blood vessel treatment. Crue decided to bait me a little. I had Clint tell her what happened to Kate and Sam. I needed to clear the air about what I will do and what I won't."

"Understood," Rachel replied. "Do you believe after what Amir did you'll be able to save him? He planned to entrap and kill Harding's crew, and as I understand it, that's what he tried to do by taking Cummings as a hostage."

"It will be delicate. Sometimes, these Middle East idiots with high sounding titles think because they have a lot of money, they can't be reached. We've already nicked them, but they don't pay attention. When they learn their offspring can be reached, they many times have a change of heart. You heard my City of Hope idea. They have people there with some medical experience, but they would need to see a doctor or surgeon in one of the nearby cities if something serious happens. Amir's kid graduated from Cal State Berkeley. Through them, he has completed his internship, and continues while a resident. I'd like to see how he feels about life without Islam."

"We heard he's an Unholy Trio fan," Gus said. "This operation will be what Johnny needs to get his YouTube channel out ranking the cat videos again."

"Yes, I was overcome by a kitten that chased its own tail for five minutes straight," Johnny admitted. "It was very embarrassing."

"Enough." Cala stood amidst loud amusement. "Play 'House of the Rising Sun', Muerto. Let's dance again, Johnny."

Johnny stood. He grasped Cala's hands while Nick sipped his iced Beam brother. "We escaped the hell of Islam. We have so much now with our child on the way. I pray we will be able to help the City of Hope."

"We will, my husband. Muerto will see to it as he has provided our escape from hell."

Nick played a long ranging interlude of monumental jazzed proportions to begin 'House of the Rising Sun', with Gus and Tina joining with Johnny and Cala. Sonny hesitantly reached for Jean's hand, dancing with her as prescribed by Rachel with only hands touching. She smiled at her husband and made Jian continue his dance lesson.

Nick met her gaze as he played, wondering if somewhere in her head she wasn't thinking about Sonny's parents. He lost his train of thought when Deke bumped against him. It was all he could do to continue with the song after noticing Deke was swinging with the music. *I shouldn't have given him that second beer.*

Nick's security system warning kicked in as he entered into his second Barry White song. After glancing at his balcony monitor, Nick hurried downstairs with .45 caliber silenced Colt in hand he had grabbed from his balcony hutch. Reaper/Dark Dragon/Unholy Trio at his back, also held weapons. A woman and her two kids stood at his doorstep. They were pre-kindergarten age. Nick swept by her, looking for targets, as his friends ushered her inside. His eyes narrowed, honed on target, decades of training, instinct, and survival kicking in as the big sedan climbed the hill toward his house. Waiting until it leveled out onto his street, Nick fired a round through the driver's head.

As the sedan meandered into the curb, Nick shot everyone in the car, rushing at it, picking his targets, and zeroing in on where he needed to hit them. The adrenaline flow cascading through his body erased his Beam buzz, and settled him into war zone mode. Johnny, Gus and Jian encircled the car, listening unaffected by the screams and cries inside. Nick ran around to the driver's side, moved the console shift into park, and pulled the dead driver out into the street. He reached in, shut off the engine, and methodically pulled the key from the ignition. Nick dragged the corpse to the trunk, opened it, and dead lifted the body inside.

Nick returned to the passengers with a big grin. "Hello there. Who wants to live? I need information. Anyone not giving me what I need gets a bullet in the head."

"I…I'm bad hurt," a tattooed gangbanger in the back cried out, blood frothing at his mouth from a lung shot.

Nick shot him through the head. "Dr. Muerto is in. Can I help anyone else who would like to be pain free immediately?"

"You can't just… execute us!"

Nick executed him immediately. "Another poor hurting soul found hell. Speak helpfully or Dr. Muerto will help you into the next dimension."

A face tattooed mobster writhing on the backseat next to the two corpses spoke in halting but accurate tone. He had been the last shot by Nick in the belly. "Anything! What do you want!"

"That's more like it. A friend of mine's family just arrived at my doorstep. I know you bunch of MS-13 gangbanging idiots know why. Tell me fast. I can keep you in pain for a week with that belly wound, asshole."

The man with the top part of his right shoulder shot to pieces groaned while struggling to contain the blood oozing in a stream down his chest. "We…we got hired to find and kill… Nick McCarty! We took Dickerson tonight… on the street… by his house… making noise… so his wife would look and see. She led us to you."

Nick smiled. The kill button had been pushed. The Terminator began to finish what he had started without the solution. A hand reached his shoulder, tentatively pulling on it.

"We need to know where Neil is, Muerto," Cala pleaded. She had seen the face of death before. Knowing the Beam led to a gap in perception, controlling the killing and maiming part of Nick's head, she acted.

Nick's finger pad eased away from the trigger. He took a deep breath. "Thanks, Reaper. You didn't drink tonight, did you?"

"No, Muerto… I am with child. I will drive to our place in the Valley."

"No time, Reaper. Speak! Where is Neil Dickerson?" Nick made the razor-sharp stiletto appear as if by magic. "Tell me now or Dr. Muerto starts surgery!"

The man with the belly wound gasped out the address, pleading for something to block the pain. Nick shot him in the head, along with the shoulder wounded man. Nick dragged them to the trunk, depositing them with Gus, Johnny, and Jian's help. The cargo compartment on the Cadillac was huge. They stuffed the bodies at odd broken angles to make them fit before closing the trunk.

"I'll get some blankets for the ride," Nick said. "You drive, Reaper. We'll settle this tonight, no matter what."

"Yes, Muerto."

"We're good to go, Nick," Gus said, as he followed Nick to the door of the house.

"I know, Gus." Rachel met Nick with a tarp in hand. She heard Nick and found a better cover. Neil's wife and kids sat on the couch in their living room. Jean and Sonny stood in front of them, knives in hand.

"Stand down, kids. Lock up behind us when I leave." Nick ran to enter the bottom floor safe-room. He retrieved MP5 submachine guns, two ET-MP grenades, and Kevlar vests, stuffing them all into his equipment bag. Nick hugged Rachel before retrieving his satellite laptop from the entryway. "Set the alarms, keep Deke nearby, and get your new Glock out. Stay away from the windows until I sort this out, babe."

Rachel kissed him. "I will."

"Nick! Please bring Neil home!"

Nick glanced at Neil's wife and kids. "I will, Linda, if it's humanly possible."

With Gus's help, Nick spread the tarp over the seats. He smoothed down the part covering the front flooring so it did not impede Cala's driving, but still covered the blood. Gus, Johnny and Jian tamped down the tarp between the seats. Nick passed the equipment bag over the seat. As they drove toward their destination, all of them glanced around, looking for neighbors taking notice.

"I used to think you keeping a weapon with silencer in multiple parts of your house was overkill," Gus said. "Silly me. Do you have a plan?"

"I'm working on it, Payaso. Get the Kevlar on. Check your weapons. Insert your earwigs. Cala will keep us on network. We get Neil back. No prisoners." Nick flitted over images of the address given to him. "There's a fenced off property across from them with trees and bushes partially hiding the short turnoff there. We'll park in the turn out opposite the house. I'll go find Neil first. I'm hoping they haven't been here long enough to have dogs. If they do have dogs, my plan changes. Pass me the grenades, Payaso. I'll stick with my Colt. Dig out my extra magazines too."

When they arrived at the street, Plumas Road in Seaside, Cala turned off the headlights, easing the Cadillac into the turnoff Nick mentioned. Before getting out of the Cadillac, Nick checked his network connection. He pointed down the road the way they had come.

"I'll head that way, circle back, and slip along the wide driveway to the rear of the house. If I find Neil, I will make a final assessment then. We're in luck. It's on a hill with unfenced front access. The house faces away from us. The brush on the hill should make it nearly impossible to see my approach from the house unless someone actually comes out to check."

Nick slipped quickly from the Cadillac, staying crouched next to it for a moment while watching the dimly lit house across the street. Nothing stirred there. Nick hurried along the underbrush for fifty yards, crossed the street, and stopped before the driveway entrance. He instead trekked upward over the rough brush, where a bare path had been worn in the sloping terrain leading to the house. Nick paused before he became visible over the slope, taking out his night-vision ocular. He scanned the grounds on the left side of the house with garage under it. Nothing prevented access to the house rear grounds. In one way, the wild brush helped conceal his approach, but because of the noise factor, Nick stayed at the edge of the cement driveway.

Hurrying to the under-the-house attached garage's side, Nick slipped alongside the garage wall to the rear. With his night-vision ocular, he scanned the uncut rear tangled brush lawn. No sign of anyone, either person or animal, showed during his area scan. The front windows, where a porch and stairway access enabled entrance, had been closed off by heavy blinds. Nick checked the darkened windows of the garage. Although drape covered, he could see the inside through the gap with his ocular. A body, tied and gagged, was anchored tightly with a chain to the middle garage support beam. Nick took the screen out of each window, his gloved hands feeling for any gap between the frame and window. The rearmost window slid open sideways, not having been locked into position.

Uncaring now who heard what, Nick scrambled over the window frame, keeping as silent as possible. His first priority shifted to getting between the body and the entrance into the house from the garage. Nick turned the body so he could look into the person's face. Neil's groggy, half lidded stare widened slightly with recognition. Nick made shushing gestures at Neil while cutting away his bonds.

"I have Neil," Nick whispered into the network. "Do you read?"

"Loud and clear, Muerto," Gus said.

"Good. I'm sure you saw me approach the house. Go up the same path to the side of the garage. Kabong watches with MP5 while I hand Neil to you and Dragon Breath, Gus. Take him to the car, while Reaper keeps watch on the house. She can keep Neil steady in the car while we finish this."

"You shall pay for insulting Dark Dragon, Muerto!"

Nick grinned, carrying Neil with arm draped over his shoulder, to the opened garage window. He never lost line of sight with the house entrance. His hand holding the silenced Colt never moved from the door. Gus and Jian reached in to help Nick ease Neil through the opening noiselessly. Without a word, Gus and Jian hurried Neil down to the Cadillac, where Cala waited at the rear door away from the house. She opened it and Gus helped Neil inside.

Johnny kept watch with the MP5 at the ready until his friends returned. The three then waited at the ready in front of the garage near the stairwell to the porch.

"We're in position, Muerto," Gus said.

"The only reason I don't blow the house up right now is they may have other hostages. Plus, I want to learn whose idea this was. We cleaned these suckers out. No way should the damn government have allowed any importation of more, so we also need to find out how they got in the country. The idiots are wearing labels across their faces. How hard can it be to round these pricks up?"

"A discussion for another time," Gus replied.

"Right you are. Stay put. I'll see how close I can get to these guys."

Nick slowly turned the knob on the entryway door to the house, while standing clear of the door on the landing. It opened as he gently applied pressure. He could hear a TV blaring inside which he knew would cover any noise the door made. Automatic weapons fire blew the center of the door apart. The moment the weapon stopped, Nick put his Colt through the hole in the door and fired three shots into the stomach of the man aiming an AK47 at the door. He fell screaming to the floor, hands clutching his spilling entrails. Nick shot him in the head.

"Hold guys. I'm good. Get anyone running out the front. Wound if possible."

"Understood," Gus acknowledged.

Nick waited by the door, only partially exposed by the door jamb. He sighted through the blown-out hole. Two more gang-members ran around the corner toward him, both with hand weapons. Nick shot them both in the shoulder of their shooting arms. He heard shots at the front before a huge guy rounded the corner of the bedroom at the house's rear most part of the hallway. Nick shot him in both knees. The knife he rushed down the hallway with clattered to the floor. Nick inspected it, and pocketed it. He restrained the big guy at ankles and wrists.

"If they ran out the front, guys, c'mon in. I'm working the back."

"Understood. Two down in front," Gus said. "We'll drag them in. They're both living, but unhappy."

"I'm checking the bedrooms now," Nick replied. "Hold in position, ready for anything at your end. Wait one."

Nick kicked the now screaming one with bad knees in the head, silencing him. "Sorry. I was having trouble concentrating. I'll clear the bedrooms and be back with you in a few minutes."

Nick moved from shabby bedroom to shabby bedroom. They were all empty, until he reached the one the big guy attacked him from. A girl in her early teens lay tied to the bedframe, her eyes only blinking slightly as she saw Nick enter the room. He cleared the room with care, only then lowering his Colt.

"Please! Please… don't kill me," the girl pleaded.

Nick freed her while making shushing sounds. "No one will hurt you. You're a bit of an inconvenience, but we'll get you back to your family somehow. I'll tell you who I am, but my solution to your problem won't be part of strict law enforcement. I will make sure you get back where you belong, but the people here in this house who took you won't be going to trial."

A grim aspect settled over the girl's features. "I understand. If…if I can get home… I don't want to know who you are. I will deal… thank you."

"No thanks necessary. C'mon, we have a few unpleasant things to do in here. I will take you to my associate, Cala. She'll take excellent care of you until we finish in here, okay?"

The girl hugged him.

Nick held her for a moment and then patted her shoulder. "You need to put some clothes on first though."

Nick turned around. "What's your name?"

"Dierdre Fulmington. I…I did something really stupid. I went to a Rave down in LA. The next thing I knew… I was tied to this bed." Dierdre collapsed on the bed, sobbing with gut wrenching cries of anguish.

Nick glanced back to make sure she had clothes on. Once he noted she had on a blouse and jeans, he turned to comfort her, thinking of Jean, who was probably only a few years younger. He gripped her shoulders. "No time for that right now, Dierdre. No one will ever know what happened here. My crew will say nothing and every person who laid a hand on you will be dead."

The girl nodded, shuddered, and turned to continue putting on her footwear. Nick escorted her by the dead and soon to be dead. His crew smiled at the young Dierdre, mouthing all the right things. Nick knew she would either succumb to self-pity and the victim syndrome so popular today, or get ready to rumble. As he walked her over to the waiting Cadillac, Nick talked to her gently about the future.

"No one listens to me anyway, but let me give you a piece of advice, kid. Put this all behind you in a locked part of your mind. Draw on it only when you are tempted to do something else foolish or deadly. We all make bad errors in judgement. When given a second chance with real life logic, what we do with the knowledge makes all the difference in the world. I know just how I'll cover for you on this. How much or how little you say after that will be up to you, okay?"

"I can handle it. Who...who are you guys. That MS-13 gang... they're the most terrifying people... I'd ever seen. They didn't have a prayer against you."

"We're the people they call when all else fails. When we are asked to intervene, we don't take bad guys to court. We make sure they never do bad things again."

Dierdre smiled as Cala left the Cadillac to greet her. "I can handle that."

Nick patted her shoulder. "I'll get one of my crew to go with Cala to take you to my house with my police lieutenant friend. Once my business is finished, I'll take you home. My wife will help you get cleaned up and find some clothes for you."

"Sure... that would be great."

"I'm Cala." Dierdre shook hands with Cala. "Ride in the front with me."

"I'll get Johnny to ride with you and drop Neil and Dierdre at my house. Bring my Ford and the Cadillac back."

"Yes, Muerto. You'll wait for us, right? No neighbors stuck their noses out. They must know the MS-13 boys like to rock and roll. Tonight, they got rolled. Tell Johnny to get a move on. I want to be at the interrogation."

Nick grinned. "I see your being pregnant hasn't mellowed you out much, Reaper."

"Heh...heh... not hardly."

* * *

"Here's the deal guys," Nick stated, walking amongst the tethered MS-13 gang. "We're not here to rehabilitate you, deport you, or hear your views on life. I'm Dr. Muerto. My associates are Dr. Payaso, Kabong, Dark Dragon, and Reaper. I brought a scalpel and this big bottle of Clorox that was under the sink. Answer my questions and you all get to go into the afterlife without much pain. Now, let's start off with my first-"

"I ain't tellin' you shit," one of the men who Gus, Johnny and Jian captured stated while spitting on the floor.

"We have a volunteer already! That's great. I'm sure your buddies will learn by your example. Gag him, Payaso."

After being gagged and restrained more tightly in a chair, Nick tore away the man's clothing, baring his chest, belly, and upper groin area. With practiced ease, Nick sliced him from sternum to groin deep enough to bulge the intestines. Johnny poured Clorox over the visible intestines. Gus anchored the chair with Nick's help while the man bucked in place, squealing through his gag until he passed out. The begging and pleading started immediately from the man's cohorts. Nick shushed them.

"I think we have answered the question of whether you will help us or not. I should give all of you Dr. Muerto's intestinal cleaning treatment for what you did to that young girl. Let's start with who hired you idiots to do this?"

"Our... boss... Tito Salento!" One of the men answered immediately with his companions shaking their heads in the affirmative.

"Where can I find him?"

"He...he's the guy in the hall you killed."

"Tito's not dead yet. I blew away his knees. Why would Tito want to come after me, and kidnap the police lieutenant?"

"You killed his brother. Tito find out... that lieutenant had something to do with it. We asked around hard about you and Dickerson. When he gets problems, Dickerson calls you. Tito took the chance if we grabbed him, the wife would go to you instead of the police."

The speaker's face revealed he thought maybe the rest of his gang had the woman and her kids. "They went after you. I bet they got her and the kids. Maybe… we can get them back for you."

"You idiot," Cala said. "Muerto killed them all. The lieutenant's family is at Muerto's house. The gangbangers are outside, stuffed in the back of your gang's Cadillac. Do you have another vehicle?"

Silence.

"Uh oh… it's best not to hold out on Muerto," Cala continued. "He will give all of you an intestinal cleaning like your friend."

"Blue Dodge van on the street. Tito has the keys."

"How did you bunch get in the country?" Nick moved closer to the speaker.

"Los Zetas smuggled us in before the border crackdown. Tito's brother was an enforcer with them."

"Ah oh… another damn continuation," Nick said to his friends. "What's his name. I think I could guess but I'd rather hear it from you."

"Raul… Raul Zeron. Raul changed his name from Pedro Salento when he went to work with the Zetas. Tito waited when he heard another Zeta guy was going to check on your crew as suspects. When they disappeared, Tito checked your past. He knew you did it. After Vasco and his crew disappeared, the Zetas didn't want any more to do with you. Bangers in Salinas know you and Dickerson are tight. They told us to stay away. Tito wouldn't listen."

"They were smart. Tito's not," Nick replied.

"Let us go, man! We don't ever come back."

"Not happening. Some mistakes you don't walk away from. You guys earned your shot of happiness. Don't piss me off and go down the Dr. Muerto road like your buddy."

Nick injected each one. When it was over, he and Johnny dragged Tito to one of the vacated chairs, cinching him tightly in place. Gus threw some water in Tito's face, bringing him to sputtering consciousness. Tito screamed when the awakened pain in his knees knifed into his skull. Nick slapped him hard in the face until Tito got the message and shut up.

"Hi there. I heard you were looking for me. Your mysteries are solved. Yes, I'm Nick McCarty and yes, I blew your brother's head off with a .50 caliber depleted uranium slug. He was down in Texas, killing Americans."

"I...I will kill you for this. One day, I will get out. You are a dead man!"

Gus, Johnny, Jian and Cala all enjoyed Tito's declaration, with Cala clapping her hands. Nick patted Tito's face. "You are a funny guy. I knew you would be. This is just as well. You're far too stupid for this gig."

Nick's face grew solemn with the task ahead. "I don't know how you think this will end, but when you raped the little girl, you earned a different ending than your crew got."

"Nobody touches Tito! The Zetas will hunt you down."

Nick sliced the clothing from Tito's front with his knife, spreading the clothing out. He then showed Tito his scalpel. "Would you like to say a prayer or something before I begin? You won't be able to say much once I start."

"Fuck you, poser!"

"Oh yeah," Nick whispered. He put the gag in place over Tito's mouth. Nick sliced through tissue like a born surgeon. "Doctor Muerto is in the house!"

Over the next hour, nothing saved Tito's sanity or life. He stroked out in the middle of his third round through the intestinal cleansing. Nick sighed, glancing at his friends. "Well, now for the boring part. Let's get the van loaded. I have a case of magnesium flares in the Ford. I hate to say this, but it would probably be better if we pack the bodies in the Ford for the freezer. We'll prep them after our gig in the North. We'll torch their vehicles in the sand between here and Route 156. We'll need to keep them tarped at the Carmel Valley house. No one will miss this bunch. No need to put a rush on them tonight."

"Good," Cala said. "After we finish, you can drive back to the 'Grove' with Jian and Gus. I know Neil won't say much besides thanks, but do you have a plan to get Diedre home without a lot of problems?"

"That's the reason for the stashed vehicles and bodies. I'll deliver her to a couple of happy parents and do my US Marshal ploy. I'll tell them because the MS-13 gang members were all illegal aliens, we took them into federal custody with the possibility they will be detained on terrorism charges too. Gus, Jian, and I will put on our US Marshal Kevlar vests like we just came from the raid."

"The story has holes, but not much can be done about them," Gus added. "I hope Diedre will be okay in her head after that ordeal."

"She seemed tough enough to handle it, but we can't fix everything. You'll be with me when we deliver her home. All we can do is look for signs she may need help coping. We can talk later. I'll go get the van and back it to the door."

"I wish we could have done a cartoon video. I lose ground to the cat videos daily," Johnny remarked. "I dropped under a cat hopping on a cucumber this morning."

"I'm certain we'll do better in Oakland," Nick replied after an amused break. "We must be masked or both Amir and his son will have to die. This crap may be too complex anyway."

"The City of Hope needs him, Muerto," Cala stated, following Nick to the door.

"I know. A growing city with a resort will need many more like Jared. He may have talent for organization too. Eventually, a hospital will need to be built with someone to run it and recruit. Later for all this talk. We have bodies to move, this house to wipe down, cops to awaken from their drugged sleep, and young girls to return home."

"I see a couple of Bushmills on the deck later, Muerto," Johnny said.

"Amen to that."

"Don't forget you'll need to walk Deke," Gus called out after him.

"Damn it! Thanks, Payaso… you prick!"

Gus chuckled. "Anytime."

* * *

Linda hugged Nick and Gus after they helped put Neil to bed. "Will he be okay?"

"Don't worry, Linda. Neil will be fine," Nick promised. "I will be over tomorrow to talk with him. Remember not to let him talk about this to anyone until he speaks to me."

"I'll make sure of it. This used to be the quietest town."

"People are saying that in a lot of towns," Nick replied. "The globalists have been throwing open the borders to third world terrorists and low life thugs as a way to control our populace. They believe if you import the lowest common denominator of violent hordes, the world will all be under a one world order police state."

"Do you really think that's true?"

"Nick's theory is the only one that fits this weirdo descent into darkness," Gus answered. "Why in the world would nations be importing malcontents who drain our economies dry? Anyhow, Nick and I need to take Dierdre home."

Linda turned her attention to the young girl smiling at the doorway. "You have my phone number, honey. If you need to talk with anyone, call me."

"I promise, Linda." Dierdre shook her hand. "Rachel and Tina told me the same thing. If I can't get a grip on this, I will call."

* * *

Nick and Gus walked away from Dierdre's home with some uneasiness. The dad wanted vengeance and the mom wanted to sue everyone in existence. They had been tearfully joyous to have Dierdre back, but Nick's explanations of vague justice did not sit well with either parent. Nick had finally needed to explain Dierdre's rapist was killed during the action, which was quickly corroborated by Dierdre. The conversation went downhill from there.

Only Dierdre bursting into tears and hugging Nick ended the verbal retribution he and Gus listened to. "They saved my life! They can't change what happened!"

Dierdre's outburst quieted the parents finally, allowing Nick and Gus to leave the family with the promise they would stay in touch.

"Wow, that went well," Gus said.

"It probably went better than it should have. I could put myself in the dad's shoes. The only thing making the conversation bearable was remembering Tito's passing."

"Yeah... he paid for his crimes here on earth. It's only eleven. I think I'll have a Bushmills with you after we walk Deke. Tina only had a glass of wine before dinner. She won't mind driving if you play a little piano."

"I can do that. Sipping and playing will be very comforting after tonight. I can't do it too late. The kids have school tomorrow. I'm walking them with Deke. Want to have an Irish morning at the 'Point'?"

"Hell yeah. We need a nice easy morning with Johnny and Jian before our trip North. An Irish coffee conference fits our schedule for figuring on a form of action taking Amir's kid too. I sure hope he can be made to understand. It's hard to believe he's an Unholy Trio fan."

"We have no way of knowing if he is or not," Nick replied. "It could be the videos stir him into jihadi action figure territory. He could be plotting some way to get at us for Amir. It's my imagination conjuring him into a City of Hope surgeon and hospital administrator. At least we're not handling the details for this snatch and grab kidnapping. John knows the North much better than I do. Since forming his Oaktown Cartel, John's information network is impressive."

"I wonder how much notoriety he accrued during the UK intervention with his incredible win over Carl Logan. He beat the undefeated Heavyweight Boxing Champ. That, in tandem with his YouTube video matches, military, CIA, and FBI connections, probably make it impossible for him to go unnoticed anywhere. The speech he gave in the UK went viral with you singing 'God Bless the Queen'. Anonymity will no longer be a problem for you two."

"The media buried most of the sensationalism because they want what we did to fail miserably. The globalists are none too pleased with our operations. They know who revamped Cafrey's Isle of Darkness. Success with the City of Hope will have them screaming for our heads. Unfortunately for them, we have those memory discs in our hands. Paul let me know he and Denny have made it plain any action by the leaders in that idiotic one world order movement will mean disaster for them. This time we have the CIA Director on our side with video, financial, and hard copy proof with what we scavenged from Cafrey's island. Paul warned me they would like to do a drone strike on us."

"We saved a family and a young girl tonight."

"I hope I can frame that in a way with Neil tomorrow where he might overlook the part about Tito and his MS-13 gang looking for revenge mostly on me."

"My advice is let Neil ask the questions. You form the answers in a way our rescue tonight was a heroic action rather than self-defense."

"I'll make a note. What if he asks the wrong questions?"

"Use the phrase 'I don't recall'. It works for the politicos."

* * *

Neil drove his squad car next to the small group of Nick, Jean, Sonny, Jay, and Deke the dog. Nick's head turned to scan the area with his peripheral vision constantly. He caught sight of Lieutenant Dickerson and waved. He stopped everyone and handed Deke's leash to Jean.

"I need to talk with Neil for a moment."

"Okay, Dad."

"Hey… no Quinn this morning?"

"He's teething. His nose is running so much I was afraid we'd need to put a scarf around it. I'll walk him down to the beach with the rest of the cartoons. It'll take his mind off it and the salt air might do him some good. How are you doing?"

"A little confused but it'll pass. I don't know what to say except thanks. I'm pretty sure it had something to do with our actions against the gangs. I don't know exactly why. Maybe that's for the best. I should never have been blindsided like they did to me. I imagine no one will ever hear from them again, huh?"

"Not without a medium and a séance."

"Linda told me they held a young girl captive."

"The leader, Tito, did it. He paid for his crimes."

"Yuck."

"That's not exactly what he said. I texted the address to you this morning where they stayed. You'll find trace of them there, plus all their phones. They didn't have anything else. Johnny downloaded everything on them so you can do what you like with them."

"I'll be more careful from now on, Nick."

"Maybe now would be a good time to kick free of me, my friend. You've probably seen my gang mixed in with John Harding's crew up North, fighting terrorists and building cities. We're moving up everyone's list of people the globalists want dead."

"It's too late for that, Nick. Call me if you find out anything I need to know."

"It's your funeral. I believe Linda may want this to end."

"Doin' right ain't got no end!" Neil drove off before Nick could respond to his favorite smartass remark fed back to him.

Nick grinned and returned to where the kids were stifling laughter. "Not funny, big ears. I guess I won't need to stop by Neil's place now. I know I've been away and that usually means trouble. Do you three have any information not passed on to my lovely wife?"

"You mean other than your father is a racist, Islamophobe," Jean asked sweetly.

"Really? Is someone picking on you because of the recent news?"

Jean smirked at Nick as he took Deke's leash again. "No one picks on the three of us… no one. Everyone stays away from us except the kids who do get picked on. We take them into protective custody until it stops."

"Well done. You've obviously handled it discreetly or your mom would have been wringing me out to dry."

"Wringing you out to… oh… you mean like twisting a wet towel? You need to get new lines, Dad," Jean advised.

"Why? You've never heard them. So, who is it saying this? Remember, Islam is not a race or a religion. It is a Sharia Law

Death Cult, hell bent on conquering the world, while torturing and killing anyone who does not believe as they do. How do we put that in Snowflake terms, children?"

"Islam is not a race or a religion. It is a political ideology, based on subjugation of others," the three kids intoned together as taught.

"Excellent."

"We tried that on him," Jean said. "I thought his head would explode. He's the fiancé of a six-grade teacher. You know the type. She's blonde, blue-eyed, and probably carries one of those signs in demonstrations I've seen on Facebook, with 'I open my legs for the refugees'."

Nick lost all train of thought, intents for admonition, and breath for the next few moments, as Jean high-fived her minions. "Oh... my... God... you girl, are a treasure. Okay... this airhead teacher thinks Sharia Law does not apply to her, and the boyfriend coddles her infidel mind with what, kids?"

"Taquiyya, the allowance by Islam to lie to the infidels," the three answered.

"That's the one. How did this incident happen and what's the fallout?"

"No fallout, Dad," Jean answered. "We waited for mom on the inside of the door to the school while you were away. She was a little late because Quinn's car-seat busted. She had to wait for Tina to get there before coming after us. The teacher, Brittany Weber, tried to hurry past us, but the boyfriend stopped her. He pointed at us and asked, 'are these the children'. She got a scared look on her face for a moment, but nodded yes. That's when he slandered you. Brit had to grab him after we answered him correctly together."

Nick took a deep breath. "Gee, the offended Muslim - picks out kids, insults the father of one of the kids, and then gets ready to kick the crap out of them when he's answered the way he should be answered. You had your knives, right?"

"We had them out the moment he moved toward us, behind our leg where they couldn't be seen, ready to thrust," Sonny answered. "We work on it together all the time, Sir. I'm the tallest. I strike high, Jay strikes middle, Jean gives the victim what she calls the Cruella Deville haircut."

Another pause while Nick enjoyed yet another dead pan gem. "I…I swear. You kids are missing your calling. Stand-up comedy should be in your future. I have to tell Crue that one when I see her."

Jean giggled. "I texted it to her, describing our training strike method. She texted back with one of those wide-eyed emojis with 'Oh no you didn't just label the groin strike a Cruella Deville haircut'. I wrote back, 'yep, for all time'. She loved it."

"I'll bet she did." Nick walked along, signaling Deke into different commands with his hand, as he had been training his beer buddy intensely during off-times.

The kids watched with fascination as they approached the school. Deke would alternately move, ready to strike between Nick's legs, prance next to him, side by side touching his leg, or launch in front, moving side to side in front of Nick. The kids gasped at Nick's drop of the leash and hatchet like command with his hand held in chopping form. Deke streaked forward twenty feet, snarling and growling, while moving back and forth sideways. A two-toned short whistle from Nick brought him back.

"Deke's as smart as Clint's dog, Tonto. Dogs love training, treats, and performing. After a time, they do whatever you teach them because they love and respect you. Me and Deke are mates, right Deke?"

Deke leaped into Nick's arms at a single gesture. Nick cradled him and he pretended to be sleeping to the wonderment of the kids. Nick laid him gently down, then whistled again. Deke strode at his side, brushing against his leg.

"That is so cool," Jean exclaimed. "We'll work with him too. Deke… the wonder dog."

Deke's ears perked up, waiting for follow through, but let out a 'grumpf' when not directed as expected.

They approached the school with all out concentration. The military aspect made Nick smile. He remembered his training. In many ways, people train like dogs when danger threatens. If reaction falls short of solution, a soldier dies. Sonny's description of a planned mode of attack honed both concentration and thwarted a combat flaw: hesitation. Nick noted far too many adolescents meandering around, unaware of danger, while they texted, gamed, or vaped out in some other way mentally. Survival instinct in today's generation dropped right off in the face of a new text message. The only time he ever saw Jean, Sonny, or Jay with phone or tablet out involved crime scenes and important facts they observed needing recorded.

Nick installed one rule with anyone chauffeuring the kids anywhere – make sure to walk them to the door or very close to it. Because of his size, Nick walked Deke to the outer curb around the entrance and waited until the kids entered the school before leaving. Today would not be a day for leaving right away. He saw the kids accosted by a Middle Eastern man at the entrance with a security guard. Nick knew most of the security guards but did not recognize this one. He smiled as Jean took lead, listening intently to what the guy blabbered about. When he finished, Jean pointed at Nick and walked by with Sonny and Jay in tow.

Nick watched the guy frothing at the mouth to grab Jean, but even he wasn't stupid enough to lay hands on an underage girl, at least not until his Sharia Law travesty became the law of the land. *I won't need to worry about that*, Nick thought, *because I'll be dead.* The man motioned the security guard to follow him out to confront Nick.

"This man is an Islamophobe! He has murdered and pillaged true believers overseas. He brainwashes children into believing Islam to be a cult, and disrespects the Prophet Muhammed! He should be detained for the police. I know for a fact he has a weapon. This unclean animal does not belong anywhere near a school, or in public, for that matter!"

The security guard listened with uneasiness. Nick showed him his US Marshal and FBI identification. "There must be some mistake. As a federal agent, I am permitted and even ordered to be armed. I never disrespected the Prophet Muhammed. He did that on his own long ago by marrying a six-year-old little girl and consummating his marriage when she was nine. How in the world could I say anything that gets lower in respect than Muhammed's pedophilia in real life? Islam is a cult and a political ideology of conquest. The only things Islam is famous for are misogyny with female genital mutilation, stonings, and Muslim honor killings of their own children. They continue to rape, murder, and pillage across the world, while at the same time pulling the victim card of being 'offended', whatever that means to a sixth century, Sharia Law loving mutant."

The security guard listened with suppressed amusement. Nick could tell this guy had been in combat somewhere for America against just what Nick described. He wore no rose-colored glasses in relation to Islam. The accuser was ready to launch. The trimmed half beard and wide-eyed outraged look signaled the discussion ended probably after Nick's first statement. He gestured wildly at Nick.

"You see! You hear the disrespect!"

A meandering group of parents were congregating nearby. They knew Nick very well and the fact he was a killer. They didn't need to read it in the paper. They had seen him in action on school grounds. They merely remained at a respectful distance.

The young security guard turned to his companion with a sigh. "According to you and Ms. Weller, the children practically attacked you and Marshal McCarty personally caused it all. As to what Islam is or isn't has nothing to do with the school. I served two years in Afghanistan. We stopped Muslims within our purview from doing exactly what Marshal McCarty stated: pedophilia with underage kids, female genital mutilation, honor killings, and stonings. I've read the Quran. I know it is stated in the books of Hadith, Aisha married the Prophet Muhammed at age six and the marriage consummated at her age of nine. I don't know about your definition of pedophilia, but that fits mine."

A loud cheering affirmation of the security guard's reply drove his offended companion over the edge. He tried to sucker punch the security guard, but Nick caught his wrist. With a simple twist, the man writhed at Nick's feet, squealing in pain.

The security guard smiled at Nick. "Thank you, but let him up, Sir."

Nick released the man and stepped back by Deke. The security guard helped the man to his feet and then faced off with him.

"You tried to sucker-punch me. Want to do it face to face when I'm ready?"

One look at the security guard's features and the man gestured no while stepping away. "I...I will-"

Nick watched the man closely while he gestured in surrender with his left hand, but reached behind him with his right. The flash under his shirt of a holstered automatic brought an instant command from Nick to Deke.

"Weapon, Deke!" Nick pointed at the man.

Deke tore the man to the ground by his right arm, shifting to his throat while watching Nick. Kneeling next to the man, Nick extracted the hideaway automatic with his handkerchief, a Glock 9mm. He set it on the walkway. "We'd better bag this. Let's get him restrained. Then, you can have him arrested. I will back up your testimony so we can put this idiot in jail."

"You cannot arrest me! I will sue this school for discrimination! Get this beast away from me!"

"Attention, Deke," Nick ordered. Deke popped into a sitting position. Nick flipped their prisoner over and the security guard handcuffed him.

"You had better save your money for a lawyer. You brought a loaded weapon into a school. That alone is a felony, Sir," the security guard explained. "Trying to draw it on a federal officer and school security guard carries another felony. Concealing the weapon on your person within a thousand feet of a school carries a five-year prison sentence and five-thousand-dollar fine."

"You will die for this outrage!"

Nick smiled. "Threatening the life of a federal officer is also a felony. If you keep talking, I don't see you getting out of prison before you're eighty."

Nick held on to the man's arm, handing the guard a pair of Nitrile gloves. "Go ahead and frisk him. I'll keep him still until you put his belongings into a bag for the police."

The security guard frisked the man as Nick suggested, bagging everything as another security guard hurriedly joined them. "Did you guys just start here at the school?"

"Yeah, the other guys got on the Monterey police force. I'm Ed Jergins and this is Larry Marin."

Nick showed Marin his US Marshal's identification and shook hands with both men. "What's this guy's name?"

"Yala Arian, Marshal," Larry replied. "I called the police. They'll be here shortly."

A blonde woman ran from the school building, her face red with rage. Jergins blocked her from invading Nick's airspace. "Hold on, Ms. Weber. This does not concern you."

"The hell it doesn't. You have my fiancé in handcuffs! What's this about. McCarty should be the one in handcuffs."

"Mr. Arian attacked us and is in possession of a loaded firearm," Ed told her. "He will be arrested and charged with multiple felonies."

"Call a lawyer, Brit! This persecution is a hate crime against Muslims."

Arian's statement drew laughter and catcalls from the parents observing the confrontation. Jergins waved at them. "Please leave your name and phone number with me if you witnessed this attack and arrest."

Weber hung on to Arian's arm, shaking her head. "Say nothing, Yala. I will contact a lawyer. This is your fault, McCarty!"

"How is it my fault your boyfriend brought a loaded weapon into the school and attacked Officer Jergins and me? We certainly didn't make him do it."

"They entrapped me!"

Nick handed Jergins his card. "Call me anytime. I will testify. Lieutenant Dickerson on the Pacific Grove police force is an associate of mine."

"Thanks, Marshal. We'll handle it. Your dog sure is well trained."

"Deke loves entertaining. Take care, guys. Ms. Weber? If you have any thought of taking this out on my daughter Jean and her friends, think again. I have lawyers too. That you allowed your fiancé inside the school, knowing he was armed and unstable, can also lead to criminal prosecution. Keep those facts in mind."

Weber wisely clamped her mouth shut as Nick walked off with Deke, pausing to shake hands and exchange pleasantries with the other parents remaining to give their names.

"We know what you've done for the school in the past, Nick," a woman he knew by the first name of Jennette said as Nick walked on. "You should have shot the prick."

"I'm trying to quit, Jenn. Marshal Deke the Dog handles all my light work now."

Chapter Five: Rattler Rescue

"Rough day in the water, Cheese." Lynn, Clint, and Clint Jr. joined us at our table. Clint Jr. waved at us happily from his mom's arms.

I shrugged. "I phoned it in and got whooped. The workout keeps me in the greatest shape of my life. Like all of you, I'm a bit addicted to the glamor of Las Vegas."

"Tommy said you were only a split-second off on your timing," Clint replied. "Did Dev tell you Carl Logan's rehab for his hip pointer proceeded better than expected. He's already talking crap to the media, calling you a chicken for not signing on for a boxing match instead of MMA."

"Yep… that's me… Mr. Chicken. That will not happen. For one thing, I've been fighting MMA for so long, I'd do a leg kick by accident during the match and get disqualified. I don't need the money. If we get Eugene back, maybe I'll see how he feels about a straight up boxing match with Logan. I'd even spar with him. It would improve my boxing skills and put him in line for a great payday."

"Do you think he's still alive, John."

I covered Lora's hand with mine. "We all think he is. Amir's using him for bait. He's no good as bait if he's dead. We did think Amir would have contacted us by now."

"I hated Rattler when he beat you, Dad," Al chimed in. "He gave you your Cheeseburger nickname."

Al elicited amusement for my nickname's origin. The Rattler turned my face to mush, hence the 'Hamburger' nickname first, followed by 'Cheeseburger'. "He did it fair and square, Al. I don't hold grudges against other fighters in the cage. He has a wife and kid. We will try to bring him home in one piece so he can be with them again."

"I understand. He was always nice when he comes in here. I hoped you wouldn't need to fight him again, but the way Uncle Tommy talked, he did great in the fight against the 'Destroyer', even though he had to fight him overseas."

"He deserves another shot at the title," I agreed. "Besides, I gave him my word he'd get the next fight."

"There's Mr. Fiialkov." Al pointed at the side entrance to the Warehouse. "He doesn't look happy."

Alexi, indeed did not look happy. He said hi to his bride to be, Marla. They would be married soon.

"I better go to the bar and greet him. Alexi seems like he wants a conference. I'll be back." I walked to the bar.

Alexi shook hands with me. Marla brought me over the brothers Beam and Bud. "Thank you for coming over to the bar, John. Darius would like a meeting with you. I feel it will be regarding Eugene. He arrived yesterday and called me. I asked him straight out if he knew what happened to Eugene. He smiled and said Eugene was fine and not to worry. We both know what that means."

"Where does he want to meet? Obviously, he didn't want to come here."

"He wants you to meet him in his hotel suite at the Waterfront Hotel."

I grinned. I may look like a troll but I'm not stupid. "Tell him I'll meet him at the bar in Scott's. I'll bring backup and he can bring backup."

"I will call him now and see if that's acceptable. I see in your manner you believe this is a trap."

"I wouldn't know, Alexi. I doubt blowing me away on his suite floor could be considered a good idea. Maybe I should go to his suite. I can bring Clint along. He's an army of one. We need to know about Eugene. I have a plan in the works to offset this

Amir's taking of Eugene. We're nearing the final stage. That's why Clint and Lynn met us for dinner tonight."

I paused to sip some Beam brother. "I'll do it. Call him. I'll meet Darius at his suite."

"I'll go with you."

"Nope. I can't have someone around me in danger that's not trained. You're a tough old coot, Alexi, but I need a Monster with me. If we met in here, I'd call Tommy, and we'd play this fight game cover deal in a perfectly safe place."

"You are my best man at the wedding, John. I can have an army surrounding the hotel in half an hour. This is a dangerous meeting. I know you will not be blackmailed into fighting him in Abu Dhabi to save Eugene. I would like to pay some of my people to go over and blow him up in his suite. I hate being played. I thought the fight would be legitimate in Abu Dhabi, and it was. When Eugene disappeared, I knew I had been screwed. That was bad business, typical of these Islamic sadists. Your friend, Nick, made me consider everything in a different light with the experiment your Monsters helped with in the City of Hope."

No doubt about that. "He forged City of Hope together into an alternative to Islam. It's working because the people now know they can believe in God without the Sharia Law travesty. What we accomplished overseas haunts us. We prepared for it with our notoriety and visibility problems. Amir taking Eugene threw us a bit, but we're on it. Call him, Alexi. I will meet with this poser and find out how many people we need to kill."

Alexi chuckled. "Excuse me, while I go outside and see this done."

"Of course." I returned to my table and informed them of what was happening.

"Hell yeah! I go with you brother," Clint stated. "They won't mix it up in a hotel suite, as you've surmised. This deals with Eugene. Darius playing coy with Alexi is a dead giveaway. He's a pug... just like you."

Everyone, including me, enjoyed that zinger a little too much. Alexi reentered the bar, and gestured me to him. Marla had guarded our spots, replenishing my Beam brother.

"He agreed to meet you at the suite with Clint. Are you sure this meeting should take place, John?"

"It has to, Alexi. No one knows what we have planned as a bartering chip. If I avoid the meeting, Amir may get suspicious. I need to hear what Darius has to say."

"If Lora will watch Clint Jr, I'll come too. There may be more happening than you think," Lynn said. "I'll wander around the hotel. I may be able to spot something going on concerning Darius's entourage. It won't be difficult for me to learn whether he has an army of guys around."

"I'd love to watch the baby," Lora offered.

"I like the idea. What suite is Darius in, Alexi?" I had another more ominous thought.

"A waterfront bay suite."

"I've had clients stay in bay view suites. There are a lot of windows. We need to stay away from them if the curtains are open, Clint."

"That could be a good ice breaker in the conversation," Clint replied. "Someone escorts us in. We see all the curtains are open and we request they be closed. Watching their reactions will give us some perspective. I've trained Lynn to recognize the best spot for a sniper attack. I brought my satellite laptop along. With the room number, I'll find the plans for the hotel and Lynn can check for anything fishy at the most likely spots."

"We have our equipment bag in the Toyota. I'll drive while Clint checks the building plans and surrounding area in view of the room." Lynn passed the baby to Lora. "We have those new dot type ear inserts too that are undetectable. We'll take Alexi along in the Highlander with us. He can monitor the network on Clint's satellite and tip you guys if something said is off in some way."

"I would be happy to do it," Alexi agreed.

* * *

"Testing," Lynn said. "I'm on the waterfront now. It's a crystal-clear night. Every building across the water with good visibility on the hotel can be seen from my position. Once you make sure the curtains are closed, I'll go blend into the scenery inside. If I see anything, I'll let you know."

"You're loud and clear, Lynn," I answered. "We're entering the hotel now. Are we clear to you, Alexi?"

"Yes. After seeing the size of those inserts, I cannot believe the range and clarity. We are good to go. I will be recording everything."

Outside the waterfront suite, Clint knocked on the door. A well-dressed professional opened the door. Although dressed casually, I could tell his slacks and shirt were expensively tailored just for him. A little over six feet tall, his shirt did nothing to hide the holstered sidearm. His trim, black, half beard rounded his lean face into the trimmed short haircut, giving him an austere featured appearance. He gestured us inside, where two more men of similar appearance stood near the cornered balcony. The curtains were open. Darius sat on one of the cushioned chairs.

Darius stood to greet us.

Although my height, Darius carried a little more bulk. I could tell it wasn't steroid induced. This was a big guy. Rattler went toe to toe with him at many instances during their fight. They fought five tough rounds. I would have judged the fight to be a Eugene Cummings win because he was the aggressor. He was probably lucky to get a draw in Abu Dhabi. Clean shaven with buzz-cut black hair, Darius wore black slacks and white pullover sweater. He shook hands with both of us with a slight smile.

"This is an associate of mine, Clint Dostiene. Alexi told me tonight you needed to talk with me. I hope it is news about finding where Eugene Cummings has been taken."

"Actually, I have no idea where Cummings is. I have heard he broke a rule in Abu Dhabi and was taken into custody because of the offense. My associate Amir Mohammed Kostler believes he may be able to bargain for Cummings release if you would agree to fight me in Abu Dhabi. Such circumstances are unfortunate, but can be approached in a civilized manner."

"Before we proceed any further, would you please shut the curtains?" The slightly startled look on Darius's face turned to tightlipped angst at my request.

"I have paid a lot of money for the view. I would rather they remain open. Why is it you want them closed?"

"Superstition. Is there a reason my request cannot be granted?"

"Very well." Darius nodded at his greeter buddy. The curtains were quickly closed.

"Got him," Lynn said in our ears. "He perked up when you guys entered the room. I saw the flash of his scope. He's on the Target building across the channel. I'm taking Alexi with me, so if the network cuts out for a time, you'll know why."

"I am searching for the Target building plans as we speak," Alexi said.

Clint cleared his throat which was our acknowledgement sign.

"Since we have no view now," Darius said, "we may as well sit at the table in the kitchenette. Would either of you care for something to drink?"

"No thanks," I replied, as did Clint. The two of us sat at the table. Clint remained standing where he could see all three of the bodyguards.

"Would you consider a fight in Abu Dhabi in the next month?"

"I don't see that happening. I'm sure you are aware of an action my team of special agents acted on in the UK at the

103

invitation of the government. It means I cannot travel safely into Islamic countries ruled by Sharia Law."

"I am well aware of your team's execution of many true believers. Your safety would be guaranteed if you agree to the match. Although transferring refugees to a gulag of death should be rewarded with torturous death, you and your handlers would be granted safe passage into and out of Abu Dhabi. Eugene Cummings' charges would be dismissed and he would be returned home with you."

"You should check the actual pictures and videos on Facebook from the new City of Hope we helped the refugees start. They have thrown off Sharia Law. Their businesses, crops, and trade have already attracted investment and resort hotel interest. They no longer rape, pillage and murder on behalf of Islam."

My words had the desired effect. Darius launched toward me, his hands reaching for my neck. I caught his wrists, even after a couple of the brothers Beam and Bud, forcing him against the kitchenette table top. Before the other three men could blink or react, Clint drew his Colt, gesturing them over against the wall.

"Grab your shirt lapels," Clint directed in Arabic. "Anyone who releases them will be shot in the head. Grab now, and acknowledge."

They did as ordered. Darius tried figuring a way to get released from across the broad table with his elbows and upper arms forced against the surface. I kept his wrists bent at an angle toward him. The pain when he tried to move his body or legs became excruciating each time he moved. I kept it up until Darius quit moving.

"I will release you. Please don't do anything else stupid." I released him back into his chair. I knew for a fact his arms would be numb for a while. He did too.

Darius rubbed circulation into his arms with movements a person does when in cold temperatures. "You will die slowly for this outrage, Harding!"

"If I do, it won't be by your hand."

"Damn…" Lynn said in my ear. "I wish I would have seen that. I'm moving into position now. Clear your throat if you're still hearing me as I hear you, Clint."

Clint cleared his throat.

"Good. You're doing a great job, Alexi," Lynn said.

"I am using the hotel's signal to bolster our network. Who says old cannot do some new tricks? Your path through Target to the roof is on your phone, Lynn. They do not guard that passage. The sniper must have used the same route."

"Excellent. We will give the turd a little surprise."

I grinned at that remark. Lynn would need a slight distraction for her visit. I turned to Clint. "I don't care anymore. If Darius the Destroyer moves, shoot him in the head. I need to give Lynn a little cover."

"Understood. Your arms are okay now, Destroyer. Grab your shirt lapels and don't let them go. I give only one warning."

I left Clint to go play with the curtains, knowing not one of the four he watched would live if one of them disobeyed his orders.

* * *

Rahm Sotar cursed under his breath as the curtains in his target room closed. He waited. His orders were clear. Hold position for a shot at Harding. He had glimpsed the big man enter the room with one other. They were to be positioned on the chairs near the window, enjoying the view. The line of sight was perfect for the shot. The curtains began to move. Finally, Rahm thought, I will have my shot at the murderous kafir.

* * *

"Perfect, Cheese. Open the curtain and wave at him," Lynn whispered.

Lynn straddled the sniper in her bare foot approach without any recognition from him. She slipped the Glock 9mm trained on the sniper's head into the back holster underneath her top. The next split second, her razor-sharp butterfly knife appeared as if by magic in her hand. She watched the curtains spread. John waved bye-bye to the sniper as Lynn slit his throat.

"I hope he appreciated the wave goodbye, Cheese. I'll be down in the Toyota with Alexi whenever you finish the visit." Lynn knelt on the convulsing body while cleaning her knife on his clothing. She patted the top of his head. "Well, Betty... that's how it's done. See ya'."

* * *

I took a deep breath as I admired the waterfront view. This was one fine place to stay. I rejoined Clint and his audience. I spoke Arabic so there would be no mistake made by anyone. "Here is how this meeting will proceed. I will frisk each one of you, confiscate your illegal weapons, then say goodbye. Although you planned to murder me here, and claim not to know about how such a thing could happen, we will leave you four alive to figure out what to do with your sniper's body."

I frisked each man, relieving him of his weapon. Darius wasn't armed. Yeah... I thought about snapping his neck for the hell of it. I knew Clint would need to shoot the other three. Instead of a nice clean operation, we'd have a mess. "You are one lucky man, D. Clint and I do not leave many enemies alive at our backs. Consider this a warning. Await my decision on the fight and stay away from us. We kill on sight from now on. I want Eugene back. I should take you hostage to get him, but now is not the time. I will be in touch."

"You are afraid to face me in the cage, kafir!"

Okay... that was about it for the posers tonight.

"I don't have Dev here to bring the rain, John," Clint warned with a smile.

"I'm good. Stand up, Destroyer. I trained in the Bay today, had a couple of adult beverages, and I still can pick off your best attack, Betty." I heard Lynn enjoying my stealing of her line. I threw the table aside. "Show me what you got, poser."

106

Darius threw what he thought was a lightning fast strike at my head with an overhand right. I blocked it easily and nailed him with a solar plexus punch with my right hook that hit dead on target. He fell to his knees, white-faced and clutching his chest. Unable to get enough air, Darius collapsed to his side. I kicked him in the face.

"Now that's entertainment," Clint said. "You three… down on your knees, hands clasped behind your heads. John and I will leave now. You guys take care of your boss, Betty. Anyone following us gets a bullet in the head."

We left the hotel. Lynn and Alexi awaited us at the curb. Once Clint and I settled in the back, Lynn said, "I guess we answered the question as to what they want to do. The sniper had an M107. They'll have a wonderful mystery to unravel on that roof."

"I'm glad Nick gets here tomorrow. We should have everything in preparation for taking Amir's son. We have no idea what they'll do to Eugene once Amir finds out what happened with his plan."

"Tommy will be happy to hear that even after training in the Bay, and having a couple drinks, Darius couldn't hit you," Clint said. "I take back calling you a pug."

"Gee… thanks."

* * *

Nick moved his hand over the baby grand piano in the huge recreation room of his purchased Bay Area mansion. Rachel, Jean, Sonny, and his Unholy Trio group stood near him as he admired the piano. He glanced at Clint and Lynn, waiting in anticipation for his reaction.

"This is a beauty. You two really did well picking this one." Nick played a classical piece with soft undertones. "It sounds wonderful. I guess this means I'll be entertaining after we take care of our Jared business."

"Plan on it, Muerto," Lynn said. "Tommy and Dev shadowed Amir's kid everywhere to be certain he would be home tonight. The only complication happened last night with the Darius surprise. We haven't heard a word from their camp since."

"From your description of events, I don't think the situation could have been handled any better. Darius still believes John considers the fight in Abu Dhabi to still be on the table. If we grab the kid tonight, and he's as much a fan of the Unholy Trio as we hope, I may be able to turn him to our side. The option of running his own medical center amongst a grateful city's population, and keeping his father alive, should be enough if he has had any issues with Islam."

"True enough," Clint said. "We need to be ready in case he is unwilling to consider our proposal, in which case Jared will need to be dealt with too."

"Agreed. How do you want to handle transport?"

"We will have our action van fixed as an EMT hospital vehicle. We have our EMP gun to take out his security system. We don't know how formidable the kid is. If you can get in without waking him, pop him with our joy juice. We'll sort out the details about his mindset at Pain Central," Lynn answered. "We'll be back at midnight if all goes well. Jared is a great student, and now resident. He has intern's disease. He sleeps nearly every moment away from the hospital or his extra classes. Jafar learned he worked a double shift so he could second on a new heart surgery procedure. If he's true to form, Jared will be sleeping through from an early hour."

"I like this even more," Nick replied. "Think about it. We can throw in all expense paid vacations to conferences all over the world as an incentive to work our City of Hope. Jared sounds as passionate as I'd hoped he would be."

Lynn smiled. "I have to say I'm liking this kid more and more. Your idea is golden with me now. We need to rework his tool of a father. There's no use getting too optimistic. We need to play this through until Jared reveals to us what really stirs inside his head."

"Agreed," Nick said. "I'm more enthused because of this kid's dedication to a calling like medicine. We'll go the extra yard to find out more about him. Depending on what we find, I would be willing to let him see us cartoons as real people. He will find out. More than a few of the residents there know about us. It would be useless to keep the Muerto secret identity when Jared will need to interact with Khan in close negotiations for the medical facilities. I'm all in on the City of Hope. Whatever I need to do in placing him there with Khan, I will do."

Cala grasped Lynn's hand. "Johnny and I want this so much. We will not be only about the 'Death Cult' we were born into. We escaped, and helped build a city where others can escape while showing the rest of the world it can be done."

Lynn shook Cala's hand with both hers. "I pray it be so, little sister. My dealings with Islamic mutants has soured my outlook. I see your vision, but I have enough of the pessimist inside me to wonder if it's possible for us to pull it off. I promise you this, kid. If it doesn't work, it won't be because I sabotaged it."

Cala hugged Lynn. "We just need to kill the right people, big sis."

"Amen to that, kid."

* * *

It went like clockwork. Clint popped the security system and Jafar confirmed all systems down from the electro-magnetic pulse. Jess drove away, leaving the black clad Unholy Trio to enter Jared's rented house. They had full audio and visual gear so we could watch the entire operation on the big screen inside our action van. We prepared for everything, including an outside security force. Luckily, that was not needed. The entire area remained under observation until we finished the operation.

Muerto burglarized the front door in seconds. We watched as the original Unholy Trio swept through the house with professional expertise. You can bet Lucas watched, ready to critique any movement out of place. Lucas trained me. I didn't see a single miscue. Nick and company arrived in Jared's room without a single problem, as we figured. I admit the cartoons were hell of impressive. They scavenged the entire room before awakening the nearly comatose Jared. They positioned themselves at the foot of the bed in complete character, MP5 submachine guns in sight, readily aimed in Jared's direction.

"Jared Amir Kostler! You are called by the Unholy Trio!"

I admit I'm a killer, but even I felt bad for the kid. Jared's worst nightmares materialized as if from thin air at his bedside. Nick stepped forward, separating from Payaso, the very evil clown, and El Kabong, in a seemingly seething fit of rage. They acted their parts to the max. The scene entertained with such humor, it was a good thing the action van only observed.

"I am El Muerto. This is Payaso and El Kabong. We have come to either enlist you in our endeavor to save another innocent, or to punish everyone involved."

"Oh… Lord… please don't let this happen!" Jared squeezed his eyes shut, hoping when he opened them the three figures would be gone. No such luck. "I…I have seen all your videos in your fight against the Sharia. Please don't do an intestinal cleaning on me! I am not a terrorist!"

I saw even through the full silk hood from his eyes, Nick took no pleasure from Jared's reaction. He gambled immediately, knowing he would need to kill the kid if his plans didn't work out. He removed his hood and went over to grasp Jared's shoulder.

"I'm Nick McCarty. I am also El Muerto. You have been a fan of my Unholy Trio. Why?"

Jared stared into Nick's eyes with obvious terror, intelligent enough to know when bad guys in masks identify themselves, the consequences mean death. "Please… no matter what you think… I cannot help you. I know nothing."

Jared sobbed, tears streaming down his cheeks as he covered his face with his hands. "I know… I must die now… because you removed your mask! Please kill me fast… please!"

Nick made a promise in opposition to our mission. So be it.

"You are not going to die, Jared. Your father, Amir Mohammed Kostler, has done numerous murderous actions. He took hostage a friend of the Unholy Trio. Amir holds our friend to blackmail us into betraying our nation. That will not happen. We see a lot of exceptional things from you. We are here to learn whether you live to help and cure people, or you follow the Islamic 'Death Cult' of murderous tyranny. My associate was brain washed from childhood to believe everyone who is not Muslim must convert, be enslaved, or die. We want to know how you feel."

"My father? He had my oldest sister killed! She raised me! Jana loved me. Her offense was she loved a man she met in Abu Dhabi while working in a hotel. The killers murdered her right in front of me!" Jared turned away on the bed. "I am a coward! I did nothing. They were men from my father's security guards, named Parsa and Mahad. They stabbed her to death! I am a surgeon. I do good to honor my Jana, who loved me and believed in me! Kill me, if you must!"

"Would you like to escape Islam's Death Cult, Jared? What does Amir have planned for you?"

"He wants me at his side, in case anything happens to him. My father wants a son to be there if something strikes him down who might save his life, assuming I would never betray him. I plotted to pretend helping him until he died!"

Nick smiled. "I have a way to change your life. Will you listen to my offer?"

Jared leaped from the bed with fists clenched. "Yes! I will kill my father for you. I will not take money to do it!"

Nick grasped the young man's shoulders. "We do not want you to kill anyone. We want you to save others like you and run your own medical facility."

Jared's mouth tightened. "Please do not play with me. I have already agreed to murder my own father for you."

111

"Let me show you something." Nick opened Johnny's satellite laptop. He showed Jared the City of Hope's numerous pictures and videos, explaining his own connection with its leader. "I do not want you to hurt anyone. I want you to be in charge of the new medical facility at the City of Hope. They need you to recruit doctors and nurses for a first-class hospital. We will send you to every state-of-the-art conference on new techniques or anything you feel will help you be the top of your field."

Jared sat on the edge of the bed in complete shock, imagining everything Nick offered. "What must I do to get such a life, Muerto?"

"Be a hostage against your father, so he will release our friend from his accomplices. Everything will be yours, no matter how this ends. The City of Hope is real. They need you there now. They have thrown off the chains of Islam. It will be a lifetime's dedication with benefits beyond your imaginings and rewards beyond comprehension."

Jared gripped Nick's hand in both his. "I will do all you ask without question. When your friend is safe and I am in the City of Hope, I ask only one thing – I want Parsa and Mahad killed by the hand of the Unholy Trio. They raped her in front of me before cutting her apart, laughing as they did it. My father thought to enlist me in his travesties from then on. I remained silent. You have given me the fulfillment of a dream. Can you do what I ask?"

"Absolutely. Get dressed and pack a bag. Will you have any trouble getting coverage at the hospital for a couple of days?"

"Not at all. I was given a week's vacation yesterday because I have had no time off at all in the past years. I will miss working at the hospital, but this City of Hope opportunity will free me from my father and Islam. If I may ask, how did you build such a city?"

"By force mostly," Gus answered. "If not for finding a leader determined to save his people, we would have failed. Khan Eshieh leads the city now. He will welcome you with open arms. Before we left the city, we deported all the malcontents who

112

refused to embrace life without Sharia Law to their place of origin."

"My father will hunt me down if you let him live."

"I believe we can get you to the City of Hope without his knowing," Johnny replied. "We trained the security force there. I doubt he could get to you in the city, but you are right in believing he can reach you when attending events in other nations."

Jared finished dressing and packing. "I will think it over while we await your friend's safe return. My father knows of the Unholy Trio. He has also seen the videos."

"Good," Nick replied. "We'll make sure we wear our costumes for him while presenting our case. By the way, this is our newest recruit, Jian Chen. We let him have the name Dark Dragon. Payaso is Gus Nason. El Kabong is Johnny Groves, formerly Ebi Zarin. I'm Nick McCarty. Jian and Johnny both renounced Islam."

Jared shook hands with each of them. "I am very happy to be meeting you without the intestinal cleaning."

Johnny put an arm around his shoulders. "You will enjoy life without Islam and Sharia. Did you see my video with Crusader Crue?"

"Yes, and also the Cleaner. I have heard the name Ebi Zarin spoken by my father. He believes you are dead."

"I get that a lot. Cleaner is my wife Cala. We call her Reaper now. Crusader Crue is in our vehicle and listening to us on our network. Does your father have anyone visiting you occasionally?"

"Not since I completed my internship. He awaits my residency finish. I have hidden the fact the hospital allowed me to complete my residency with extra shifts. I know he planned to take me soon."

"We will work it all out with you," Jian promised.

"You were of the Chinese Hui people… correct?"

"Yes. I have a new life now as you will soon."

"How did you become part of the Unholy Trio?"

"Muerto, the white-eye, shot me."

"Oh."

* * *

After settling Jared in at Pain Central, we agreed to meet again in the morning at 8 am to contact Amir Mohammed Kostler. I arrived early, as did Nick and his crew. I think everyone was anxious to see this negotiation through to the end. Quays Tannous had the night watch. Jared awoke early and Quays fixed him breakfast already. Jafar made certain no one could trace our phone call to Amir. Lynn directed Nick and his cartoons into position for a video scene with Jared restrained on a chair, sullenly enduring his capture.

"You're on, Muerto."

"As you can see, Amir Mohammed Kostler, no one is beyond the reach of El Muerto and his Unholy Trio. I decided because your son is a doctor, I would not cut a piece off his body to send to you. You are holding a friend of John Harding. You will set him free, see that he is out of the country with all of his belongings, and on his way to San Francisco. If he arrives within the next twenty-four hours, I will keep your son whole. If Eugene Cummings does not reach San Francisco within that time period, I will begin cutting pieces of your son off for your viewing pleasure. Here is a number for you to call after you see this video."

Nick held a placard up to the camera with a special number conjured by Jafar to be untraceable. He then uploaded the video to a Dropbox link and sent the link to Amir's email from a Saudi Arabia server Jafar hacked into. Amir called within half an hour.

"John Harding here."

"If you hurt my son, I will-"

"Shut your pie-hole! I contracted the Unholy Trio to take your son. If you want him in one piece, you better damn well get

Eugene on a plane to us with all his belongings. Anything missing on him, or damaged, and you get your son in the same way. Your son told El Muerto you have seen the Unholy Trio videos. You must know then what will happen if you do not comply."

"How will the exchange be made?"

"Your son told Muerto you have two bodyguards you trust, named Mahad and Parsa. Send them with Eugene. We will bring your son to the airport and pass him to you in the baggage claim area. Your bodyguards can call you when they have Jared with them safely."

"Very well. I will call you with the flight number of the New York to San Francisco flight they get on."

"Good. Do not screw this up, Amir." I hung up on him. "We have him. He'll phone me with the flight number for the jet from New York to San Francisco. He agreed to send the bodyguards Jared knows. What's that all about, Muerto?"

"I made a deal with Jared. I plan on keeping my end of it. US Marshals Dark Dragon, El Kabong, Payaso, and El Muerto are heading to New York. I booked a flight for us that leaves in an hour and a half. We're going to be there waiting to arrest the two bodyguards on kidnapping charges. US Marshals have jurisdiction everywhere. My friends Tim and Grace faxed me the arrest warrants before I left the house. We'll make sure Eugene gets on his flight home."

"Thank you, Muerto," Jared said.

"Why not wait until they get to San Francisco?"

"I have connections in New York, John," Nick answered. "US Marshals on official business can travel armed without question. I called my contact in New York. He'll have a van waiting for us at JFK Airport when our flight lands. We'll be there to take them the moment they get off the plane. I know a spot an hour from JFK where I can question these two before I deposit them as I promised Jared. They raped and cut his sister apart by order of Amir in front of him. They are Amir's most trusted bodyguards. I will find out all about Amir, his hopes and dreams, and his most likely places to hang out. Then, Mahad and Parsa disappear."

I smiled. "Admit it. You're bringing the costumes with you."

Silence. After a humorous moment of smiles and chuckles amongst the Monsters, Johnny spoke. "My latest YouTube channel video was passed by a giraffe eating a leaf."

We enjoyed Johnny's reasoning for recording a horrendous video of men getting an intestinal cleaning by the cartoons with a typical monstrous response of amusement. Jared's features indicated although he had watched the Unholy Trio in action, he didn't know about the dark humor involved.

"I am very glad I am on your side," Jared stated.

Lynn, who sat next to him, patted his hand. "So are we, kid."

* * *

All four US Marshals wore either a dark gray or black suit. They awaited the plane's disembarking with professional patience next to three airport security guards accompanying them. Nick saw Eugene Cummings exit as the last of the passengers entered the airport terminal. His two companions, Mahad Antar and Parsa Kalb, walked behind him with bored expressions. Nick allowed them to get beyond the outer ring of greeters. Eugene recognized him from Las Vegas. Nick motioned him over. Jian took Eugene's arm with a big smile.

"Welcome back, Eugene. Please come with me for a moment."

The two companions were surrounded immediately and hand cuffed by Johnny and Gus.

"What is the meaning of this?" Parsa blurted out a stunned bit of outrage in broken English while being restrained.

"Parsa Kalb and Mahad Antar," Nick said, while showing his US Marshal's identification. "We are US Marshals Nason,

Groves, and McCarty. You are under arrest for the kidnapping of Eugen Cummings. Please do not make a scene or you will be dealt with accordingly."

Nick then repeated it in Arabic, before turning to the security personnel. "Thank you for your assistance, officers. My men will take it from here."

After the security personnel left, Jian returned with a stunned Eugene. "He says he is fine."

"My flight doesn't leave for an hour," Eugene added. "Jian tells me John engineered my freedom. Man, I don't think I could fight him after this. I thought I'd be in that dungeon they threw me in forever. I know there was to be an exchange. I heard these two talking with their boss. I don't know Arabic, but I think they had something bad planned in San Francisco. I was going to deck them both the moment we got clear of the other passengers and make a break for it."

"That would have been a good idea," Nick told him, while handing him an iPhone. "We will find out everything they know while you fly home to your family. Call your family. John tells me they're worried sick about you."

"We will tell you nothing, kafir!"

Johnny smiled. "Yes. We have heard that song before. Come along with us. We will transport you to your destination, where you can request your embassy's help or lawyers or whatever you want."

"We will be free in hours!"

Gus patted Eugene's shoulder. "I'm more pessimistic than my companions. I was afraid we wouldn't get you back in one piece. Go get a beer and call your family. We'll make sure you'll be fine in San Francisco. Do you have money?"

"They stole everything in currency I had."

"Here." Nick gave him a thousand dollars. "Like Gus said, call your family while you sip a beer before your flight. We know you've went through hell. It's over now."

"Thank you." Eugene turned to his two captors with grim countenance. "You two are very lucky these men were here to arrest you both. I would have fucked you both up right here in the terminal."

"We will see you again soon, kafir," Parsa promised with a grin. "You Americans are all talk. Mahad and I will come collect you some time when you least expect it."

Nick nudged Eugene away. "No... you won't. Go on, Eugene. We'll take good care of your buddies."

Eugene smiled for the first time. He knew what Nick was from Las Vegas and his talks with Alexi Fiialkov. "I know you will. It is the only reason I do not rip this prick's head off right now in the middle of everything. See you guys soon."

Eugene walked away with a wave. Nick took Parsa's arm while Gus guided Mahad. "Come along quietly. You will be taken somewhere all of your complaints and requests will be heard."

"That is true, kafir," Parsa replied confidently. "Amir will hear of this outrage. For your sake, I pray his son is safe."

"He is indeed safe. Let us simply walk in quiet silence now," Nick advised in Arabic. "Being around you gives me very bad thoughts."

"It is good you think such thoughts, little man. Perhaps one day I will return the favor you have cursed us with today."

"I think not," Nick replied.

Chapter Six: Beyond Cleaning

"There's the turnoff, Gus. Follow it around to the left. It turns into a dirt road. An abandoned shack of a barn lies dead ahead. No one comes here… not even road crews."

"When did you happen along this path before, Muerto?" Gus turned off the lights and engine.

"Because I've had business in New York City, I needed to find places here in Pennsylvania where I could transport my business and still make it back to JFK for a flight, or keep going across country. This I-476 route has a few nice spots."

Muffled cries from the two gagged men in the cargo area of the van made it plain they did not like the area at all. When they began rocking up and down, Jian popped them in the head with his nightstick stun-gun.

"Our guests are unhappy." Jian waved his nightstick threateningly. The men stopped moving around.

"I'll go in the barn first. I know my way around in there. Once you see the lantern come on, bring the guys in."

Nick got out of the van with equipment bag in hand. He allowed his eyes to adjust to the darkness before picking his way carefully into the abandoned barn. With the military grade tactical LED lanterns in the corner of the barn set where he wanted them, Nick positioned his tripod and camera for the video. Gus, Johnny, and Jian entered, marching their reluctant prisoners inside. Nick retrieved two wooden backed chairs from the rear of the barn, placing them ten feet apart. They duct taped the prisoners securely in the chairs.

"I see you installed some furniture," Gus noted. "How do you want to proceed?"

"Let's get our costumes on. We'll introduce Dark Dragon before I make a couple of cuts and do the initial cleaning. The camera can keep rolling until the question and answer session begins. I won't stretch this out. We have a flight to catch back home."

With costumes on, Nick cut both men, exposing a small amount of intestine. Johnny sprayed on the Clorox. Nick let Jian speak then while the men screamed behind their gags. Jian introduced himself as Dark Dragon before announcing the crimes of the two men. Nick paused the video with his remote. After the neutralizing solution was applied, Gus removed the gags. Mahad and Parsa sobbed out entreaties for mercy. They no longer held any hope of living.

Nick spoke in Arabic to make certain there were no misunderstandings. "Now that we all know you two will not be going to Disneyland, I will ask you some questions. If I like the answers, you may proceed to hell without any further pain. If I do not like your answers, I will again introduce you to hell on earth. We are recording this question and answer session. You first, Mahad. I want you to list all the places Amir Mohammed Kostler visits or stays, including mistresses or wives. Secondly, I want to know if anyone higher than Kostler ordered this kidnapping of Eugene Cummings."

"I...I must have a doctor... the pain is too much!"

"Doctor Muerto is in the house." Gus put the gag back in place and Nick sprayed Mahad with Clorox again. He turned to Parsa. "How about you? Do you need something for the pain too?"

Parsa recited every place he had ever visited in the company of Kostler, including a Canadian mistress living in Vancouver. "He...he may be there now. Amir knows Harding has vast resources. Mahad and I stayed in Abu Dhabi with Cummings, awaiting orders."

"I noticed neither of you has a cell-phone. I imagine you were ordered not to take anything electronic with you. I need to know addresses for these places."

120

"Yes… we were to take nothing. Amir told us to buy throwaway phones when we reached the USA."

"That makes me unhappy, Parsa. You know what happens when Dr. Muerto gets unhappy."

"Wait! I know the addresses by heart except for a couple!"

"Okay… proceed," Nick told him. Mahad died a moment later during Parsa's recitation. Mahad's death quieted Parsa. He stared at Mahad's convulsing body in horror. "Don't mind your buddy. You are doing well. Continue."

Johnny and Gus checked each address, mostly overseas in Saudi Arabia or the Arab Emirates. The Vancouver, Canada address interested Nick the most. A few ideas streamed through his mind as to the Vancouver mistress. When Johnny and Gus confirmed the addresses, Nick kept the interrogation going.

"Get me the phone number for Evelyn Scott in Vancouver. Parsa is going to call there and learn whether his boss decided on visiting his mistress."

A few moments later, Gus handed Nick their satellite phone with ID blocking. "I programmed her number in."

"Thanks." Nick gave Parsa a measured shot of pain relief, watching the tense features relax. "I want you to call the girlfriend and ask if Amir is there. Identify yourself and tell her it is urgent that you speak with him. If he is there, tell him everything went wrong when the plane landed in New York. Explain to him that you and Mahad are on the run and Eugene got on the flight for San Francisco. Advise him to stay where he is until the damage is assessed and whether Jared is released."

"I can do that," Parsa agreed. Nick called, holding the phone on speaker. A woman answered. "This is Amir's bodyguard Parsa Kalb. I must speak with Amir, Ms. Scott. It is urgent."

"How… never mind… Amir? It is someone named Parsa Kalb."

"Why have you called me like this?" Kostler sounded more than a little enraged by the call. "What is so urgent, and how did you know to call me here?"

"I took a chance you were with Ms. Scott. The authorities awaited us at the airport. They allowed Cummings to continue, but held Mahad and I for a long time. I called to warn you. I advise you to stay where you are for now until Mahad and I learn what has happened with Jared."

"I will do as you advise. Get to San Francisco any way you can and find out if Jared has been released. If the opportunity arises, kill John Harding!"

"Yes, Amir."

"Excellent, Parsa. Here's a bit more for the pain." Nick gave Parsa a death dose. "That went well. Let's do the video wrap, call John, and let him know about our new wrinkle with a Vancouver mistress."

"What about the bodies?"

"Unfortunately, Jian, as Gus and Johnny will tell you, sometimes we need to do things old school."

"A burial detail? Oh great. We will look like graverobbers at the airport."

"Quit whining, Grasshopper. I'll show you where we need to bury these guys. The grounds soft. Besides, what did you think I brought shovels and lye for? There's a loam pit nearby, all soft earth, clay, sand, and lye added. I'll lead the entire time so you won't be afraid in the dark."

"I will go get the shovels and lye, white-eye. I did not know graverobbing would be one of my duties as a US Marshal."

"We're not robbing graves, Charlie Chan. We're filling them," Nick called after him.

"Racist!"

"Okay then… move your butt, Jet Li!"

Jian fired off a string of Chinese insults, which Nick answered in kind. He smiled when Jian laughed instead of answering.

Gus grasped Nick's arm. "What did Jian say to you?"

"He said my mother sucks bears' dicks in the woods."

"What did you say back?"

"I told Jian his mother picked his name by throwing him down the stairs to see what kind of sound he made."

As promised, after dragging the bodies to the spot Nick cultivated in the past, they found damp, soft, grainy earth, luckily wet from recent rains. They deposited the bodies, covered them in lye and loamy earth. Nick poured the rest of the Clorox he brought over the pit to ward off curious animals. Lastly, he covered the pit again with tree branches and rocks. Nick's companions followed in a line at his direction to the van while he used a branch to swipe away all trace of their passing.

"You guys wait in the van. I'll gather the equipment, put things in order, and swish away any sign in the barn. We'll stop at a hotel after we leave Pennsylvania. We'll get a shower and change for the flight home. I'll call John on the way to the hotel."

"You are quite the gravedigger, Muerto," Gus said.

"Thank you, Gus."

"That wasn't a compliment."

"That is of no importance. A truth stands alone, no matter its sarcastic source."

* * *

"Hi, John. We took care of business here. I uploaded the video so Jared can watch the final judgement on his sister's murderers. Amir is in Vancouver with his mistress as we speak. I made one of his minions call him and advise he stay there until contacted. I directed him to say they were taken into custody at JFK International, but they would get clear and continue to San

Francisco. Amir told him if the opportunity presented itself, kill John Harding. I assume Eugene's back home in good shape, right?"

"He's already back with his family, happy as hell to be alive. I don't think he'll ever fight me though. The first thing he told me when we picked him up at the airport was 'there ain't goin' to be no rematch'. I told him if he changed his mind we could always reschedule."

"Did you talk to him about fighting Carl Logan?"

"No. I figured I'd hold off on that until he shook off being in captivity."

"Good idea," Nick agreed. "I believe this might be a great time to take a cruise to Vancouver on the Ranger. Now would be a good time for Jared to talk with his father. I do not believe we can save him."

"I'll talk with Jared and put him through to Amir. He can tell him of his intent to start a medical facility in the City of Hope. I believe we will be able to gauge the cruise to Vancouver by how the conversation progresses after that, Nick. I'm not afraid of Amir. I'm willing to go along with your effort to keep him alive."

"Listen, brother… Amir is dangerous. He's after you. Forget Jared and the conversation. Let them talk and say goodbye, no matter the feelings about Jared going to the City of Hope. He could kill Lora or Al when you least expect it. We've been in the Sand. Sharia Law Mutants will turn on you like rabid dogs at any time they get the opportunity. He said, 'kill John Harding' – end of story. We fly, drive, or sail to Vancouver right now and make sure Amir only has one last thought – how to die without pain. Get Lynn. Her toy is intact and waiting. I have a formidable contact in the region. I trust her enough to take some precautions with local authorities. We all know how dangerous action in Canada against Islam's terrorist horde is at this time, with the asshole traitor they have in charge."

Silence reigned for a moment of consideration by Harding.

"You're right, Muerto. I'll raise the forces of darkness while you make your way home. I want you with us. Lucas and Gus can pilot the Ranger. We can even bring the dependents on board. No one will be in danger aboard the Ranger, at sea, or in port. We have enough fire power aboard our combat ship to make war. We won't, of course, but I am glad you have a contact who may be able to intercede on our behalf if Amir extermination doesn't go strictly by plan."

"Agreed," Nick said. "See you soon."

Nick called his contact in Canada next. Robyn MacEachern worked with Homeland Security, and coordinated operations on the border with Canada Border Services Agency.

"MacEachern here."

"Robyn. This is Nick McCarty."

"I've kept updated on your exploits, Marshal McCarty. I'm not sure how the hell you get into everything you do and not be dead or in prison. I know you didn't call me just to pass the time and say hello. What can I do for you."

"I check your whereabouts because of our past connection. The latest information I have places you in Vancouver, acting as liaison with Canada Border Services. Are you still stationed there?"

"Yes. I'm acting director of our office. Because of Canada importing so many unvetted refugees, I send daily reports to Director Gilbrech. Why? Are you coming for a visit?"

Nick briefed her on Amir Mohammed Kostler, his mistress's name and address, along with a summary of his recent hostage taking. "He placed a contract on a federal agent: John Harding."

"The UFC Heavyweight Champion who works for CIA, FBI, and Homeland Security? He would be the last person on earth I'd ever hire killed. If I'm reading between the lines correctly, you'll be coming to Vancouver to personally deal with Mr. Kostler, correct?"

"John and I discussed sailing to Vancouver and taking Mr. Kostler on board for a cruise to never/never land."

"Arriving by boat would be an excellent approach, Nick. Local annoyance level with our Muslim refugee population has never been higher. A lot of citizens would probably stuff your Amir on the yacht for you, and pay to have the privilege. The Vancouver Metro area was saddled with thousands of Syrian refugees. Nearly all of them are still on the government dole, in other words, the citizens' dole. I will facilitate anything you need and keep an eye on Amir for you. Let me know when you dock."

"I will, Robyn. Thanks for your help. There will be a big bonus in it for you. If you can find a house for us to rent at an exorbitant price near Amir's mistress, price is no object."

"I won't turn down a bonus, Nick. I'll work on the house rental right away in my name. Talk at you soon."

"Damn," Gus exclaimed happily after Nick disconnected. "We're finally sailing the Ranger on a mission, huh?"

"We sure are, brother. My contact believes it's the best approach too. Although there are plenty of wilderness sites to ditch Amir in, bringing him aboard the Ranger and sailing off into the sunset would be ideal. Robyn confirmed thousands of refugees have been imported into the area. You can bet many have already been aligned with Amir since he has a Vancouver mistress. It will be interesting to learn her story. Do you know anything about the Vancouver area, Johnny?"

"I was given the names of three Masjids there, aiding any Muslim on the jihadi trek. You know the way it is, Muerto. They lie, enable, and deny. The fools who refuse to know Sharia Law betray our nations daily. The Syrian refugee crisis represents the dumbest con job ever perpetrated on Western Civilization. They arrive unvetted, all male in prime soldiers' ages, with cell-phones and designer clothes. The idiots greeting them with open arms and crocodile tears all cry out 'come in, come in, you poor things'. It is truly disgusting how easily our governments import these murderous swine into our midst without explanation or accountability."

"We're stuck with the situation," Nick agreed. "We put out small fires and pray our city building effort acts as a beacon in the Muslim world. An entire city of former Muslims throwing off Sharia Law and Islam, while succeeding in production, trade, and tourism, will go further than anything to defeat the Caliphate."

"Nuking Mecca from orbit is also a good choice," Jian added.

Nick breathed in deeply. "Let's not start pondering that road, Dragon. We missed our chance after 9/11 to decimate the Middle East with a real message of violent resolve. Now, we're stuck for the time being, kissing their asses. If people were offered the choice of bombing the mutants until it was once again safe to fly anywhere without more than a few minutes to board a plane, what do you think would be the voting outcome?"

"The bombers would already be fueled awaiting election day," Gus said. "The Snowflakes get accosted by TSA agents the same as everyone else. Muerto tamed Chicago for a time. It's taking them a long time to get their gang kill ratio up to pre-Muerto holocaust levels."

"I have no optimistic dreams for that cesspool," Nick replied. "Paul's stepdaughter and grandkid are still doing okay, but he's worried all the time. As long as a liberal idiot is in charge of Chicago, there will be no peace, law, or sanity. They will return to the killing fields soon unless the populace votes in a law and order mayor who allows the people to be armed. Conceal/Carry would reduce crime and murder in Chicago within weeks. Open season on gangbangers will work everywhere it's tried."

"You sure showed them the advantageous use of grenades, Muerto."

"Thank you, Gus."

"That was not a compliment."

"That is still of no matter."

* * *

127

Nick entertained at his huge recreation room's piano. We danced, sang along, and generally lost all train of thought about what we were. Nick stripped away the Monsters down to elemental human enjoyment. I envied his talent. In the meantime, I dance with Lora amongst many of my Monster couples. The babies played away in their playpen together, rocking in their own way to Nick's music. He ended his Barry White tune with typical flare and went over to start the jukebox in the corner playing tunes. Everyone was there for the party, even our soon to be wed Alexi Fiialkov and Marla Tomlinson. The family of Monsters, Unholy Trio, and Snow Whites gathered to enjoy the short respite from the unending terror war.

Rachel hugged and kissed Nick. "I have an iced Beam over at the table for you with your name on it. You are incredible tonight."

"I second that, Nick." He was in fine form and my Monsters and Snow Whites were very appreciative with loud backup for Rachel's expression. "That's an amazing spread of food too, Rachel. Thank you for hosting us all."

"Once I calculated what it would take to feed an army, it was easy. In the land of giants, it's best to overachieve on food prep," Rachel replied in good spirits. She pointed at Jess. "And you, Jesse Brown, it's a good thing you need to work with the Dark Lord every day, or you would be a 'Jenny Craig' candidate within weeks."

"Damn, Mrs." Jess looked around sheepishly as the others piled on. "I missed breakfast this morning."

"You're good with me, but I don't know how Rochelle keeps you fed," Rachel replied, sitting down with Nick.

"I make him eat out," Rochelle joked. "His idea of missing breakfast is six eggs and a loaf of bread."

"Don't disrespect me, woman. I'll have Dev cast the Latin on you. It'll rain over your head everywhere you go. You'll be like that little guy in the 'Peanuts' cartoon with the dark cloud of dirt following him everywhere. Instead of a nickname like 'Pigpen', yours will be 'Wet-Noodle'."

As everyone enjoyed Jess's zinger, including Rochelle, Quays popped in with his side of the story. The minions take care of food and beverages at Pain Central. "We buy a month's supply of food for Pain Central. If Jess makes one visit, we're down to two weeks supply instantly."

"Hey! What happens at Pain Central stays at Pain Central, brother." Jess enjoyed the attention. He knew it was all true. "We're working every softball practice and game, right 'Chelle? She pitched fastpitch softball in college. Al's team will win the championship this year."

"I think the parents asked for John and Lynn because no one argues from the other side when they see the Monsters in the bleachers," Lora said. "I've seen the fights between the parents at the game before us. The girls have a lot more fun when the parents and coaches aren't screaming at each other. Are you and Sonny thinking about playing any sports, Jean."

"We were thinking about trying soccer and maybe lacrosse," Jean answered, glancing at Sonny.

"You are?" That news perked Nick up. "You and Sonny could get on a baseball team together if you want."

"I think I'd like to try soccer. It starts at the end of May. Mom signed us up already. We didn't have a chance to tell you about signing yet."

"That's great, Jean. I'll help all I can."

"I signed you up already to fill in as a coach or assistant. I don't think they'll even contact you because so many of the kids have played before. Parents with coaching experience are in position already."

"They always need parents for shagging balls, carrying equipment, and scrimmaging," Nick said. "I can do that."

"We want to see one of Al's tournaments, Dad," Jean said.

"You do?" Al was in heaven. "Sure… I'll text you the schedule. I'd love to have you visit for a tournament. There might even be one in Santa Cruz. We could mess around at the amusement park there after the tournament."

"I'll make it happen," Nick promised.

"Before Nick entertains again, we need to talk about a cruise we're making together to Vancouver," I explained. "It's not all pleasure, but it will be on our superyacht, the Ranger. You've all seen it – 240 footer with everything you can think of for luxury. Although outfitted for war and combat on the seas, we'll have one of our UH-60 helicopter gunships on board. I doubt we'll need worry about trouble on the ocean or in port. All the Monsters, Snow Whites, and Nick's cartoons are shipping out on board for our maiden voyage. We'll handle all shipboard duties, but the voyage will not be like it was on the skyscraper cruise ship we protected. All dependents are welcome to come. Think it over. We will be leaving soon."

Jean turned on Nick immediately. "Can Sonny and I go, Dad?"

"Yep. Even if your mom's not interested in taking Quinn, I'll take you, Sonny, and Deke with me. How about it, babe?"

"I'm in," Rachel said. "As long as I don't have to swab decks or cook for the crew, I'm going. That's why you were checking on extra-large doggy grass potties."

Nick shrugged. "I like having Deke with me. Tonto and Naji are coming too. Those three together are like an entertainment system. After a couple hours, they all start to move and act like a pack. It's funny as hell. Their heads cock at the same angles. Besides, I'm thinking of walking Deke in front of Amir's house to do close recon. We don't want to drive around there. He has a small army providing protection. My contact in Vancouver will rent us a house in the area to operate out of near the mistress."

"I found a marina that will take the Ranger," Lucas said. "Have you ever been to the Coal Harbour Marina, Gus? It takes superyachts over 300 feet in length."

"I wondered about whether we would need to anchor the Ranger out in the bay," Gus answered. "In answer to your question, I've anchored in St. John's Bay on the other coast but never on the Pacific side of Canada. The Ranger's a dream to handle. We'll port her fine. A ship the Ranger's size needs a little tug help, depending on the harbor. It will be a pleasure copiloting her with you, Lucas. It's a shame to spend all the money we do to keep the fleet operating without using them."

"Amen to that," Lucas replied. "We've confiscated so much money from the pedophiles that were on Cafrey's Isle of Darkness, it took away the pain of having the Ranger docked all the time with nothing but maintenance expenses. We own our own island now with deep water dock, but she still has to be maintained by a group out of Washington state to service her. We had to vet them like secret agents because of the armament changes we made aboard her."

"The timing couldn't be better for this. The kids are off on Spring Break next week," Nick said. "They had a piano on board the ship when it was the 'Tempest'. It didn't get damaged either."

"You're right, Nick! There was a baby grand in the barroom/entertainment deck," Lucas said. "I am definitely into this business/pleasure type endeavor. The Ranger also has indoor hot tubs and swimming pools. The cabins compete with the nicest resort hotel rooms too. Come along with us, Sarah. I know you hate what I do and you don't want the kids along. They can visit your folks for the week."

"I'm going, Sarah," Casey's wife, Anna, said. "I'm bringing little Lucas along too. Lynn's bringing Dannie and Amara with her to help watch over the babies. You're going too, aren't you, Sam?"

"Oh yes," Samira answered. "I am bringing Mia along."

Sarah hugged Lucas. "I'm in. My folks would love to have the kids for the week."

"There are twenty-six cabins," Casey added. "The kids will have their own cabins in the crew quarters. They were built to accommodate two crewmembers each. I'm glad we all went through the passport crap when we went on the last voyage. Quays... you have a goofy look on your face, as do the other minions. Your wives are avoiding even looking at us."

"Our wives want no part in this. They know we need to crew along with you all aboard so big a ship. The training cruise to Monster Island with Gus teaching us our roles on board was a lot of fun. We learned everyone's job by switching during training. Gus told us the Ranger runs a full crew of thirty, but we did very well with twenty."

"My husband is correct." Celia shifted her newborn, holding little Quays momentarily. "This bugger will need to be a lot older before we do anything like the Ranger cruise. It will be cold as an iceberg this time of year."

"Rhonda and I know you have two motorized Panga boats in the hold of the ship, and a damn helicopter transport," Celia added. "I'm sure it's as safe as can be, but we've decided to stick with the skyscrapers of the seas if we go cruising."

"Sonny and I will help crew the boat," Jean said. "This is going to be great!"

"I'm going," Laredo stated, taking his wife Sybil's hand. "Sybil wants to stick with ocean going skyscrapers too."

"I know you all will keep Dannie safe," Sybil added. "I'm queasy about the ocean. With you bunch on board though, it will be safe in every other way imaginable."

"Maria and I will be in DC," Denny said. "I will be in place with the Director to intercede in any way we can. Nick has Robyn MacEachern to smooth the edges locally. Paul knows her and has worked with her in the past, as Nick also has done. Amir concerns me because of the numbers of unvetted Syrian refugees in the area. It's obvious if he has a Canadian mistress, Amir probably employs an army there."

"Did you just insult us, Denny," Lynn asked, which made for an amusing moment. No one in the room, including Denny, thought an army of Syrian refugees could overwhelm the force sailing on the Ranger.

"I believe Denny is referring to armed combat on Canadian soil between a paramilitary bunch like ours, and those poor refugees, imported to hasten what the idiot Prime Minister wants: one world order."

"Precisely," Denny agreed. "This will be a delicate operation. Only you bunch would sail off on board a ship with dependents, partying on the way to nab a known terrorist, surrounded by who knows how many Sharia Law Mutants."

"We're not taking this lightly," Nick said. "Robyn's renting us a house near the mistress. We'll recon the operation from the house. Amir will not have heard from his two trusted bodyguards in over a week by the time we dock. He will talk with his son tomorrow which should relax him a bit. I believe Amir will do as I told his bodyguard to recommend: stay with the mistress. I doubt he'll have an army staying in the mistress's neighborhood."

"Nick's right," I added. "Amir would draw more attention to himself housing a bunch of refugees at his house. I think we have everything covered we can until we dock the Ranger. Let's enjoy the rest of the evening. Nick's caught the bug of entertaining. He's hooked us so we may as well dance the night away."

Nick moved back to the piano. "I would ask for requests. Unfortunately, there are people with a twisted sense of humor in this room, so I'll be picking my own tunes."

"What? You mean you won't be doing 'Tiptoe Through the Tulips'?"

"Sit down or get on the dance floor, Dr. Deville. I will never... ever... sing the 'Tulip' song." Nick didn't wait for a reply. He launched into 'California Dreaming'.

Clint took Lynn into his arms. "Don't bait the maestro, babe. We have a voyage of singing and dancing ahead."

"I second that, Sis," I mentioned with Lora in my arms. "I hope Gus and Lucas can make the voyage as smooth as possible. We'll be bucking the California currents going North this time of year. Vancouver will be cold, probably in the low fifties and upper forties."

"The Ranger employs the latest stabilizer technology," Gus added, while dancing with Tina. "We'll make it a smooth voyage, even heading into the currents. As John said though, it will be cold."

"I was listening." Laredo moved with Sybil nearer. "With the range of the UH-60, I can fly anyone inland if things are not working out on the ocean for anyone. It's only a two-night voyage anyway, right Gus?"

"Yes, and that's at smooth steaming speeds. I wouldn't have minded going with Lucas to Seattle and steaming Ranger down here to port ourselves. We could have done it with a skeleton crew like when we ported her in the North at Monster Island."

"You guys can still do that after the mission cruise," I told him. "We'll have plenty of guys to put together a skeleton crew and steam Ranger to home port at Monster Island. After we check things out on the island, we can fly back home from Seattle."

Many murmurings of agreement sounded from the other dancers as Nick ended the song.

"That's enough steamboat talk," Tina said. "I want to dance without you guys drowning out the entertainment."

"That reminds me. Hey, Nick, do 'Brandy' for Lucas and Sarah."

Nick put a fist up. "Good one, John. Lucas has Sarah with him tonight."

"You told them about 'Brandy'." Sarah held on tight to Lucas. "You old romantic."

Lucas kissed her. "At least you're here with me this time."

Nick sang 'Brandy' with first class piano accompaniment, giving Lucas and Sarah an extended version the rest of us could tell moved them. That particular song moved Deke too. He comically head swayed with his front paws on Nick's piano bench. Nick noticed, shifting to sway with Deke while playing and singing. It was hilarious.

* * *

Nick stood with Jean, Sonny, and Al. They all wore rain gear as the Ranger plunged along into a very cold squall. The blackened sky seemed to stretch on into eternity with only the white capped waves reflecting the lights from Ranger. Nick grinned down at his two adventurous charges. They asked to see the storm and seas at the third deck railing after going with Nick to batten down the hatches. They helped him check everything that could not be stowed inside. Deke insisted on joining them, although his canine brothers, Tonto and Naji, elected to stay dry inside. Deke leaned into Nick at each deck movement while he too watched the sky.

"This is incredible, Dad! Have you ever seen it like this before?"

"I've been in typhoons at sea with Gus on past missions. We were in a much smaller craft. At times, we would disappear under the waves, even with Gus steering her into the storm's calmest channels. If you're on a boat at sea, you want guys like Gus and Lucas handling the piloting duties."

"Are we in danger?" Nick could see the excited anticipation on Jean's face.

"On the ocean, human beings are always in danger, much like in an aircraft. Anything mechanical or weather-wise changes everything. The larger a ship is, the less the danger, but only if piloted correctly. Gus and Lucas need to change course instantly in shifting stormy seas. The ocean changes its face in a storm from lapping gentle waves into crushing monstrous walls of water, capable of capsizing anything."

"Do you get scared out at sea, Sir," Sonny asked, glancing at Nick's face.

"When I'm with you kids in unknown circumstances, I'm always wary of what might happen. A parent's nightmare involves only one recurring theme, a child perishing before their eyes."

"Are you still glad you traded for life with Mom, me, and Deke?"

"Every moment," Nick admitted. "I had only death then."

* * *

Nick walked Deke, nearing the mistress's house. He practiced Deke's movements, drilling his beer buddy through a series of commands, while complimenting him effusively with every followed command. Two men, obviously of Middle Eastern origin, strode out to the sidewalk in barely suppressed rage.

"Take that unclean animal away from here!"

"Relax. I have a dog waste bag," Nick reasoned, holding up his leash with attached doggy bag pouch. "If Deke does anything in your yard, I'll pick it right up."

The second man poked Nick to emphasize something he wanted to say. Deke tore him to the ground by his wrist, maneuvering to his throat. The first man reached for a weapon. Nick pistol whipped him to the sidewalk.

"So much for recon," Nick said, dragging the first man toward the house, releasing Deke's leash. "Hold, Deke!"

A van drove to the curb with Cala driving. Johnny ran to join Nick while Gus and Jian stuffed Deke's quarry inside, restraining and gagging him. Deke draped over the man with a rolling growl. The door the two men had exited from stood partially open. Nick streaked through the door, firing .45 caliber rounds center mass into the two remaining shocked bodyguards. The mistress appeared with a machine pistol in hand. Nick shot her through the head. Nick ran down the hall with Johnny at his back after securing the first bodyguard. The bedroom door at the end of the hallway slammed shut. Nick and Johnny then professionally cleared the rest of the house while always having eyes on the bedroom. Ascertaining the house was clear of other assailants, Nick and Johnny positioned themselves on either side of the bedroom door. Nick knocked.

"Hello, Amir. This can go a couple of ways. Surrender, and I won't throw this grenade I have in my hand into your bedroom. Play hard to get and I pull the pin for your last moments on earth."

"You are bluffing, kafir! I would be a fool to surrender. Let me talk with my woman."

"Sorry, Amir… you'd need that kid who talks to dead people for that to happen. I'll count to three and then kick the door open. An ET-MP grenade will be thrown into the room. There won't be a single place in there safe from its blast. Ready or not, here we go. One… two… three!"

Nick started pulling the pin on the ET-MP grenade with Johnny gesturing wildly for him not to do it. With a big disappointed sigh, Nick kicked free the door and tossed the grenade inside. Amir screamed like a three-year-old child with a tarantula on its arm. He ran out the doorway, only to be clotheslined by Johnny and restrained. Nick walked in, picked up his grenade with another sigh, and pocketed it.

"Sorry, John. We have Amir, but we'll need four body-bags and an empty equipment bag."

"On our way, Muerto."

"The first one is still alive, Muerto," Johnny told him as they dragged Amir to the front room.

Nick knelt next to the only surviving bodyguard. He gripped his neck for a few minutes, shutting off air and life. "Not anymore, Kabong. Damn… I thought the walking the dog recon was a real gem. Now… I have another mess to clean. Such is life, Kabong."

Johnny had been chuckling away while restraining Amir, along with the rest of the network. "On mission with you, Muerto, there is very little life anyway."

"I will help you clean, Muerto," Cala volunteered.

"Nope. Stay in the van, Reaper. You drive. We'll load. Keep an eye on the neighbors. Let me know if anyone investigates."

"Understood," Cala agreed. "Tommy drove behind me with the body detail."

"The good news is they have the new laminated flooring," Nick announced.

"Yeah... that's the good news," Gus said. "What happened to situational control, Muerto?"

"Don't be a hater, Payaso. This is an inexact science."

"He was going to pull the pin on the grenade, Payaso."

"Shut up, Kabong."

Cala chuckled and drove away.

* * *

Casey, Jess, Dev, and I carried the body-bags in from our second van. We all pitched in to get our new room temperature traveling companions into bags for their cruise transport. Johnny gave Amir a shot to keep him unconscious. We put him in a bag anyway. While we loaded, Nick worked at the cleaning. He retrieved cleaning supplies from the mistress's cupboard, working hard to remove most, if not all, of our visit.

"We'll be in the van, watching for attention, Nick."

"Don't stay, John. All of Amir's belongings are in the suitcases by the door. I threw his minions stuff in there I found too. I don't think they were staying at the house. I advise you to take the bodies and surviving Crue toys to the Ranger. I'll keep cleaning and then walk to the house Robyn rented for us. I'll call you when I need a ride. I don't want the locals stopping the vans loaded with killers and bodies."

"That'll work, brother. You weren't really going to pull the pin on a grenade, right?"

"I figure if I can make Kabong think I am, then the ploy will work on the target. I would never do such a horrible thing."

Oh boy... we enjoyed that lie all the way through the loading, including Kabong.

* * *

Nick methodically went over the house with nitrile gloves on after cleaning the major mess and depositing everything in a plastic garbage bag. His break in through the bedroom door only chipped the doorjamb, rather than damaged it. He made all the beds neatly, picking up and either hanging clothes or folding them into drawers, belonging to the mistress. Nick used the laminated floor polish to cover his floor cleaning. One last look around, and Nick deposited his cleaning rags into the empty equipment bag, after putting away the supplies where he found them. He locked the door from the inside, making sure the knob on the outside was in the locked position. When he walked to the rented house, Nick found his crew and Deke waiting for him inside.

"We dropped off the people and came back for you," Gus said. "How did the cleaning go?"

"Great. Only a professional CSI team could find trace we ever were there. No one was supposed to know about Amir's mistress in Canada. They will be listed when someone checks as missing, at least the girlfriend will. If Evelyn hadn't come out of the bedroom with a weapon, she'd be detained by my contact for questioning. The Canadian authorities would have been involved as to her fate."

"What are you going to tell Robyn when she asks about Evelyn Scott," Johnny asked.

"She sleeps with the fishes."

After a moment of hilarity, Gus said, "she'll love that."

"She'll understand. We had our video cams on. I'll show her Evelyn charging from the hallway, weapon in hand, which is illegal to own in Canada."

"So was the Colt you shot her with."

"Shut up, Kabong. Let's check over the house and then head for the ship. I think we need to head for the high seas."

"Dr. Deville told us to only save Amir for interrogation," Jian said. "Gus and I gave them their one-way ticket to eternity on the way to the Ranger. Robyn cleared our way to the ship. Apparently, she has some very good contacts at the ports too."

"She works with the Canada Border Services," Nick mentioned. "I'm certain there are a lot of Canadian citizens and law enforcement that are fed up with this terrorist coddling."

"Lucas started the checkoff sheet for leaving port. I'm glad our families were able to go ashore for at least a day in Vancouver."

"Except for the storm, the scenery made them all happy," Nick replied. "The kids even loved the storm."

"Speaking of storms. The Cruella Deville podiatry clinic is already in operation." Cala took over the driver's seat.

"John told us Jared already talked with his father. At first, Amir proclaimed great happiness," Johnny said, as they entered the van. "When he mentioned dedicating himself to establishing his own medical wing at the City of Hope, Amir threatened to have his two bodyguards torture him to death if he did not return. Jared kept his composure, resisting the urge to tell his father what actually happened to the bodyguards. He ended the call with Amir still screaming at him."

"Once Crue gets Amir to pay us for this very expensive excursion, I'm certain we will be able to give Jared the money to establish the best hospital in the Middle East," Nick replied. "Such an endeavor will also brighten the already bright future of our pet city."

"I'm certain once Dr. Deville explains what wonderful advances Amir's contributions will make to the City of Hope's health care system, he will be ecstatic with his donation."

"Exactly, Cala," Nick agreed. "I'll bet Amir jumps on board with Jared right after his introduction to Dr. Deville."

Chapter Seven: Senator Trouble

Amir screamed behind his gag, issuing a muted blurt of noise, as Lynn initiated his first podiatry exam. Because we planned to confiscate every fortune we could, Lynn provided her patient with the utmost care so he wouldn't quit breathing during her exam. She varied voltage and heat with the expertise learned through many applications of her fabulous learning tool. Amir passed out as Lynn shut down our interrogation equipment.

"Are you ready, Jafar. I doubt we'll be able to slow him down once he starts talking again?"

"I am ready, Crue. I will record it too."

"Wake him, Cheese. We'll be leaving port soon, thanks to Muerto's adlib with Deke the dog. Reception for Jafar to transfer funds may get interrupted."

I grinned at Clint and the minions in various positions while restraining Amir. Our facilities aboard the Ranger adequately supplied us with everything for the cruise except restraints. I forgot to mention transferring one of our gurneys from Pain Central. No one else thought to do it either, but the Cheeseburger gets barbequed for it. Silvio created a workable table for the interrogation. It required extra help though during Crue's longer educational moments. I slapped Amir lightly to get him into full groaning consciousness.

"Listen closely, Amir," Lynn warned him. "If you don't, it will mean a lot more pain. We don't want that, do we?"

A virulent negative headshake, accompanied by a mewling muffled please, convinced Lynn he understood the consequences.

"Good. When we remove your gag, you will tell us the account numbers for all your wealth. We will use it to build Jared a hospital with all the trimmings in our new City of Hope. Won't that be wonderful? If you do not start helping in the transfer, I will need to reeducate you with another ten minutes of unbelievable pain."

Once I removed his gag, Amir rattled off everything but the account numbers. I gestured for Lynn to halt the second procedure for a moment. I slapped Amir hard enough to jolt his brain back into place. "Account numbers first, Amir. We'll get to the other questions later."

We finished with the accounts a half hour later when Jafar signaled completion. "Definitely enough to build and stock a hospital, John. You already signed the construction firm we need to start the project. Would you like me to transfer the funds?"

"Yep. The sooner the better. Tell them we want a small quickie medical office with all the things on the list Jared gave us when we didn't know how soon the hospital could be built."

"On it."

"Okay, my very helpful friend, we need to delve into your need to end my life. What or who put you in the mood to see me and my crew dead?"

"I did it… out of revenge. I thought you could be lured to Abu Dhabi. When… you refused, I settled for your friend."

"You thought I would try and rescue him in the Emirates?"

"Yes. All the kafirs who seek to destroy Islam with this kafir city. I…I would kill my own son rather than see him there working, even in his own hospital."

"Wow, that's very modern age of you," Lynn said. "We will now build the hospital for your son. He will run the entire operation, including recruitment of other likeminded doctors willing to work in the new city medical center. It will be the chance of a lifetime for him. It's too bad you're so small minded you can't even be proud of him."

"He is helping to destroy my religion! Islam must be preserved at all cost. People in the Middle East are all talking about this new city. We nearly assimilated all of Europe and the

143

UK before the action by your…" Amir shut up, remembering what would happen if he trekked down that trail. "Jared was meant to be with me in the Emirates. The only thing he will accomplish in that blasphemous place you are sending him is turning people against the Prophet and Islam. That is a death sentence in our faith!"

"So, this whole vendetta against us has to do with your warped religion? There's no one else on the perimeter of this stupid idea of yours pulling your puppet strings?" I found it hard to believe, but Amir nearly had me convinced.

"There is no one else. I wanted you all dead, and the city eventually attacked and destroyed as a lesson."

"Put his gag back in, Cheese. I ain't buyin' it," Lynn said. "He needed backing to get the Emirates to join in on an ambush of the magnitude he's talking about."

I did as instructed. Amir tried to scream. I gave him a short chop to the throat that would not kill him but it would limit his ability to scream.

Lynn cranked the juice up for a varying fifteen minutes of nightmare, nearly enough to fry his brain. She backed off before he passed out. I waited another few moments for his brain to unscramble. He needed to know what would happen if Lynn didn't get something new and interesting. It would not be a bluff, even if Amir was telling the truth. Lynn didn't like being called a kafir.

"Listen closely again. I want to hear something new come out of your mouth this time, or I will throw the switches and burn the brain right out of your skull. Are we clear? Do you understand? When you address me, you will say yes, Mistress of the Dark."

Amir was so prepped, he began sobbing with real tears while shaking his head violently in the affirmative. I removed his gag.

"Benny Danders!"

Lynn slapped him with comical nuance. "Amir! You can do better than that idiot communist in the Senate. The moron has never held a real job in his entire life. He's never held an original thought in his head. The Senate screwed the veterans by allowing the pervert on that committee. What the hell committee that he's on would interest you Islamic assholes, other than the fact he's on the Saudi payroll? Don't make me crank you up for the final time. You won't like it!"

"Wait…wait!" Amir stopped himself from crying with visible effort. "Danders is on the Health, Education, Labor and Pensions Committee'! He tweaks law having to do with Islam in the schools, and finds ways for us to launder money through the Labor and Pensions Committee. My money recruited him. My agent… in Washington, DC confers with him regularly. Because of my connection to Danders, I was given permission to try and draw your team to the Emirates."

"Shit!" Lynn walked away from the table. "Good Lord almighty! Do these assholes own everyone in the Senate and House? We knew Danders and his wife scam everything and everyone in contact with them… but this? I'm thinking retirement to Monster Island, guys."

"What the hell fun would that be," Clint asked, gripping her from behind. "We war, babe. It's what we do. No one in the blue-collar citizen population has a voice. They barely have time from jobs and kids to understand anything about the political prostitutes they elect. We're their voice. We act outside the law because the liberals have perverted it to a point where only criminals have a voice in it."

Lynn shuddered under the touch of her soulmate in all things. "Sorry. I got lost for a moment."

Lynn returned to the table with fire in her eyes. She grabbed Amir's chin in her hands. "Belt it all out, Pooky. Everything you know about Danders, I want recorded. Speak carefully and completely about every business deal he has ever been in on that you know about. Think! We will give you time for this traitor. Then, I want to know where we can get hard evidence. I want your agent's name in Washington DC, along with his address!"

Having stared for the last few moments into Lynn's face, Amir had only one response: yes… Mistress of the Dark!"

After Amir completed his answers and began stuttering into repeats, Denny spoke for the first time from DC. Jafar networked with him during the entire interrogation. "I ask that because of your desire to help his son establish a medical center in the City of Hope, consider giving Amir to me. We need to get Danders. I'll send Clyde Bacall to bring him here for further questioning and holding until I can place him with my intelligence gathering group."

"It will be Important to keep Amir under lock and key if we let you take him, Denny," I stated when Lynn simply shrugged.

"Of course, John. You won't regret this." Denny's excitement caused some amusement amongst our network. "Will it be okay with Nick?"

"What? You don't want to piss off the number one assassin in the world," Lynn replied.

"Nor the number one interrogator, Lynn. I'm trying to stay alive to watch my kid grow up. There may be people in this business who take the teams they work with lightly. Paul and I do not. You've already proven the taking of Amir was the right call. We did not have Senator Danders on our radar other than as another coin operated fraud. Is Nick with you?"

"No," I answered. "He's meeting to thank his contact, Robyn. I believe you and Paul know her."

"Yep. She's one of us. Jafar updated me with the video taken in Amir's snatch and grab. The cleanup work Nick did was his usual excellence in detail. It was unfortunate about Evelyn Scott, but she left Nick with no choice. If he has any qualms about Amir, tell him to call me. Although Jared wanted him dead, having your father killed even when he deserves it, is something I would like to spare the kid."

Plus, you get Amir, Spawn. By the chuckles on our network I was certain I had company with that train of thought. "I believe Nick feels the same way, not that he wouldn't kill both of them without blinking."

Denny took a deep audible breath. "That's how I figured it too."

* * *

Nick straightened a bit at the coffee shop booth as Robyn MacEachern entered. She nodded and joined him. Nick handed her the house keys for the rented place he used for only a day. "Thanks for all your help Robyn."

"You got me good with the twenty-thousand-dollar bonus in my offshore account. I never expected an amount like that. Then, I began wondering if you ran into problems."

"Evelyn Scott's dead. Amir's four henchmen also went the way of the dodo." Nick cued the video in muted mode, with the scene of Evelyn attacking from the hallway with weapon in hand. He also showed her the pictures of the cleaned houses. "We planned to turn her over to Canadian authorities. I didn't want you to think I was tying up loose ends."

Robyn shrugged. "It looks like you did a great CSI cleaning. She chose her side. I'll be okay. I'm certain no one will hear of her again. The family will eventually get around to checking on her. There will be an investigation. It will end as a missing persons case. I involved no one else in my work on this. There were no casualties on our side. That's what counts."

Robyn stood and shook hands with Nick. "Finish your coffee. I need to get back to work. Thanks again for the lovely bonus. No one will find Evelyn, right Nick?"

"Absolutely not."

* * *

Nick and Johnny helped Cala prepare the bodies for deposit in the ocean down in the Panga boat launch section, as Gus and Lucas steamed out of port. They loaded each of the prepared bodies, stripped and disemboweled on top of a tarp already lining the boat. When they finished, Nick flipped the tarp over the corpses. They washed the bags with saltwater thoroughly. The bags would need to be dried at the fantail.

"Gus will steer us out further than need be," Nick said. "We'll take the Panga out tonight when we anchor for the evening. Until then, we'll need to watch my snoopy young charges. Although this area will be locked down, we can never be sure what devilment Jean will get into. She saw us board Amir and deposit the bags down here. She and Sonny aren't ghouls, but they'll be curious. If it weren't for the fact Rachel's head would explode, I would have let the kids see the bodies before we prepared them for the ocean."

"Get ahead of it, Muerto," Cala advised. "Tell Jean and Sonny what we've done so she doesn't get a crowbar to break into this area."

Nick thought it over. "I'll tell Rachel first and get her in the loop. The kids are chasing the dogs around the decks so I'll have a little time. Lynn has Amir drugged in one of the crew cabins with her minions taking turns guarding and looking in on him."

"Are you surprised they let him live," Johnny asked.

"A little. I don't think he'll cause any trouble where Denny takes him. Although his motive isn't pure, Denny's right about Jared going on with his life knowing he had no part in killing his father. In his new life building a hospital medical facility in the City of Hope, he can avoid his relatives, who will surely be wondering what happened to Amir and his fortune."

"I'm excited about tonight after we go boating with the bait," Cala said. "You'll be singing and playing piano again as we planned. Johnny and I will dance the night away. When do we discuss the new political storm?"

"Denny's investigating it. Clyde's meeting us in port to take Amir into custody. It will be good to see him."

"He and Dannie have something going on," Johnny said. "I hope it works out for him. Lynn won't want to lose her trusted assistant."

"Dannie will be finishing college first. You're right about one thing though, she's already been with him in DC. Lynn said Dannie's hooked on the Washington DC power structure. She knows the depths of depravity there, but the glitz of parties, dinners, and Clyde's role as the CIA Director's Chief of Staff has left their mark on Dannie. Anyway, if we have a part in busting Senator Danders, John will let us know. I believe we'll be on the Otter's Point beach, sipping in the mornings again, for a while after we get home."

"I am ready for that," Johnny stated. "We did not get much of a break after the City of Hope venture. This cruise has been fun and informative. I had no idea the number of duties to be carried out aboard a ship like this."

"We all did more this time out with regular passengers to work around. Except for Jean and Sonny, the rest of our guests treated this as a pleasure cruise. How did I do as chef?"

"No complaints, except from Tina, which is to be expected," Cala replied. "I want to go on the cruise to take the Ranger to Monster Island again after we drop off the guests."

"You would be welcome, considering the number of crew it takes. If we get back in time, I'll take Jean and Sonny too. They loved the cruise. They did as much deckhand work as any of the adults. Even Lucas was impressed with them. I know Gus was. They only had to be told the right way once on anything they did. Let's go air out these bags on the fantail."

   * * *

Nick, with Deke sitting next to him, shook hands with Clyde Bacall. "It's good seeing you, Clyde."

"Paul sends his regards." Clyde searched beyond the dock landing where passengers disembarked from the Ranger. Dannie appeared, waving at him energetically. He waved back. "Ah... it's good to see you too, Nick. Would you mind watching Amir for me while I say hello to Dannie?"

"Sure. Amir is a new man since meeting Dr. Deville, right buddy?"

149

Amir, standing next to Nick, kept his eyes on the pier. "Yes. If I may find a place never to see her again, I will do anything... anything."

"That's the spirit. Go on, Clyde. We'll wait for you here. Do you need me to go back with you?"

"No, but thanks, Nick. I have two of Denny's men with me. Excuse me."

Clyde went on to meet Dannie. The meeting, passionate and uncaring about who saw what, went on for a few moments as others streamed by them. Nick turned again to Amir. "You have a great opportunity to become a real man and father instead of a brainwashed lunatic. Denny will get you in touch with Jared regularly. Once you've thrown off the Islamic mutant yoke, maybe you will be allowed to visit him at his new City of Hope medical facility."

"I will never visit the city of blasphemy!"

Nick grinned because Amir spoke while staring at his feet. "It's good you've learned humility. It will serve you well. Jared will far exceed anything you've ever done in your putrid life of Sharia Law Mutant enabling. If you ever find a way to hurt him or belittle him in any way, I will hunt you down and do you old school. I will slice you from your peanut dick to your chest until your intestines bulge out. Then, I give you an old school intestinal cleaning. Remember my warning when you talk with your son, Amir."

Nick spotted an agent he knew, striding towards him. "Deke. Hold."

Deke instantly crouched at Amir's feet, hackles up, and growling through fang filled mouth. Amir stood stock still.

"Ken Carter?" Nick shook the man's hand. "I thought you would have retired with the sum of money from our last journey into night."

"You know how it is. I can pretend I want to retire, but truth is, it would kill me. I get to soldier on this way until I can't do it physically. Paul and Clyde still trust me. I get to stay on the edge. I didn't approach to bore you with my life. Phil Salvatore called me, if you can believe that. He needs a bodyguard he can trust in a meeting with Senator Bethany Barren from Massachusetts."

Nick smiled. "You mean Bethany 'Littlebull' Barren, the one who claims to be one-thirty-second Cherokee, who has made a fortune pretending to be of Native American background?"

"That's the one. 'Littlebull' is tied up into some bigtime gangsters in Massachusetts, she can't shake. She promised them a number of things which they recorded. The dimwit thought she could play the Native American Card, along with laundering money through a charitable foundation supposedly for the homeless. On top of that, according to your nemesis, Phil, 'Littlebull' skimmed money. She believes they will kill her, or more likely, expose her to prosecution and eventually prison."

"I get it, Ken. 'Littlebull' approached the only passport dealing authority open to larceny in existence at this time. She knows what he's done in the past and wonders 'wow, how did he get away with it'. 'Littlebull' paid him in advance, and she wants the passport to escape under a phony name right now."

Ken nodded with grim smile. "You got it, chief. 'Littlebull' wants a meeting in guess where?"

"Pacific Grove, where our munchkin, Phil, lives. I guess Barren doesn't know I live there too. I nailed a number of Congressional toads recently." Nick paused, thinking over the fact Barren probably was aware Nick lived in Pacific Grove. "I'm beginning to wonder if maybe Barren does know I live in Pacific Grove. If she were hoping Phil would bring me in on the meeting, the pieces would fit together. Where did the chump agree to meet her... or her associates?"

"They want to come to his house," Ken replied. "You may be on to something. They also requested Sonny be there. The only reason he contacted me was because the con-artists are working out of the same place they live. They need protection. They also know asking you for it will mean unintended consequences, but

Barren doesn't know that. I had to renew my passport this year. Three guesses how Phil found me."

"He's a tool. No doubt about that, Ken. If we can nail Senator Barren, we'll do it on the spot. This may be an ambush, Ken. I may be on the menu rather than Phil. I have a feeling 'Littlebull' isn't leading this parade of imbeciles. I'm wondering if maybe I should call on our interrogator supreme to have a few words with Amir. Lynn possibly gave up on the question and answer session too soon, when Amir confessed to owning Benny Danders."

"Danders, huh? Good Lord... an outright commie like that piece of shit, with a wife double-dealing on the side, ripping off countless people with bank fraud while acting as a college president. I thought the FBI was already on the trail of those larcenous assholes."

"They are. Once you allow the Saudis and billionaire globalists to form a cabal of one world order anarchists, the game they play becomes nearly impossible to beat without forces outside the law. Danders and Barren could be on the same string. Barren may have branched out too far with her schemes into a partnership with people who don't play by anyone's rules. I'm getting real interested in these gangsters Barren supposedly screwed. How did you handle Phil's approach?"

"He called me yesterday. We tangled first on how he managed to get my private phone number. I admit my first thought was to twist his head off."

"Been there, brother." Nick told Ken what he had done to the couple in the night, giving them special haircuts they were still hiding. Nick smiled, seeing Ken express wild amusement at Nick's dark night attitude adjustment.

"Nick... you are... the best. I didn't tell him no, because I knew I would be meeting with you today. I'll play the hand all the way if you want to sit in."

"I do. This illustrates the fact those two will need to be watched throughout their lives. They never stop, no matter what danger they put themselves into. Phil's nearly been killed or imprisoned more times than I like to think about. If he wasn't the father of my daughter's best friend I would have killed him. Thanks for bringing this to me. When you find out the details of this new scheme, call me. Since we snatched Amir, I should be sitting around my house writing pulp fiction."

"Clyde told me you're taking contracts on the 'Dark Web' again. Maybe it would be a good idea to stick with the novel writing."

"The last time I tried retirement from it, I lost an edge I can't afford to lose. You're a fine one to talk, Agent Carter."

"Baby steps," Ken deadpanned. "Let me load Amir for Clyde after you try your word trap. Clyde's in love. I want him to take as much time as he wants with his girlfriend. Dannie's quite a lady. She survived the gangs, Harding's interrogator supreme, and turned her life around. I heard how close to death Clyde came when he thought this Company gig was a game he could walk away from. They make a great pair."

Nick motioned Ken to come with him. "Good idea. Amir's not completely civilized, but he's subdued. Don't turn your back on him for a second."

Ken grinned at Amir, taking him by the arm as Deke rejoined Nick at his side. He opened the word game for Nick. "We'll get along fine. I'll be talking with you soon, Nick. Do you want me to brief Paul on this thing with Senator Barren?"

"Absolutely. I want him and Denny in on that from the start in case it becomes clear Barren and Danders take money from the same source." Nick watched Amir jolt slightly and glance up momentarily before returning his gaze to the ground. "You're lucky I'm in a good mood, Amir. You confirmed my suspicion with body language. Say it out loud for me or I call over Dr. Deville."

Amir tensed, looking around the pier for any sign of Lynn. "Please... do not! Barren has taken my money. My operative in Washington DC acts as my liaison for both Senators."

"Your operative you mentioned to Dr. Deville, named Fuma Sabedin, did she report to you about the trouble Barren got into with gangsters?"

Amir gasped, while looking beyond Nick, seeing Lynn walk onto the pier with Clint and the baby. They stopped to talk with Clyde and Dannie. Amir shook his head in the negative with violent emphasis. "No... no... we obtained information about anything related to spreading Islam, laundering money for projects connected with the Muslim Brotherhood and C.A.I.R., who in turn spread our investment over the network we have built. Fuma suspected Barren was dealing with someone else. She is on prime committees we need updated on."

"That makes sense, Nick. Senator Barren sits on the Banking, Housing, Urban Affairs Committee," Ken said. "She's on a strategic subcommittee on the Armed Forces Committee. I would guess her other committee assignment would be a bonanza for Amir too. The Committee on Health, Education, Labor, and Pensions would be a monumental plus, interpreting law where vast amounts of money can be mishandled, redirected, and disappear. Fuma Sabedin is 'Littlebull' Barren's personal assistant."

"Take this prick before I shoot him in the head. Please update Clyde, Paul, and Denny on all this crap. I'll try and learn what group or gang Barren has been dealing with on the side. I have an idea this may be political rather than gang related. If I find Danders went on the hook right after Barren, it may be they were tipped off by a past target of mine: former Senator Diane Cameron. I remember that Fuma woman worked for Cameron. Diane has a big grudge against me. I forced her resignation and emptied her bank accounts. I heard she landed on her feet giving idiot speeches for half a mil a year."

"Here comes 'Don Juan' Bacall now," Ken said. "He has Dannie with him. Maybe Lynn gave her time off to come with us. She already has a bag."

"Dannie's coming with us, Ken. I'll drive. You and Tucker can sit with Amir in the back, okay?"

"Sure. Hi, Dannie. Good to see you." Ken hugged Dannie. "We have Paul's ride this trip. You'll like the trip to DC in it."

"You look a lot happier since deciding not to retire, Ken," Dannie replied. She turned to Nick. "You're amazing, Nick. You need to perform on one of those reality shows. I'm making Clyde attend the next piano man concert."

"I look forward to it, Dannie. Have a nice trip. You can fill in Clyde in the car, Ken. Dannie's cleared all the way into Top Secret territory."

"Good to know," Ken replied. "That's what happens when you hang out with Monsters."

"Yes, but they're my Monsters now, Ken. If you had been on board being entertained by Muerto, you'd think twice about the Monster tag. We'll get you a date to attend with Clyde and me on the next outing."

"I'm in," Ken agreed. "Just so Muerto doesn't do any Rap music."

They walked off chuckling over Ken's joking line. In answer, Nick launched into a spot-on MC Hammer 'U Can't Touch This'. In moments, no one on the pier could speak. To say shock and hilarity prevailed amongst the Monsters would be understating to the extreme. Jess ran over to join him. The duo turned the pier into a hand clapping accompaniment, with Nick doing both the music sound effects and duo dancing in perfect sync with Jess, including hand waves, hops, and moon-walk. They ended their performance to wild cheers and applause. Jess shoulder hugged the much smaller Nick.

"You good to go, brother! Where the hell did you pick all that up at?"

"In France, when I did the gig as a nightclub performer. I did a couple of Michael Jackson tunes, alternating between dancing, playing, and singing. It took the longest time for me to mimic Hammer. You are incredible, Jess. You have the moves, brother."

"Man, I did Hammer all the damn time when I was a kid."

"We'll work it in when I play for us all next time," Nick promised. "My crew and I need to get in the air back to the 'Grove'. We have a date on my favorite beach tomorrow morning, sipping the Irish, and toning down a bit."

"Until I wind your clock again, Muerto," Ken called out while walking away.

Nick took a deep breath as Rachel with Quinn in her arms, Jean, Sonny, and Deke the dog moved to be near him. "Until then, Agent Carter... until then. Don't bother calling tomorrow."

Ken waved his understanding.

"What clock are we talking about winding, Muerto," Rachel asked with furrowed brow.

"I'll tell you all about it on our deck back home with an iced Beam brother and the piano keys under my fingers."

"Okay, but this clock winding better not include a Phil and Clarice involvement."

Silence.

"Uh oh," Jean said, yanking on Sonny's arm. "Jay had the Phil and Clarice watch. He didn't text us about anything."

"I'll go home and find out what's going on," a dejected Sonny replied. "I'm sure it's bad."

"Stay over at our place until I get it sorted out, as much as you're allowed, kid," Nick advised. "There may be some dangerous elements to this I need to investigate before you can hang around your folks for more than short periods of time. You have the Muerto alarm button if someone dangerous arrives at the house. I'll see about getting a safe-room added at your home. It seems we can't talk sense to your folks no matter what we do. Keeping them alive is becoming a fulltime job."

Rachel walked away. "I won't need to kill Clarice. I'll just beat her into a coma. No… I'll go old school with the stun-gun nightstick… or maybe-"

"We better go after her and get Kong, Dad. I think mom's rode the wave into the rocks."

"Yep. I think you're right." Nick hurried to Rachel's side, taking Quinn from her.

Jean turned to Sonny. "First thing is check on Jay."

"Agreed. Do you think maybe I really was stolen at the hospital?"

"Maybe. We'll talk dad into forging documents making it true."

"That'll work."

* * *

Nick finished two hours of line edits on the deck while sipping an iced Beam brother. Jean and Sonny sat near him, working feverishly on the Phil and Clarice tapes while texting with Jay. Sonny installed the tracking device Nick gave him which recorded the destinations Phil visited. Deke slept with his head on Nick's shoe. Rachel entered with a veggie tray and dip.

"Quinn's down for the evening. I figured you three would be ready for a snack, especially you, Hemingway. Didn't I read somewhere that the real Ernest Hemingway advised 'write drunk, edit sober'."

"That's a misquote," Nick corrected her. "Besides, I believe moderation in all things to be the golden rule."

"I have the link to some very bad videos illustrating the opposite, Muerto," Rachel replied. "You promised an explanation into this new event. Did you have a chance to investigate what's going on and why Phil felt the need to pay a bodyguard to attend a fake passport meeting?"

"They covered their tracks at the house, which left Jay with nothing to report. The tracker recorded Phil going to his office in San Francisco more than he has done since starting work there. The kids began a detailed search of the videos made from the security cams at the house."

"We haven't found anything," Jean admitted. "They're careful in the house. We're all trying to figure out why they would schedule a meeting at home when they know dad has the place under surveillance."

"I did find the story claiming Senator 'Littlebull' Barren fears some shadowy gang she defrauded to be 'big bull'," Nick added. "I hacked into her phone records and email account. I also investigated Diane Cameron. She conducted video conferencing, phone calls, and a torrent of emails under a pseudo name she didn't know I knew about from my last investigation when I busted her."

"I get it," Rachel replied. "Cameron figures she can make her move on you now with this whacky idea to enlist Barren's help setting the ambush. Unlike you naïve children, I know why the meeting is at Phil and Clarice's house. They want you dead more than Cameron does. To understand this crap, you need to think like those two toads. This elaborate scheme involving Ken Carter involves something about Ken too."

Nick leaned back with the kids watching him speculatively. He smiled. "Ken treated Phil like the fraud and would be traitor he is the last time we needed to keep Phil under guard. Your thesis fits the scheme perfectly. As Jean said, they know we have the house under surveillance. We have a way to confirm what you suspect. After Ken agrees to the deal, if Phil and Clarice start talking about it, we'll know it's to draw me into the ambush. Ken talked about a stipulation Sonny had to be there. There's just too many loose ends. I'll play some piano and entertain for a while. It helps me think."

"Want another Beam?"

"Thanks. I believe I will."

* * *

158

Nick walked Deke, pondering the complexity of a plot so convoluted as to make no sense at all. Phil and Clarice hated him, but ambushing him in their own house made no sense at all. The scheme hinged on Nick taking the bait. His phone buzzed. It was Ken Carter.

"Phil wants to meet with us tomorrow, Nick. He's given up all pretense. When Barren told Phil that Sonny had to be there too, he decided to come clean and get you involved too. Phil inadvertently intercepted emails between Danders, Barren, Diane Cameron, Fuma Sabedin, and Tark Ruban, the billionaire supposed philanthropist. They describe a massive money laundering scheme, camouflaging funds from Ruban and the Saudis into political action committees to elect Muslims into key state positions in Michigan. The funds will be to buy judicial positions for Sharia Law activists in the state too. They're grooming a Muslim for the Governorship, and eventually the Presidency. Their plan is to run Benny Danders as President, with Abu El-Tayed as Vice President. El-Tayed would be next in line."

"Gee, there's some good news. I'm beginning to wish it was an ambush to kill me. How in hell did Phil intercept the emails and how much was he trying to blackmail them for?"

"Sabedin was careless with her laptop. She left it on the front seat of her car. Someone who knew who she was, broke in and stole it. The thief worked for Phil when he was bigtime in DC. He called Phil and asked for twenty-thousand for the laptop. Phil told him no way, unless he could get past the security password. Phil wanted a sample. The thief paid to have it hacked and sold it to a very enthusiastic Phil."

"Now we're getting closer to a Phil scam. How much?"

"Phil demanded five million. They agreed after some deliberation. Barren wanting a meeting at his house for the exchange, with Sonny there, finally set off the alarms in Phil's head. Last night, Darin Soledad, the laptop thief, was found strapped to a chair inside an abandoned warehouse with a bullet through the back of his head."

"So, heavyweight king makers, foreign governments, Senators, and billionaire anarchists, bound together in an illuminati type cabal, unafraid to erase anyone who gets in their way, huh? Phil should have asked for less. They would have given him half a million." After Ken's revelation, Nick talked with his attention on the area around him, paying close attention to Deke's sense of danger. "They have something huge planned, but short of blowing the house up with the Salvatore family in it, what would they figure on doing?"

"The wildcard is you, Nick. Phil stated they don't know anything about you being tied in with him in any way. Diane Cameron wants you dead, The Saudis want you dead. Danders, Barren, and Sabedin will soon want you dead. The good news is they think they're going against Phil and probably a security guard."

"They'll go for overkill with numbers. It will be difficult to ascertain what they have planned at this stage. It would be a clean snatch and grab to simply take you all hostage while they tear Phil's place apart, keeping a gun or knife at Sonny's throat until they make sure of having all potential blackmail items. Knowing Phil, he would claim to have multiple files ready to be released if something happens to him. He doesn't have the brains, even after what I've done to him, to realize they'll make him tell them everything."

"I like your thinking on the hostage taking," Ken agreed. "We know they won't give the jerk five million dollars. That leaves only killing Phil's family and gambling it's a bluff, or taking us all hostage until they find his blackmailing tools. What's our counter?"

"Kill them all, except one, to explain the situation."

"Simple, yet elegant. We'll need the cartoons in on this."

"That we will, Ken. I'll recruit them tomorrow morning. Pick a hotel in Monterey to stay at when you fly in. I will meet with you and Phil there. By then, he'll have a tail, making sure of his whereabouts at all times. It may be possible for me to snatch the guy following him."

"I bet he'd be glad to tell you what they have planned, Muerto."

"Absolutely."

* * *

"Tell me again why we're following this clown." The man kept three cars back from their target. "We should grab the wife and kid right now. Make 'em scream until this ass-wipe tells us everything."

"The Senator thinks this guy is cute enough to really have a dead man release on the files," his companion answered. "You heard him on the phone. He's meeting with some dunce he hired for protection. We'll see where the guy's staying. One of us will take him out before the meeting."

Gordon Cantor and Fitz Burnington worked under the guise of campaign advisors for Senator Bethany Barren. In reality, they were contract killers, working as enforcers when their real boss, Tark Ruban's business dealings, required protection or enforcement. They left small messages of terror for people who crossed Ruban's associates.

Flashing lights behind them caused Cantor to curse, while glancing into his rearview mirror. "What the fuck is this. I'm in the middle of a stream of traffic."

"Pull over, G. It can't be any big deal. Maybe we have a taillight out or something."

Cantor stopped at the curb. "Hey, these guys are wearing US Marshal vests! What the hell would the Marshals be stopping us for."

"Don't know, but I don't like it. We may need to pull the plug on this gig. Tark will have our asses on pikes if we get jammed."

"Give me the registration, Fitz." Cantor took the registration given him while opening the window of their rental SUV. The man approaching his window smiled. "Oh shit!"

161

* * *

Nick pressed the stun-gun into Cantor's temple while firing the Taser needles from the gun in his left hand into Fitz at full charge. Cantor slumped unconscious sideways while Fitz did the dance electric for a few more moments. Nick hit the unlock button. Johnny and Jian yanked Fitz out of the passenger seat. They deposited him in the rear seat and restrained his hands behind his back quickly. Nick tossed Cantor over the center console for Jian and Johnny to restrain in the rear seat. Nick slipped into the driver's seat with Johnny beside him. Jian closed the doors and ran back with Gus in the Ford. Johnny used knockout syringes on both men, on their way to Carmel Valley. Johnny called Ken.

"Two in the rear seat, on their way for hell to greet."

Ken chuckled. "You've been hanging with Muerto too much, Johnny. I'll talk things over with Phil. Call me if you learn anything we need to discuss right away. Muerto was right. This was a snatch and grab. They followed him to find out where I was. My shelf-life was due to be less than a snow-cone on a Las Vegas street corner in August."

"I will call with anything new, Frosty," Johnny replied, ending the call while hearing Ken's amusement with Johnny's tag.

Cantor struggled to sit first, squinting at Nick. He shook his head and remained silent. Burnington groaned his way into a sitting position, glancing at his partner.

"What is it, G?"

"We're dead men, Fitz. That's Nick McCarty driving."

"The guy… the Saudi guys are scared shitless of?"

"Yep. How did we cross you, McCarty?"

"It's a long story, G," Nick replied, using the man's initial like his companion did. "We're all men of the world here. Why talk politics at a time like this? You guys work for a traitorous gasbag with a lot of money. He's slowly flaying America's skin off with his BLM, Antifa, and La Raza thug army. We're the

162

resistance – the first guys you want to see at your side in a fight, and the last you ever want to see facing you. I won't bore you guys. We need questions answered. Do we need to go over the rules? Johnny has a helpful video montage where the guys we questioned ignored the rules."

"I know the rules," Cantor said. "What is it you want to know?"

"That's the spirit."

* * *

"Where the fuck are those two idiots hired to be with us, Al," Danders asked. He nervously paced the hotel suite where four other armed men waited to attend the meeting with Danders and Barren. "Do you think they waited to ambush the guy Salvatore hired?"

"I can't say, Sir. They're not answering their phones. They may have gone dark to handle him, but I don't know why they would have."

"These four guys can handle that pussy, Salvatore," Barren stated. "We'll keep one outside on watch in case the security guard shows up. Cantor was right. We should have grabbed the wife and kid while Salvatore met with his guardian, for all the good it was going to do him. Five minutes with him and he'll be begging to tell us everything."

"Don't get your Cherokee blood in an uproar, 'Littlebull'," Danders retorted. "We're on site. Nothing can go wrong or we are in deep shit."

"Listen, Crazy Benny." Barren poked her finger in Danders' chest. "Even God couldn't get you reelected in your bankrupt state after the crap you and your wife pulled, you weasel! I agreed to this shit so we could get Tark out of harm's way before this nobody, Salvatore, released Fuma's files. The guy's delusional, demanding five million. I wonder how he liked his thief buddy getting a .22 caliber bullet in the back of the head."

"Speaking of Fuma, this whole debacle happened because of her carelessness. Tark then has to send two sitting Senators to gather what was lost with his hirelings to make certain the information never gets out."

"Fuma is protected through the Muslim Brotherhood, with contacts in Saudi Arabia and the Emirates," Barren replied. "Besides, admit it. We're here to make sure the two of us stay out of each other's files. I don't want you leaking shit to the press if I run against you in the future. You can't be trusted. You have no honor."

"Honor? Really? A tick on your sacred buffalo's ass has more honor than you do, 'Littlebull'. We're here to do a job. Tark must be protected. He's our last huge contributor able to fund our projects and get the people bused or flown where we need them. Cafrey Rothstein and Michael Moronas disappeared. Even Tark doesn't know what happened to them. There are rumors mercenaries snatched them on his island. I've heard they have a military governor there now, and the island treats medical emergencies, along with providing care for orphans."

"Senators? We need to do the meeting or abort. Gordon and Fitz are missing in action," Al told them. "What is your decision?"

Danders gestured at the surrounding luxurious living room. "Tark let us use his estate here in Monterey. We flew in on his private jet. No one knows this place. We could wait this out. Salvatore will contact us again. You guys could track down Cantor and Burnington."

"We were to get this done and fly back to DC by tonight, Sir," Al said.

"Listen, Bolero." Barren stood with pursed lips and hands on hips. "We've interrupted everything to come here. Call Mr. Ruban."

"I can't do that, Ma'am." Al Bolero moved closer to the two Senators, speaking in a quieter tone. "Mr. Ruban ordered me not to contact him under any circumstances. My advice is we abort this."

"Surely, the four of you could-"

Four men in US Marshal's vests rushed into the room with MP5 submachine guns already pointing at targets.

* * *

Nick finished injecting Burnington with a lethal dose of his eternity shot. "You guys have been very helpful, G. It makes everything a bit easier since Ruban loaned the team and Senators his estate in Monterey. That Paseo Vista Place must be beautiful. With your keycard, my guys and I can surprise those idiot Senators. I have a little plan for their special demise."

"I guess we couldn't make a deal, huh Nick? I could testify against everybody."

Nick gripped Cantor's shoulder. "Sorry, G. No can do. It's bad business at our level to leave pros alive we've crossed paths with in a bad way."

"It was worth a try." Cantor shut his eyes as the syringe needle expelled the death serum into his neck.

Nick straightened. "You were sure right about emptying out the freezer the moment we returned, Reaper. After this, we'll need to make another fish food flight tomorrow."

"What is the plan you mentioned to Cantor?"

"It depends on us being able to capture the killers alive for non-bloody disposal, Gus. We have forty minutes before the proposed meeting. I know the area Ruban's estate is in. Cala drives. She can let us out near the estate. We'll trek in quiet and see if we can take them by surprise. This is a gamble of sorts, but it will work perfectly in the scheme of things, especially at an estate owned by Ruban."

"I called Ken," Johnny said. "He had a little trouble with Phil at the hotel. Phil wanted to hang on to the laptop. Ken had to get physical with him."

"Good. How did we do on damaging evidence?"

Johnny grinned. "Everything we hoped for. Will you be arresting the Senators for Tim and Grace to do a US Marshal transfer?"

"Nope. They're going to kill each other," Nick replied.

Jian stared at Nick uncomprehendingly. "They are?"

Gus took a deep breath. "You haven't seen that Muerto scene yet, Dragon. I'm picturing it. Like Muerto says, we need to get their contract killers without a mess."

"How do you make two Senators kill each other, Muerto? Do you hypnotize them?"

"You'll see," Nick told him. "It's a very delicate process."

"Oh brother," Gus said.

"We need to leave for our appointment." Nick headed for the stairs leading out of their underground torture center. "We don't have time to freeze G and Fitz."

Chapter Eight: Political Correction

Nick smiled at Gus as Cantor's keycard opened the entrance door. "Follow me, boys."

Inside, Nick heard voices yammering at each other in less than cordial tones. He stayed along the wall, moving toward the voices. At the entrance to the living room area, Nick strode through with Gus, Johnny, and Jian spreading out at his sides, MP5s at the ready.

"On the floor! Now! Make a move and we rake you with a 9mm hollow point burst!"

The four killers thought about reaching. In custody, the killers had no clue if they would be bound over for past crimes. Barren started sobbing. Danders peed his pants and dived for the floor, face down.

"Okay... go for it," Nick said. "My burst hits across you guys at your balls level. My friends will aim high. Before you die, you'll all know how it feels not to have a dick."

"Fine. You'd best hope we don't get free, Marshal," Al told him. Al got face down on the floor, as did his companions.

"Lock your hands behind your heads." Nick pointed at Barren as Jian began restraining the men while Johnny and Gus covered them. "Quit your crying and get face down on the floor, 'Littlebull'. If you don't do it, I'll do it for you."

Barren knelt carefully. "Who...who are you?"

"I'm US Marshal Nick McCarty. With me are Marshals Nason, Groves, and Chen. Face down, Senator. That's it. Lock those fingers behind your liberal head."

"I'll have your badge for this, McCarty! Why does your name sound familiar?"

"I put one of your cohorts out of business: Diane Cameron. She sold out to the Sharia Law Mutants just like you and 'Crazy Benny'. I busted her ass out of the Senate."

"Yes! I know you now. You're nothing but a prejudiced asshole!"

"Spoken like a true fraud, 'Chief Littlebull'. I have more Cherokee blood in the heel of my shoe than you do in your entire line of miscreants, poser. Because we allowed the leftist, politically correct morons like you destroy the English language, a great word like prejudice disappeared from normal vocabulary and descriptive phrases. In past times, anyone of any race, creed, or color could be legitimately prejudiced against someone or something. For instance, I'm prejudiced against people without logical thinking capability and common sense - like you. I'm prejudiced against BLM/Antifa/La Raza goon squads. I'm prejudiced against liberal anarchist nitwits, striving to destroy the foundation of America – like you. I'm prejudiced against people incapable of hearing or reading a simple statement, without distorting the literal meaning, with whatever twisted morass of nonsense happens to be flowing in their own heads – like you. From now on when someone accuses me of being prejudiced, I'll just say 'thank you'. They still won't know what the meaning of the word is, but I will."

Nick restrained Barren at ankles and wrists as she cried out in anguish at her harsh treatment. Nick patted her down professionally. "Calm down, 'Littlebull'."

"Cala is in the front with the Ford," Johnny said. "Great speech, Muerto."

Nick grinned at his friends chuckling appreciation of his expansive reaction to 'Chief Little Bull'. Amusement for speeches to a dead person fit right in with their gig, as he restrained Danders in the same manner. "I know… I know… I get tired being lectured to by outright traitors, con-artists, and Sharia Law Mutant enablers. 'Crazy Benny' has good instincts. He knows to keep his mouth shut."

"We'll load our prisoners and give them something to relax their nerves," Gus said. "Wait for us to come in and help with the scene. You keep an eye on the Senators in case they say something that triggers another lecture, El Muerto."

"I'm done," Nick admitted. "I'm either preaching to the choir or casting pearls before the swine... oh wait a minute... you Sharia Law enablers hate pork, huh Benny?"

Nick nudged the very uncomfortable Benny Danders with his foot.

It worked. "We'll get you for this, McCarty! You can play all the angles, but you're dead meat! Our lawyers will strip away your entire life, asshole!"

Nick bent down to pinch Benny's cheek as his crew marched the killers out to their Ford. "Ah... alas... my poor 'Crazy Benny', none of what you hope or believe will happen. We have you two so completely, we can rig any ending we want for you."

"What?! You can't execute us! Are you insane?" Benny's wild and wooly gray head arched to tell Nick how wrong he was. "We're United States Senators, for God's sake! Let us go free and we will make all of this right."

"No... Benny boy... you won't," Nick said. "I do have a great ending to this scene. I'll see how Senator Barren feels about this. I think she's beginning to realize from her silence, the two of you are not walking out of here. See... the four thugs you had with you... they're dead already and stuffed in the luggage compartment of my very big SUV. I need to make a scene with you two of epic proportions. This scene, you two will be part of, may define political activism into the next century for all other leftist assholes."

Gus, Johnny, and Jian rejoined Nick. "Gus pointed at the tiny video cam attached to his vest. "Cala wanted a live remote shot of this so I'm staying back to give her a good recording."

"That's good. I'll help set the scene and direct. Director Deville will be so jealous." Nick helped the sobbing Barren to her feet and onto a lounge chair across from a large couch. "Relax here for a moment, 'Littlebull'. Do you know any Cherokee death chants?"

In response, Barren cried harder. Johnny and Jian had already yanked Benny to his feet, avoiding the puddle from his accidental discharge. Nick directed them to place him on the couch across from Barren. He then did a gloved hands inspection of Barren's large purse and Danders' briefcase, humorously surprised at what he found, but also glad he would not need to give up two of his unmarked weapons. He held his discoveries so his friends could see.

"Look what we have here, guys. These anti-gun nuts both own heat which works out well for my scene." Nick placed the 9mm Taurus handgun on the couch where Benny sat. "Shame on you, 'Crazy' Benny, and especially you, 'Littlebull'. You two own handguns while trying to deprive Second Amendment rights from the rest of our citizenry."

Nick made comical shaming gestures at the two after placing Barren's .32 caliber Beretta next to her. "Oh… you little hypocrite. You've been screaming for gun confiscation all these years and here you are packin' heat. This does make it very nice for me though."

Nick went to the expansive bar. He put ice in two glasses and filled them from a Bushmills bottle. He gave one of the glasses to Jian. "Help Benny sip his whiskey until it's gone. I advise you to drink it, Benny. You'll need a little buzz going."

Jian followed Nick's directions. Benny sipped at his enthusiastically without hesitation. Nick cut the restraint on Bethany Barren's wrists, but left the one on her ankles. He sat down beside Barren and helped her hold onto the whiskey glass with shaking hands, steadying her grip.

"Down the hatch, 'Littlebull'."

"I…I should throw it in your face… you murderer!" Instead, Barren with the steadying help of Nick's iron grip, drained her glass. Barren's petulant look returned with her glasses perched at the tip of her nose with mouth open, and eyes in wide glaring fashion. "Give me another whiskey and let me wipe my face."

"Absolutely." Nick gave over the glass to Johnny who took it to the bar with Danders' empty glass. "Want another, Benny?"

Johnny refilled both with a grin at Danders' enthusiastic head shake in the affirmative. Nick gave Barren a handkerchief from her purse. She wiped her face and blew her nose. Throwing aside the handkerchief, Bethany drained her second whiskey without Nick's help. He took the glass rather than have it thrown at him.

"One more?" Nick jiggled the glass.

A bleary-eyed Barren nodded. "Sure… why not?"

Both Danders and Barren sipped their third one more slowly. Nick handed off Barren's empty. He placed the Beretta in her right hand while blocking access to the trigger, and holding her in an iron grip around the chest from behind.

"Hold Benny still, guys."

Jian and Johnny gripped Danders' shoulders on each side while keeping as far away from him as possible.

Barren giggled. "I've dreamed of… shootin'… this old fraud."

"Bitch!" Danders was none too happy. "I see how this… plays out. I hope… I'm alive… to blast that bug-eyed look… right off your face."

As it was only necessary to make sure Barren showed gun powder residue on her hand, Nick slipped his finger onto the trigger. "This will hurt a bit, Benny. I need to wound you too. No one would expect two drunks to shoot expertly at each other."

Nick fired a couple of rounds through the couch near Danders. He shot a round through Dander's shoulder before spotting one near his heart. Barren jumped but giggled with each hit. "We need to switch places guys. Come hold onto Barren."

The men exchanged places after Nick restrained Barren's wrists behind her once again. He cut loose the gasping Danders.

Blood frothing at Benny's mouth meant the second shot hit his lung.

"Hurry... I want... a shot."

"Good thing... the bastard's helpin' you aim... you old commie!" Barren struggled slightly under Johnny and Jian's grips at her shoulders.

"Did you hear that, Benny? Let her go after the kill shot, guys." Nick cut off Danders' restraint at the wrists. He only needed to put the Taurus in his right hand while blocking access to the trigger. Nick had shot him on the left side so his movements were minimal.

Benny coughed blood as Nick squeezed off one shot into the couch.

"Missed me... you wanker!"

Nick stifled amusement, firing again into Barren's upper left chest, and then her forehead in rapid succession. Johnny and Jian allowed her to collapse and fall off the couch. Jian cut her restraints off. Nick held onto Danders with the Taurus still in Benny's hand while he passed away, his lung filling with blood.

"Good shot, Benny. You got her right between the eyes."

Danders' chuckle turned into a bloody death rattle as Nick allowed him and the Taurus to collapse on the couch. Nick patted his shoulder. "Perfect, Benny."

Nick studied Barren's position. Her right arm was up, so Nick pushed it gently forward. Her right hand rested then on the carpet. Nick put her Beretta a little past her hand. He then backed away, taking in the scene from different angles, finally straightening with a satisfied nod.

"This looks great. It's a damn shame when leftist liberals don't get along. Murdering each other like this though... horrible... simply horrible. There's a lesson in this for all of us," Nick lectured straight-faced and with big sighs.

"Don't mess with Muerto's the only lesson I see," Johnny replied.

"I was going with 'can't we all just get along'," Nick said.

"Oh barf! You are one sick puppy," Gus retorted.

"Can you do a Kabuki dance with one of the dead ones in the Ford," Jian asked.

"Not funny, Dragon breath! Don't encourage him. He's already in 'Hannibal Lecter' territory now."

"What a terrible thing to say, Payaso," Nick replied with shocked tone. "I have never cooked and eaten anyone."

"It's only a matter of time."

"Now, you're just being mean."

* * *

Gus awaited Nick and Cala at their hangar. They had prepped and loaded all the bodies in their UH-60M before dark. Nick let Cala fly out into an area, fifteen-miles offshore, which they found in the past to be an active shark area. The bodies, naked and sliced open with intestines open to avoid gas bubbles, usually attracted hits right away. This night had been no exception.

"That didn't take long at all," Gus greeted them.

"It turned into a fish feed frenzy," Cala said. "We were only there minutes. Muerto had not finished throwing out the fourth body and they struck hard."

"I confess I've been avoiding the news," Gus said. "Ken took the laptop with him back to DC. He says Paul will find a way to release what's on it to the media. Your shooting scene will be more believable once some of the laptop evidence hits the airwaves. Ken told us there is definitely enough on there to get the rats running around like they were on an electrical charged grid. Are you telling Rachel about your intention to pay Phil tonight?"

"I need to get it out in the open. If she finds out about it secondhand I'll be in the soup then. Law enforcement agencies have paid informants. They're in many cases sleaze-balls like Phil and Clarice. This way, I may at least be able to get them thinking about selling stuff to me, rather than to the enemy."

"Not five-million-dollars worth of stuff," Gus replied as he drove toward Nick's house. "I guess Ken really had to reeducate Phil on his position in all this. He told us Phil may have a cracked rib."

Nick grinned and sighed with content. "That may be enough to keep me off the hotplate with Rachel. It's hard to believe Phil would think he could play us for money. Out of curiosity, what did the weasel think he should get?"

"A million."

It took many moments for the three companions to rein in the hilarity they shared over Phil's attempted demands of Ken Carter.

"No wonder Ken worked the weasel over," Nick said finally. "Phil comes to us because he and Clarice try to extort five million dollars from a billionaire and his Senate minions so above the law they immediately hatch a plan to exterminate his family. Then, after realizing the facts, he comes to us for saving."

Nick paused while again loudly enjoying the moment. "He...he then tries to demand a million from his own nation's law enforcement agency because his traitorous extortion plot failed. Oh my... I will need to reveal this to Rachel in private. Sonny can take the truth, but not in front of everyone. He's tough enough for that too, but I ain't doing it that way."

"Perhaps Rachel will understand, Muerto," Cala offered.

Gus nearly drove to the side of the road as he and Nick enjoyed Cala's hoped for Rachel response. "Never underestimate Rachel's intense feelings toward Phil and Clarice, Reaper."

"It is really that bad, huh?"

"Yeah, it's really that bad," Nick answered. "I will need a couple of Bushmills before speaking to her on any level about Phil and Clarice. Her head will explode as it is with the amount I'm planning to pay them. We would never have gotten that laptop without them."

"How much, Muerto," Cala asked.

"I'm paying Ken fifty thousand for his part in this. He'll figure I shouldn't give him anything. I'm giving our dastardly duo a hundred thousand so they'll hopefully consider doing what's right in the future. Whether they do or not is anyone's guess."

"That is not so bad," Cala replied. "I am sure Rachel will understand."

Nick leaned back in his seat. "I don't think so, but she will need to. In any case, I will have at least two Bushmills in me before I even discuss it with her."

Cala laughed and clapped her hands. "This is so entertaining, watching the number one assassin in the world groveling at the feet of his wife."

Cala smacked her hands over her mouth, blurting out in muffled form, "Sorry...sorry... did I say that out loud?"

"Loud and clear, Cleaner... loud and clear."

"I am Reaper, Muerto."

"Not anymore."

* * *

"You're doing what! Good Lord in heaven, Muerto! Grow a pair for God's sake! A hundred thousand dollars hush money to keep a government official from betraying his own country? Where in the sane universe could that possibly be considered an option?"

Nick sipped his third Bushmills in the private chat with Rachel, with everyone else up on the deck. "I can't kill them. I can't imprison them. Sonny means more to me than anything his parents do. They will plot for anything to get money. I need to get them considering coming to me first with anything of the

175

magnitude garnered off the laptop they bought. I treat them like pet rattlesnakes. Calm down, Rach. I know how you feel towards-"

"No! You don't! I want them dead. How much? You're taking contracts again. I want those two dead by morning!"

Nick's almost blowing his Bushmill's out his nose was enough to get Rachel off the plateau of death. She chuckled at him snorting and trying to not go into a choking episode. They were speaking in the safe-room downstairs. Nick suddenly ripped Rachel's slacks and underwear down. He gripped her thighs, keeping her rolled into a tucked position, completely exposed. He grinned at her through the gap in Rachel's pulled down slacks. Nick kissed the insides of her thighs in exploratory form.

"Don't...don't you dare... oh God... no... oh Muerto!"

* * *

Deke greeted Nick and Rachel at the deck door.

"I know." Nick stroked Deke's head. "You've been waiting patiently for your beer ration."

"You're still alive, Muerto. I assume Phil and Clarice will live another day," Gus said.

"You two were gone a long time," Tina added.

"We negotiated peace in our time." Nick poured a beer into Deke's bowl. "Where's Jian?"

"He had a date tonight," Johnny said. "Joe introduced him to Joan at the Monte Café. You were working that day, weren't you, Rachel?"

"No. Joe mentioned something about it. A woman named Joan Tuan drove down from San Francisco. She has a degree in hotel management. She and Joe hit it off right away. When Jian stopped in for breakfast, Joe introduced them. Joan told Joe she interviewed for a manager's job at the Monterey Marriott. When Joan found out Jian's US Marshal status, she invited him to have breakfast with her."

"Interesting meeting," Nick commented.

"Don't get any ideas, Gomez." Tina pointed a warning finger at Nick. "Now and then, people do meet."

"Not with our Unholy Trio crew," Johnny said. "I will see what I can find on Joan. We all know there are a lot of hotels in San Francisco. The Monterey/Carmel area probably has nearly the same number though. Chance meetings in our business need to be taken seriously, Tina. Joan's interest in Jian's Marshal status could be legitimate, or there could be something more to it than attraction."

"Johnny's not planning on waterboarding her, Hon," Gus added. "He'll do a background check to make sure Joan is down here for a job interview at the Marriott. The other question would be how she made her way to a little place like the Monte Café instead of picking one of the restaurants at Fisherman's Wharf or in the Marriott itself."

"If Dad doesn't act like everyone's out to get us, someone will," Jean stated. "We don't hurt anyone's feelings on purpose, but we can't ignore stuff and get killed."

"Jean has it right, Tina," Nick agreed. "We can't pretend everything's great. We make sure it is. Jian has good instincts. His impressions count too."

"How about a few slow dances, Gomez," Tina suggested. "We can play at our 'Addam's Family Values' game another time after Jian talks about his date."

"Sure. I'll sip a beer and play." Nick retrieved a beer from the deck refrigerator and headed for the piano. His phone vibrated as he arrived at his bench. "Hey… it's Cassie."

"Nick! I've read the first draft of 'Hell Zone' three times already. This one will be red meat for the fans. I received a call from the Book Works, right in Pacific Grove. They know you live in Pacific Grove. Would you like to do a book signing there?"

"I don't see why not. I remember driving past it on Lighthouse Avenue. I should have stopped in before. They have like a little café inside it serving coffee, tea, and pastries, right?"

"That's the one. I'm glad you're familiar with it. Here's the catch. They want you to fill in tomorrow, doing a talk on writing, read a chapter of 'Blood Beach', and stay for a book signing. The event they planned fell through after weeks of advertising. One of your rivals who lives in Carmel promised to do it, but canceled at the last minute."

"Sounds like fun. Do they have any of my novels in stock?"

"The manager said she did. She promised to get a bunch on consignment from other bookstores in the area if you'll agree to do it."

"Who am I filling in for?"

"Hardin Travers."

Nick had to put his beer down while having a moment of hilarity.

"I know... I know," Cassie said. "He's the guy who had a troll army do book killings on your first novel after it became a bestseller. Travers moved to Carmel at the beginning of the year. You guys are in all the same categories in action and adventure."

"Sorry... Cass... his troll army introduced me to the meaning of what the term 'book killer' meant. He screwed himself up when they all ended their tirade against me with a plug for him as an author, not to mention using nearly the identical wording in their one-star hit pieces. His fans won't appreciate my replacing him. Hardin's protagonist, Ren Caulfield, a supposed special forces operative, gets into one goofball situation after another, doing stupid stuff no professional would ever do. It is the typical ploy though in literature: dig holes for your character to claw their way out of at the last second to avoid disaster."

"Sounds like you have your writing subject," Cassie pointed out.

"True. Good input, Cass. It will give me an opportunity to politely call attention to the differences in style, so we don't have a bunch of unhappy people expecting Ren Caulfield type action, but getting a cold-blooded killer like Diego."

"Thanks for doing this. The incredible publicity you've been getting from your endeavors overseas, and here in America, have you in the number one position amongst all authors. Hell… your real-life adventures are beginning to eclipse Diego's fiction ones. The manager told me the local media will be covering the event. She only asked one thing – please don't kill anyone."

"I'll try not to," Nick played along, "but I make no promises."

"I'll check on you tomorrow. Get some sleep. The event is at 11 am."

"Did you just insult me?"

"Bye, Nick."

Nick put away his phone. "I have a book signing tomorrow here in Pacific Grove. Anyone interested, be ready to arrive at the store by 10:30. It's not mandatory for anyone. I'm filling in for an author so different from me, I'll be giving a talk on the differences, so the readers attending won't be expecting one thing and getting another."

"In other words, the readers at the store will probably not know anything about Jed and Leo, huh?"

"That would be my guess, Payaso," Nick answered. "Travers style and mine are so different, his readers may have tried my novels, and hated my style. I would introduce you guys if it is a big crowd. I know the store had to send out a notice that Travers had cancelled. He may have had fans coming from as far North as San Francisco, and who knows how far South."

"I want to come, Dad," Jean said. "Even if there are only a few people, I'd like to see the Book Works store. I heard you say it was on Lighthouse Avenue. That's within walking distance of us. It would be fun."

"I'd like to go too, Sir," Sonny added. "I like studying the people. If what you describe is true about Travers' fans, it will be really interesting to see how they react to you. Jean and I will study Hardin Travers' background. We can read the reviews he gets and read some of his 'Look Inside' previews of his books."

Nick stared right at Rachel with a big smile.

"Okay... okay... Sonny's a jewel," Rachel admitted. "We need to keep his folks alive."

"What my lovely wife is trying to say is that's good thinking, Sonny," Nick told him. "You and Jean on the prep work will get us ready to face any readers super perturbed their favorite author isn't there."

"Jed's going," Gus said. "Like Jean said, we're in walking distance of home."

"Leo, of course will be there," Johnny promised. "We've taken care of our local problems. We could all walk down together, have a breakfast roll and coffee in the bookstore. I heard you mention they have a small café inside."

"That sounds like fun," Rachel said. "Tina, Cala, and I will bring Quinn down to the Book Works in the Ford for coffee and a roll. That way, you can walk Deke too. We'll drive down to check out the bookstore and take Deke back with us."

"I like it." Nick did a riff on the piano keys. He launched into Louis Armstrong's 'It's a Wonderful World'.

＊ ＊ ＊

"This is a setup of some kind, Sonny." Jean pointed at her screen excitedly. "There are no notices of Travers even being scheduled to do a book signing at the Book Works on their own website. They have a surprise event scheduled with a mystery author. Wow... what do you think this means?"

"I don't know. We've read all of Travers' 'Look Inside' previews. They seem bland compared to your Dad's. Travers' novels sink like a stone with a lot of critical reviews wondering if he has someone else writing them. He has the usual release with bought and paid for reviews. After the first couple of weeks, the new release fades quickly as the negative reviews pile up. The tie-in I see is your Dad's agent, Cassie. She'll know who contacted her. Whoever it is might be a manager Cassie knows. We need to bring your dad in on this now."

Jean clenched her fists, resisting the wild urge to play the new scene out without telling Nick anything about it. The adrenaline rush of being amongst adults who thought they could take on the Unholy Trio nearly buried her moral creed.

"I do what you say in all things, Jean," Sonny said uneasily. "You know better than to hide this. Do you want me to tell him?"

Jean took a deep breath. She gripped Sonny's hand. "You do it, Cracker. It was your idea. I need to take a step back."

Sonny covered her hand. "We're partners... forever. I will remind you of duty and honor. If you decide something different, I follow your lead no matter what."

"Let's go get this over with." Jean listened to the pounding piano upstairs, hearing Nick's voice belting out 'House of the Rising Sun'. "I know it's wrong, but sometimes I fear letting the Terminator know stuff."

"I hear you. It's worse if you keep the information away from him and he ends up in the middle of it. Your dad will kill everyone involved in a heartbeat, even in public. This may be something petty having to do with this Travers' jealousy of your dad. We can't determine what your dad will do if he gets dumped into something unknown."

"You're right. He needs to know without me playing kid's games."

* * *

Nick's mouth tightened. He had been enjoying the late evening more than he could express in words. The passion he performed with, reflected his joy in entertaining. Nick's return to music restored something in his soul. He gripped Sonny's shoulders. "Thanks, kid. We'll scope the situation out. I'll call my agent now and learn who at Book Works called her. I'm hoping this is just a cheap shot at me by Travers. It may not be good for you kids to go tomorrow."

Jean gripped Nick's hand. "Please don't leave us out of this, Dad. Sonny and I can take care of ourselves. With you and the Unholy Trio crew, there's no chance of anyone ambushing us now."

Nick hugged Jean. "You have not yet learned the rule of unintended consequences, Viper. Picture what would happen if someone simply blew the Book Works into the next dimension."

Jean giggled. "Don't project, Dad." Her jab provoked amusement amongst the others.

The little twerp and her accomplice pay too much attention to the news. Nick knew Jean joked about his propensity for using grenades, as did his crew. "I hope you understand I would never do that with my fellow American citizens innocently in the target zone."

"I know that," Jean stated. "Call Cassie. We'll get to the bottom of this quick."

Nick smiled. "Your will… my hand, Viper."

Nick woke Cassie up in New York time. She answered with mumbled greetings.

"Nick?"

"I need to know who contacted you, Cass. Travers never signed on to do anything at Book Works. I will show for the 'Mystery Author' book signing tomorrow, but I do need to know what the hell is going on."

"Rhonda Ceries. I've met her at agents and publishers' gatherings. She's a real person. What is it you suspect?"

"I'm not sure what to suspect. I guess it could be a gag or a roundabout way to get me to do a book signing. That doesn't make sense either, since all they had to do was call. Think about it. Why would anyone call you with a ploy to get me filling in for a famous author at a small bookstore in out of the way Pacific Grove?"

"I...I don't have a clue, Nick."

"That's clear enough. Don't call or contact anyone until this so-called book signing is in the past and we find out what prompted it, Cass. It may be something humorous like leaving me sitting in an empty bookstore."

"Understood. Rhonda sold me on her sincerity. Please call me with what you find out. I'm sorry about this, Nick."

"No need to be. This wasn't your fault. Talk at you tomorrow." Nick disconnected. "Cass knew the manager who called. Her name is Rhonda Ceries. I think we're done for the night. The kids and I will do one last check on the situation."

"This does seem more like a joke than something sinister," Rachel said.

"You've told us about seeing authors with their books piled on a table at a book signing with no one around," Gus said. "Would someone want to snap pictures of the great author sitting in an empty bookstore?"

"Maybe. This should be a fun Saturday morning adventure," Nick replied. "It's like one of those cozy mysteries you hear about."

"Yeah... because cute little things like that always happen around you, Gomez," Tina said. "More likely, it's a trap with a cartel army waiting to give you a Columbian Necktie."

"I will call Jian in the morning," Johnny offered. "He loved the last book signing. We will then have a full crew on hand for anything."

"This book signing sounds interesting enough for me to have a coffee and roll," Cala added. "With the morning sickness, I may not be able to enjoy coffee and a roll soon."

"Goodnight, everyone," Nick said. "I'll go investigate a few things with the kids and take Deke for a walk."

Deke began leaping straight up and down.

"Strike that. First I walk Deke the pogo-stick."

* * *

"At least Rhonda works for the bookstore." Nick found the bookstore's employee list with Jean and Sonny sitting on either side of him. "I could probably ruin this cute mystery with a single call to her tomorrow."

"It will be fun, Dad. We'll arrive for the book signing. If it's weird, we'll leave. We're less than a mile away from it."

"Okay… but I want to go on record as hating surprises or mysteries."

* * *

"This is a great looking building." Nick stood with Deke sitting next to him on the Park Street side of the bookstore with Gus, Jian, Johnny, Cala, Sonny, and Jean. "I'm beginning to hope this signing happens even in an empty store."

Rachel parked their Ford on the Lighthouse side of the corner, in front of the bookstore. Nick walked Deke to the Ford. Rachel and Tina exited the SUV while Nick undid Quinn from his car-seat. Rachel handed Nick the beef bone for Deke to munch on in the Ford. "It's chilly this morning. April in paradise."

Nick left the Ford windows partially down in the front. "Yep. The ocean breeze howled between the houses on our way down the street too. If this isn't a hoax, we may get a good crowd in here. I'm ready to play out any episode."

Gus pointed at Nick's equipment. "Ready in what way, Muerto?"

Nick stopped. "No grenades or explosives of any kind, Payaso. I brought proof of who I am… at least my background in the military, and the agencies I consult with. I brought my writers' credentials and proof I own my place in Pacific Grove."

Jian looked confused. "I do not understand. Do you need to prove who you are to do a book signing where they already know who you are?"

"Sort of," Nick answered, moving toward the door again. "We're only appearing here today for fun. If it becomes a problem, we'll walk the hell out of here. The mystery will be solved shortly."

Nick led the way inside. A dark-haired woman matching the picture in the employee files for Ronda Ceries approached at a hurried gait in black slacks, white blouse, and high heels that brought her to about Rachel's height in tennis shoes. She stuck her hand out to Nick with a big smile.

"I'm so glad you came Mr. McCarty. Hardin told me you and he were old friends. This will be such a blast with two pulp fiction, bestselling legends here for our mystery author event."

"Why did you tell my agent I would be filling in for Travers?"

"Hardin told me it was a bit of a prank, and you two do it to each other all the time." Rhonda appeared genuinely confused at Nick's clueless look. "Did I misunderstand?"

"I don't know Hardin Travers personally or professionally. I'm here because I genuinely wanted to see the inside of your bookstore and hopefully fill in adequately for Travers. Does this mean he'll be here too?"

"Yes. Oh my… I'm sorry, Mr. McCarty. Why would he do such a thing?"

Nick patted her shoulder. "We'll find out soon. We're going over to have coffee, tea, and pastry rolls until opening. Is that okay?"

"Of course. Thank you for your understanding. Then you really don't know Hardin Travers?"

"I know who he is. I am not his friend. It will be interesting to learn what this dual author signing meant to him. I don't see this as a misunderstanding other than a yet to be determined ploy by Travers for a yet unknown reason. I will give the talk, answer questions, and sign anyone's book upon request. Is it okay if my friends and family have a coffee and roll together?"

"Of course. Thank you for coming. Please help yourself to anything you like in our café section. I would never have participated in anything like this if I'd known you two had never met."

"It's okay, Rhonda. I love your bookstore. I can't say I hate Amazon's digital store. I get the majority of my sales through Amazon's digital marketplace. I like your idea for a book exchange and used book section. That, coupled with your instore café will help you to compete. I'll do book signings here anytime you invite me."

"That's great, Nick! This is a rough business. It was the main reason when Hardin called to suggest this ploy, I was happy to do it."

"Do you have security in place for this?"

Rhonda blushed. "No… I should have, but the expense is very steep. I know you've had problems at other book signings. I figured since no one knew you would be attending our surprise author gettogether, there wouldn't be any difficulties."

"You're probably right," Nick replied. "Were you able to get a consignment of books?

"I did. We are stocked in Nick McCarty's novels."

"Excellent. Let me know in advance and I'll try and stop in for a couple of hours anytime you want me to."

"Joe from the Monte Café talks about you any time he stops in for a book. I'm sworn to secrecy as to what his favorite series of books is."

"Thank you for that. Joe's been busting my chops for many years over pulp fiction. It will be our secret. Joe is a very good friend of mine. My wife, Rachel, works at the Monte."

Rachel shook hands with Rhonda. "I'm glad you didn't know anything about this deal with Travers. I love your café/bookstore. I'll coerce my friends Tina and Cala to walk with me to visit with my baby Quinn."

"That would be wonderful, Rachel!"

"I'd like that," Tina said. "I'll take a cab up the hill to home though."

"I will walk with you, Rachel." Cala moved near Rachel. "We must pressure the T-Rex into walking more, especially uphill. She's been filling out into the same tail proportions as her namesake."

"You can't bait me, Reaper. Just wait until you're in the middle of postpartum depression and you need me to comfort you while helping with the baby. I'll say, 'hey… just walk down to the bookstore'."

"Wait a minute! Postpartum what?" Cala hurried after a chuckling Tina with Rachel following. Jean and Sonny, enjoying the adult digs, kept pace with Rachel and Quinn.

"They're just trading shots," Nick told Rhonda. "Want me a half hour from now?"

"That will work fine, Nick. Hardin turned down all my requests for book signing appearances until he saw the mystery author event. He called me then with this scheme. I'll see you a little later." Rhonda walked toward the counter.

Gus nudged Nick. "This Travers guy wants a piece, huh?"

"I guess so. If he's coming to the party we may find out what the hell his intentions were. It's no big deal. We're attending a book signing, not a cage match with John Harding."

"Uh… you have killed men at your book signings," Johnny reminded Nick.

"Shut up, Kabong."

Chapter Nine: Book Signing Stolen Valor

"Oh my." Cala pointed at the entrance. Nick's crew busily fixed their sales table with books, including signed cards, and autographed newsletters advertising his soon to be released 'Hell Zone'.

Nick glanced from his autographing task. Hardin Travers arrived with three large chin beard Isis types. They scowled at anyone who looked at them. The main attraction, Hardin Travers, wore a dress blues Marine uniform that form fitted his rotund but huge six-foot, four-inch stature. His darkly trimmed beard stuck out from the collar of the Marine uniform with authority. An energized group of fans bounced around him. Travers glared at Nick, who smiled and waved. Travers turned away.

"Why are you being so friendly with Travers, Dad? Is it because he's a Marine?"

"He was never in the Marine Corps. I saw his picture early this morning on the Internet wearing the Marine uniform. He's only fifty years old, but he's wearing a Vietnam service medal. Unless they let him into the Corps right out of kindergarten, I'm afraid he's a phony."

"He has a lot of ribbons on his chest. Where did he get them?"

"I don't know, Jean... maybe a pawn shop. It's okay. We're having fun. That was a great café experience with the smell of pastries, books and coffee. I think I could make this place my headquarters."

Sonny brightened. "Yes! That's exactly it. The odors were indescribably good."

Jean wasn't happy with what she learned about Travers. "He's lucky Lucas Blake isn't here. He'd make that guy eat those ribbons."

Nick enjoyed that word picture in hushed but energetic mirth. "Oh… God… if I had known this jackass would arrive in Marine Corps dress blues with the Force Recon patch, I would have flown North to get him for this event. Hey… what are you doing, Jean?"

"I'm streaming this to Lucas's instant messaging," Jean answered, moving her iPad with the progress of Travers.

Nick covered his head. "Oh, good Lord… I'm in the soup now. Hep me, Gus… hep me."

"Pray Lucas doesn't see Jean's stream of this guy, Muerto." Gus's immediate seriousness shut off the mirth Johnny and Jian at first displayed. Nick's iPhone buzzed. "Oh shit! Tell me… it isn't Ahab."

Nick raised his phone screen for Gus's viewing of Lucas in his Marine combat gear from Vietnam with face camouflaged. Nick put him on speaker. *Why should I be the only one to enjoy this?* "Hi, Lucas… how the heck are-"

"Shut up, Delta Dawn! If that bearded prick walks out with that jacket on, you and I will have a moment together. It won't be pretty!"

"C'mon, brother… I'm at a book signing with the kids. Jean inadvertently thought you'd get a kick out of seeing him all decked out. I knew better."

"Lucas?" Jean popped into Lucas's view with knife in hand. "I'll cut the Marine Recon patch off for you!"

Jean grinned at Nick as Lucas came unglued. Many moments passed before he could look at the screen. Every time he did, Jean struck a new cutting pose.

"Okay!" Lucas surrendered. "Good one, Jean… you little brat. Promise me you'll hurt him if you get the chance, Dead Boy."

Nick took a deep breath. He nodded. "If it happens, will the patch do?"

"Yeah… it would be acceptable. You know what-"

"I know what Marine Recon means, brother. I'm sorry Jean gave you the visual before I could explain."

"I know what it means!" Jean barged into the screen. "Sonny and I will be Marines! That Marine Recon patch was worn by men who died for this nation. This fat turd didn't even serve. I know what stolen valor is!"

"Stand down! You did good, kid. Your passion makes an old Marine proud. Thank you." Lucas disconnected as he was getting choked up.

"Sorry, Dad. I thought Lucas would get a laugh out of the video. I knew better, but I did it anyway."

"It's the main reason when Lucas calls out to John Harding, 'Recon!', John treasures it. We strive in the service for the respect of our betters."

"You were Delta Force, Dad. Lucas respects you."

"Yep. He told me and Casey Lambert when he trained us in the CIA camp that we were almost at Marine Recon level."

Jean giggled appreciatively.

"Marines don't giggle."

"This one does," Jean retorted. "The talk on writing happens first, right?"

"Yes. I don't know if Travers and I are the only ones speaking or not. The guide for our talk Rhonda gave me lists writing style, plotting, and voice."

"What does voice mean in a novel?"

You would ask that. "Describing writer's voice will not be easy. If a reader recognizes a style of writing as either my work or Travers without any mention of our characters, we achieved distinctive writer's voice."

"I get it," Jean replied. "I always knew which author wrote what when mom read to me at night. I bet it's easier to detect writer's voice when a reader hears someone read to them."

"That's a good point. I may be able to slip that into my talk." Nick glanced around at the rapidly filling store. "It will be crowded in here today. I can tell that."

"I don't like the looks of the guys Travers brought with him," Sonny said. "It's as if he wanted to cause trouble from the start."

"Make that two of us," Gus added.

"They are not simply associates, Muerto," Johnny said.

"I am glad I came this morning."

"Just once, Jian?" Cala whispered, referring to his date with the mysterious Joan.

Jian gave Cala the shaming gesture he learned watching interactions amongst the Unholy Trio. "For shame, Cala... for shame. Johnny checked Joan out. She's golden."

Jean and Sonny looked at the adults expectantly with no explanation as Cala whispered her small verbal gem to Gus, Johnny, and Nick. All three, on cue, gave her the shaming gesture.

"We will all remain vigilant regarding the three minions," Nick said. "They eyeball us every few seconds. I believe Sonny's right. I don't think Travers would want to start something in the middle of a book signing."

"If he's petty enough to put troll army book killers on competitors' books, and pretend he was a Marine, I doubt causing a scene here would bother him," Gus said. "Here comes Rhonda."

"I have a dais setting for you and Hardin, Nick. I also have front row seats for your group. It looks like you're all set for the book signing. I'm really excited about the business."

"I think you will sell some books today, Rhonda. Lead on."

"This is going to be so fun," Jean whispered to Sonny.

"Only you would think so," Sonny replied in a whisper. "Think of the unintended consequences Nick always warns us about. Four dead bodies, one of them a New York Times

191

Bestselling Author like Travers – not counting innocent victims his idiot minions kill by accident. I don't think fun is the word for it."

"Dad won't kill the fake. You're right though," Jean admitted. "Dad has too many bad hits on his book signing gigs. We can't do much about it though except stay out of the way."

"Right. We need to get down quick so they don't worry about us and make a mistake."

* * *

Nick finished his talk, hitting on the subjects given to him, incorporating Jean's point on writer's voice being more easily detected when read out loud. He had grabbed a copy of Earnest Hemingway's 'The Old Man and the Sea', along with John Steinbeck's 'Grapes of Wrath'. Quickly picking out two subtle scenes, Nick read them aloud. Many voices called out the correct author from the two choices. His talk elicited loud applause at the close.

Travers took over the podium, agreeing with Nick about writer's voice. "Many of us skilled hands at this art, employ a more literary flavor in our writing, rather than the slam/bam approach. Wouldn't you agree, Nick?"

"Absolutely," Nick agreed. "I'm neither Hemingway nor Steinbeck. I admit I'm a storyteller rather than an artist."

Travers nodded, returning to his talk, which droned on past his time slightly as he regaled on the hard work needed to complete passages readers feel mistakenly to be minutiae. "In conclusion, the tapestry must be created with order and detail. Otherwise, it resembles one of those splash paint pictures."

Travers sat down to mild applause. Rhonda stepped to the microphone. "We have time for a few questions."

A lady stood in the middle of the third row of seats. "This is directed at Mr. McCarty. Talk, talk, talk – your novels need more care in plotting and a lot less conversation. They're certainly not spy novels."

Nick waited. When the woman didn't go on. "Thank you. Was there a question in there somewhere?"

Nick's response drew repressed amusement to the consternation of the young woman. "Please address my critique of your style."

Nick shrugged. "There's no need to. I love writing interaction between characters and allowing the storytelling to proceed from the characters' views. I won't be changing my style. Lastly, my character Diego is an assassin, not a spy."

"Speaking of your character, Diego," a man on the left called out as the red-faced woman sat down to a smattering of applause, "He seems too polished. Nothing ever really happens to him. He survives practically unscathed. Don't you think he should be challenged?"

"I chose writing about an assassin because I knew what I loved to read in pulp fiction novels. I changed what I didn't like about the genre. Most writers I followed in the genre used a common ploy in their writing. They threw their character into sometimes ridiculous danger, which many times led to ridiculous escapes. I wrote in the genre with a more logical approach to how a cold-blooded assassin would think. There is a reason the deadliest assassins throughout history were rarely caught: they had no connection to the victim, they researched and formulated plans for insertion, execution, and escape. Once free of the area, they were never seen again."

"So, you're saying when writers pop in illogical situations for their main character to fall into, it's a tool?"

"We all use tools," Nick answered. "One of the reasons I love the Pulp Fiction genre is I get to pick the tools."

Nick's response evoked an amused response from the audience.

A woman on the other side of the audience stood and pointed at Travers. "This question is for you. My husband died in Mosul. He was Marine Recon. You ain't no Marine, and you're wearing ribbons not in your age group, moron. You were

193

practically a baby in diapers when the Vietnam War took place. Where did you get a Vietnam campaign ribbon, the local pawn shop? What the hell gives you the right to wear a uniform, men who died for this nation served in, poser! Marine Recon patch… bullshit! You have a lot of nerve coming here today in that uniform, shithead! If my husband was alive, he'd kick the shit out of you and tear off that Marine Recon patch with his teeth!"

Dead silence reigned after the woman's spot-on assessment.

"Well… poser? Say something, you stolen valor freak!"

Sweating profusely, Hardin Travers moved to the microphone. "I…I wore this uniform as a tribute to-"

"Bullshit!" The woman pointed at him threateningly. "Take the blue jacket off or I'll take it off for you!"

"Really, madam, calm down," Travers urged, gesturing for his minions to do something. They stood to work around towards the speaker.

"You three stay where you are," Nick stood to point at them, with Gus, Johnny, Jian, and Cala rising with him. "If you approach that woman, I will remove you from either this room or this dimension. Your choice."

The three looked around at the enthusiastic, applauding audience and sat down again.

"Please remove this woman," Travers demanded, looking over at Rhonda who shook her head in the negative.

Travers pointed at Nick. "What? I try to honor fallen heroes and this real poser gets away with his crap?"

Nick stood with folder in hand. He walked to the microphone. "I didn't know if it would come into question today, but I have hard copy backup to what I am. This is my DD214, providing information to the units I've served in, along with details, including an honorable discharge with my reserve status. I served in special forces, Delta Force, and I have friends who are

194

today Marine Recon. I have here pictures of my Delta Force unit with me in it. Everything this young woman said is true."

Nick walked into Travers' airspace, pointing at a ribbon. "As she stated, this yellow green ribbon is a Vietnam Campaign ribbon. Travers never served as a Marine in Vietnam or anywhere else. I made a vow to a Marine Recon brother, that I would defend the few and proud. Take the jacket off now, or I will remove it for you."

An old, thin gnarly man stood at the back, fists clenched. "I served in Vietnam, 1st Battalion, 26th Regiment at Khe Sanh in '68. You do as McCarty tells you to do, or I'll be dead before you leave this fucking room... poser! I lost brothers there you couldn't measure up to in your wildest fucking dreams! Get the fucking jacket off now!"

Travers looked at Rhonda with wide, frightened and yet outraged eyes. Rhonda turned away. Nick smiled. "Take the coat off, or else I will take it off for you."

Travers surveyed the silent audience with outrage surging past logic. He threw a right-hand roundhouse at Nick's head. Nick caught it, snapped it to the right, forcing Travers onto his knees with a scream of pain. One of Travers' bodyguards rushed Nick, only to be met with a sidekick to his head as Johnny launched to Nick's side. Jian and Gus rushed to the reaching other bodyguards.

"Grab the lapels on your jackets and kneel, or die," Gus ordered, his Taurus 9mm half out of his holster. "We will not hesitate to kill all three of you in a heartbeat. Johnny will snap your partner's neck. Jian and I will shoot you both right between the eyes. I am US Marshal Gus Nason and this is US Marshal Jian Chen. Grab your lapels!"

The men followed Gus's order slowly and to the letter. Johnny restrained their wrists at the back. Jian dragged the unconscious bodyguard Johnny had kicked into another reality, and restrained him also.

Nick shook Travers' hand slightly. He unbuttoned the Marine dress blues jacket. "If you resist, I will hurt you. I see you

195

have a t-shirt on underneath. That's good. No one wants to see your blubber. Once you are released, take off the coat and cover, and hand them to me. Do you understand?"

Travers nodded. Nick released his hand and helped him up. Travers shakily disrobed from the jacket, handing it and his hat to Nick. The woman in the back who had accused him at the start, stood again, pointing at Travers. "A real Marine would have died rather than strip off that coat... poser!"

"We're running these guys' names, Nick," Gus told him. "They're all packing without license."

"Crap. Neil will be pleased at another McCarty adventure. Tell me what you get on them. We may simply confiscate their weapons. Sit over on your chair, Hardin. Why did you bring your three helpers with you?"

"I am in the process of converting to Islam. They attend the same mosque and were outraged at the treatment of Islam in your pulp novels."

"Getting me here was their idea, huh?"

"Yes."

"You thought you'd have more credibility wearing the uniform while attacking me about Islam. That makes sense. I can tell you've done this before without getting outed as a fraud. You can bet this event was covered in the media. It would be best if you sent your minions home if they check out. Do the book signing and stick with your original story about honoring the military."

"I'll still look like a fool."

"There are plenty of your more liberal followers here. They'll think you were mistreated. It'll work out."

"They're okay," Gus called over.

"Keep their weapons. They can pick them up at the police station." Nick turned to Hardin again. "Go ahead and get them on their way."

Hardin trudged over to where his companions were now standing. After a quiet conversation, the men left. Hardin then spoke to a concerned Rhonda. She nodded and addressed the crowd. "We have the book signing tables set up on opposite sides of the store. Nick McCarty will be on the right, and Hardin Travers on the left. That was more exciting of a talk than I prepared for. It's over. Let's get some books signed."

A round of applause greeted Rhonda's directions. As predicted by Nick, Travers drew many of his solid fans with books in hand. Nick introduced his crew, along with Jean and Sonny. His book signing line, enthusiastic and demanding, kept a running dialogue of questions about what they saw. Nick and crew answered all questions concerning the US Marshal's service, with boating, sidekicks, and romance with Diego's new love, Fatima, close seconds. So many asked to see his military picture and DD214, Nick left them on display.

"One's in line from Travers' flock," Jean whispered. "She went from happy to sullen in the few steps from his line to yours. Green blouse, mousy brown hair, five and a half feet tall, thin as a rail – she's clutching a book with both hands so tightly, I can see the white knuckles from here."

"I believe you're right." Nick greeted the next man in line, recognizing him as the Marine veteran from the Vietnam War era. "Thank you for your service, Sir."

He shook hands with Nick somewhat hesitantly. "Sorry about the foul-mouthed outburst around the children. That jerk's dress blues drove me nuts. I see you did your time."

"Still doin' my time, Gunny, just like you. As they say, there are no ex-Marines."

"You have that right. Thanks for the hours of entertainment I've gotten from your novels. I've read the Diego series over from the beginning many times. Write faster!"

"I will endeavor to do so. Take care of yourself, Gunny."

"Will do."

197

The sidekick and Fatima questions dominated the discussion as Nick autographed books, centering on his inclusion of real life in many of his plots. Nick handled those questions with care, reminding everyone Diego was a pulp fiction character. The woman Jean picked out as a Travers' emissary stalked to the table, glaring at Jean and Sonny.

"I hope this man is not influencing you two kids to do his bidding. He's a racist of the worst sort."

Well-schooled on what they were to say in reply to a verbal attack, Jean and Sonny stared directly at her with smiles. "I can tell he's brainwashed the both of you!"

"My dad taught me how to survive in a world with America hating scum," Jean replied.

The woman reached for Jean. "Why you little-"

A big hand blocked her reaching appendage.

"No touching, ma'am. Say whatever it is you want to say and then move on. If you reach for the kids again, my associate Cala will help you find the exit. Believe me... you don't want that."

"Who is-"

"That would be me." Cala slid between the woman and the signing table. "I'm Cala. As Nick asked you, say whatever you need to say and move the line. If you don't, I will remove you, with force if necessary."

"I am here to inform others of your blasphemous treatment of sacred Islam in your novels. You malign the blessed religion of nearly two billion people."

"You are an idiot," Cala stated. "There are three ex-Muslims with Nick McCarty today. He personally saved me and my cousin from honor killing relatives. Islam is a cult of pedophiles, misogynist enslavers of women and outright slavers of any who do not believe in the cult, guilty of murderous terrorism the world over, exterminators of gays, Christians, and all other true religions. You are too stupid to open your mouth in public, lady. Where is your slave costume? Cover yourself, harlot! Better yet, take your 'taquiyya, lying to the infidel' nonsense somewhere else!"

The lady tried to meet Cala's eyes, but broke into sobs instead, fleeing from the bookstore. Cala gestured dismissively at the woman's back. "Do not give her a second thought. Have any of you seen the Facebook page for the City of Hope we created with refugees turning their backs on Islam and Sharia Law?"

There were many who had, but also many who had not. Cala turned her iPad holder into a tilted base on the table by the kids, instantly generating the Facebook loop of daily updates, featuring the escapees from Islam's death cult, and their new refuge. The highlighted laughter, success, and incredible living improvements continued to generate awe as the book signing went on. Rhonda watched the iPad program through once and put it on the network within the bookstore. Travers left in a self-indulgent tirade of outrage after seeing the loop on the screen near him. By then, his line had disappeared anyway, so Nick figured it was more of an exit gimmick. Nick and company stayed well past the allotted time.

Rhonda joined them as they gathered their belongings for the walk to Nick's house. "Except for the confrontation, this has been an incredible day, Nick. We only hear the praises of Islam from the media and its sycophants. Is it true your team helped create the City of Hope?"

"We did. The City's current leader updates us daily with everything, good and bad. The only bad so far has been the malcontents sent to sabotage the progress. Kahn has a dedicated staff who prevent the setbacks before they occur and deport the criminals back to Islam run countries. They salvage more and more of the former wasteland with added desalinization plants and community additions. A huge medical facility servicing all peoples in the Western Sahara will be run by an ex-Muslim doctor we recruited here in the United States."

"I never realized what a petty, egotistical wretch Hardin was until today," Rhonda said. "I am so happy this event took place. It opened my eyes too. I've had blinders on."

Nick handed her his card. "Put this somewhere you can access it easily and keep my number on your instant contact list. If the Sharia Cult swine, Antifa, or BLM surrogates of this leftist plague trying to bury us, threatens or physically appears to disrupt your business, call me."

Nick's urging had the intended effect of making Rhonda aware of unintended consequences. "Do you think we're doomed to have another civil war, Nick?"

"My personal opinion is there aren't enough 'Snowflakes' in this country to cause a civil war. A vigilante uprising against them is far more likely."

"Is…is there any room for middle of the road folks?"

"Only if you don't mind becoming middle of the road kill, Rhonda. You said you have the blinders off now. Good… take the rose colored glasses off too while you're at it. We are already at war for the preservation of America."

"You've given me a lot to think about. I will call if I get any trouble. Thank you."

"Above everything else, we are US Marshals, sworn to uphold the Constitution against all enemies, foreign and domestic. We take our duty seriously."

* * *

As they trekked up the hill toward the McCarty domain, Jean asked something that was in the minds of everyone walking. "Do you think Rhonda will be okay, Dad?"

"She will be if she keeps her eyes open for danger. If she ignores it, then no. At some point, no matter how much we would like to protect people, the moment of danger happens when least expected. When we walk you to school, we'll walk down to Lighthouse Ave and check on the bookstore. Deke will love marking new territory. I'll head down to Lover's Point coastal path and then to Otter's Point. It's a great hike before Otter's Point libations."

"You're on the sauce too early in the morning, Dad."

"Jian has corrupted us, Jean. He's relentless. If the heathen doesn't get his Irish in the morning, we all must pay the piper in his foul moods, Chinese laundry, and pestilence."

"Pestilence?" Jian pointed warningly at his companions. "Keep this disrespectful offal cascading down upon my head and I will be forced to seek justice, white-eye!"

Gus put an arm around Jian's shoulders. "Never seek vengeance on Muerto. He is protected by the God of evil cartoons: Mothra."

The mention of a Japanese movie monster, one of the most ridiculous of all time, as a protector of Muerto sent Jian into snorting fits as he both tried to stay outraged, and also stifle amusement.

"I'm serious, Dad. One day these people will stake you and the cartoons out. Everyone in Pacific Grove knows you guys go down there nearly every morning and drink. It's pitiful, thinking about the Unholy Trio, Dark Dragon, and Reaper getting blown apart while throwing down Irish coffees."

"You placed Reaper last in the cartoon train, Jean," Cala pointed out. "That is not very insightful or respectful to put Dragon breath in front of me."

"You cartoons are getting a little needy," Jean retorted to more amusement. "Maybe we should rename you cartoons since there are five of you. It could be something with hand in it, like the 'Drunken Hand', or the 'Hand of Self-Indulgence', or the 'Blitzed Hand', or 'In Alcohol Cometh the Hand', or-"

"Or the 'Hand of Grounded Smartasses'. How does two weeks without electrical devices sound to you, little miss high and mighty?"

"Oh sure… kill the messenger."

* * *

Nick sat with Neil Dickerson in his office, having delivered the confiscated weapons, waiting as Neil jotted down serial numbers. He explained what happened, describing the incident as a publicity ploy gone bad.

"You have their names and addresses, so I'll issue citations for carrying concealed weapons in a public place without licenses. If you sign the citations, it will mean a hefty fine if they want the weapons returned. If they are the legal owners of the weapons, I will leave it at just the fine if the weapons were never used in a crime."

"I like your idea. I wish we had legal concealed carry for everyone in this state, but enforcing the law on these three is the right course. They were going to draw on us."

"Thank God they didn't. That would have been a mess. I'll have a car swing by the bookstore on a more regular basis, since the place has been jinxed with the Muerto curse."

"Muerto curse? It's called notoriety. Notoriety makes money. The Carmel bookstore I had a couple of incidents in made a lot of money. I put them on the map."

"Incidents? You killed one guy in unarmed combat mode, and shot the other one through the head. Only you would call them incidents. Did your US Marshal friends reach you? Tim called me to see if you were okay. They have real Marshal business for you cartoons."

"I saw they called. When they have something important for me, they usually text me a bulletin." Nick signed the citations Neil turned for his signature. "If you're done critiquing my actions, I'll go do some real work."

"We're done. Did you get your new novel done? I've been waiting patiently after 'Blood Beach' to see where you go with Fatima. When do I get my advanced copy?"

"Never. I've crossed you off the advanced copy list for accusations unbecoming of a policeman and I didn't want to upset your sensibilities with my violent pulp any longer."

Neil waved Nick away. "Send me my copy or the next time you need local cover for your cartoons, you'll find yourself off the cooperation list."

"You know better than to play that card."

"Send me my copy… damn it!"

Nick waved as he left the office. He called Tim while leaving the precinct building. "The cops told me you have a warrant out for my arrest."

Tim chuckled. "Grace and I are on our way to you. We have the location for two escaped felons. We tapped the lines of anyone they ever knew. One of them called an ex-girlfriend in Portland, asking if he could see her. She told him no… and hell no, but we know where he is now."

"No offense, but what do you need me for?"

"We believe Vince Talbert and his partner, Bill Cloverman, took over the farmhouse at the address. A couple lives there with two boys, ages four and six. We don't need more bodies. We need a sniper. Talbert and Cloverman killed two guards while escaping from Atwater. They had a car waiting for them. The prison officials asked the Marshal's service in on the case immediately, hoping to nab the two before they escaped the area. No such luck."

"Count me in, but you do understand the consequences, right?"

"They will kill that family if they haven't already, Nick. If you get a shot, take it. Can you do some research on the address for us?"

"I'll tap into our satellite coverage and do you one better. We can detect bodies from space now. I'll count heat signatures and let you know if we still have a family to save. I'm hoping they'll keep the family as hostages. What put them in Atwater?"

"Home invasions with rape and murder," Tim answered. "We know of five deaths the jury convicted them of without their testimony. A neighbor called the police at the scene of the fifth one we know about. The police arrived in time to get them, but not to save the older couple living there."

"We'll be ready when you get here. Come to my house."

"Will do. Thanks, Nick."

* * *

Nick and his crew, including Jean and Sonny, networked with everything from satellite coverage to farmhouse plans. Rachel showed Tim and Grace onto the deck.

"The kids too?"

"They have better instincts than either of you cardboard cutouts, Grace. We have some good news. Our satellites show four practically unmoving figures in the back bedroom of the ranch style house. The other two move around, including one of them checking on the other four periodically."

"Excellent," Grace said. "For good news of that sort, I would have expected more enthusiasm. Did I interrupt the bad news report?"

"Sort of," Nick continued. "A wavy white fence borders a driveway approach nearly a hundred yards from the house. If not for the trees lining the road, they would be able to see vehicles coming from a mile away. The area surrounding the farmhouse is completely open terrain with only a couple of small trees. I studied the topographical map in relation to the satellite shots. I found a spot where I have open access to take the shots. If they have a brain though, the windows will be covered. If the windows are covered, all the snipers in the world won't be able to help. In that case, I'll begin an approach from the left side of the farmhouse."

"Meaning what? You can't simply walk in on them with the hostages."

"Your grasp of the obvious still makes me shudder, Grace. If the windows are covered, I will approach in the dark, secure the hostages in the room they're in. We will be networked together. Once I have the room secure and the hostages away from the room entrance, everyone arrives outside the house, with sirens and the whole works. They run back to get the hostages. Done deal."

"Yes... good one, Muerto," Johnny said. "You did something similar with the Marines, Chuck and Sal. The approach will be difficult."

"I think so too," Gus agreed. "Chances are, they'll have the windows covered or even boarded. Like Johnny says, the approach will be the hard part. You'll need a first-class glass cutter, not one of those tinker toys they sell."

"I have one," Nick replied. "I'm hoping they have a chair or something in the back so I can slip in easier."

Tim and Grace remained silent after Nick's 'Done deal'. They knew what it meant. There would be no arrests or trials. Nick grinned at the two Marshals.

"Let's go save the state of California a lot of money. God knows with that jackass we have as Governor now, we need to save the actual working people some tax money. It takes a lot of money to keep murderers alive in prison. The downside is he'll probably take it and build a snow-making plant in the middle of the Mojave Desert. When what we need are desalinization plants all along the coast, what we get are bullet trains to bullshit."

"Hey... when did you get the piano?"

"When we found out Muerto's been holding out on us, Tim," Rachel said. "Be careful out there. Save the family and come back here to celebrate with our new Muerto entertainment system."

"I hope it's as easy as that," Grace said.

"Did you just insult me?"

* * *

205

"Good Lord, Muerto, these idiots don't have a clue," Gus jabbed Nick over the network. "Get your cold-blooded killer in gear. You're wasting time crawling noiselessly over barren ground those tuna you're targeting can't see anyway."

Nick entered the approach field from the right of the ranch house while Gus, Johnny, and Jian walked along Blackie Road to positions where they could see nearly all of the house. Nick grinned in appreciation of Gus's disparaging remarks about his approach. Once Nick learned Vince Talbert was a contract killer, along with being a serial house invader and murderer, he took no chances on anything.

His instincts proved true. While methodically picking his way through the brush leading to the house, he noticed tamped down sections near him: indicators of human passage – broken bushes and flattened leaves. Slipping his night-vision goggles into place, he spotted the thin wire running across the ground. Nick doubted it was hooked to explosives, but he was certain it was put there for show. Looking further, he noted a secondary trip wire. Nick passed over them without disruption or hurry, shielding any glowing sign from his goggles as he moved.

Gus hummed a humorous 'Beat the Clock' tune. Johnny, who had been assigned watcher's duty for anything near Nick, hushed Gus. "Trip wires, Payaso. Muerto just passed over a primary and secondary, attached to God knows what."

"Mothra causes this shit to happen in order to back Muerto's sloth-like approach."

Nick had to stop his approach, stifling amusement with both hands at the mention of his cartoon protector god. He took a deep breath and crawled forward carefully. Nearing his target, he wanted nothing interfering with saving the hostage family. Psychopath or not, Nick's imagination could conjure reality in the form of the family's horrifying imprisonment within their own house with ease and empathy. His lips tightened into a disappointing snarl at not being able to end Talbert and Cloverman with a cleaning.

Nick reached the rear of the ranch house without further barrier, confident Talbert would feel secure knowing he had the grounds wired. A picnic set, complete with table umbrella, supplied Nick with a hard-plastic lawn chair to stand on. He retrieved his glasscutter with vacuum attachment, and stood on the chair at the hostage room window. Without hesitation, Nick cut a large circle in the glass, pulling it free with the suction cup. He unlocked the window as he heard stirring bodies under him.

Nick made shushing sounds. "I'm here to help. If you're under the window, try and roll to the sides," he whispered.

Nick shed everything except his MP5 and pocketed extra magazines. He slowly and gently positioned the submachine gun against the inner wall. A tied and gagged man moved to hold it in place as Nick slid through the window and down onto the floor. He waved and smiled at the captives while retrieving his MP5 to be placed a few steps away.

"I am US Marshal Nick McCarty. I have a team outside. We wanted to make sure all of you were safe before we dealt with your captors," Nick whispered. "I am going to remove your restraints and gags. Please stay quiet."

Nick undid the parents' restraints and gags first. "Take the children over against the far wall. Hide their faces and your own. If the bad guys come in here, I will not give them surrender terms. Do you understand?"

"I wish I could help," the man said simply. He and his wife moved their two boys into the corner where they could not be seen from the doorway.

Nick positioned himself to the right of the doorway, at the opposite wall. "Make some noise, Marshals. We are secure in here."

"Understood," Tim said, signaling Cala to drive them in. He and Grace readied themselves. They knew both Johnny and Jian had M107 sniper rifles trained on the doorway.

Cala turned on the sirens and lights. She screeched into a tight turn approach toward the ranch house. "Ready, my love?"

"Anything sticking its head out the door will be unhappy, love," Johnny answered.

Inside the house, Vince and Bill panicked out of alcohol aided sleep, with search lights beaming onto the front of the house. Both men ran at the back bedroom, throwing open the door to get at their hostages. Two 9mm bursts pulped their chests and heads. They died before hitting the floor.

"Talbert and Cloverman have left the building... in a spiritual sense. Black wraiths vomited up from the floor to drag them down into hell. Done deal. Come around to the hostage window so I can hand the kids to you, Payaso, and help the parents exit through the window. Come with him, Johnny. I don't want to disturb the crime scene at the bedroom door."

"On our way, Muerto," Gus acknowledged.

"Tim and Grace? Enter through the front carefully. We still have a driver to catch. We need to get this part done and the family safe before waiting for the third member of this crew."

"You could have left one of them alive to question about the driver," Grace said.

"Sure, Grace, I'll leave you to use the victims as bait next time. I don't do that. When you want to pursue that line of thinking, count me out."

"And me," Gus agreed, along with everyone on the network.

"Statement retracted. Coming in the front now." Grace sighed while following Tim in combat mode.

Jian hurried in after Grace and Tim to provide backup. A man streaked around a bedroom door in the hallway, pointing an AK47 at Tim and Grace.

"US Mars-"

Jian shot the man in the head. Both the man and his weapon clattered to the floor. "Third man down."

Jian rushed ahead of Tim and Grace. "We need to clear the rest, my friends."

"Thanks, Jian," Tim said.

"No problem." Jian continued with the more energized Marshals behind him. It took only minutes to clear the rest of the house. "Clear, Muerto."

"We've been sitting behind desks too much lately," Grace said, staring down at the man in the hallway. "I was going to shout a surrender order while we got shot to death."

"Same here. That's why we called Nick," Tim replied. "Let's not beat ourselves up when the results could not be better. I'll gather the cell-phones and electronics. We'll need to make sure these three were the only ones in this crew."

"Good thinking, Tim." Nick joined the two from the front of the house. "Did you call in for a CSI team, ambulance, and meat wagon?"

"I just did it," Grace said. "Thanks for keeping the kill scene untouched. Those two with weapons dropped from their fingers in attack position will corroborate any story the family tells. We won't be returning to your house. Tim and I will be spending the night elaborating on our calling in a US Marshal's special operations team to free the hostages. We'll stick with that and only that for now. Our boss will be beamed in here to get in front of the cameras, so after the family is safe, and Tim learns whether anyone else is involved, your special ops team can leave, Muerto."

"Thanks, Grace, I'll relay your statement. No need for names to be mentioned. Hell, let your boss claim he busted in here and killed all the bad guys if it will make this easier."

"Actually, the boss is a she, about five feet tall. Tamara Blassinghill, hold over from the last administration, couldn't break into a Girl Scout cookie box. Tamara would take credit for the whole thing if she could. The new Attorney General already told her he expects her resignation on his desk by May 1st. I wish we could stay and hear you perform on the deck."

"Next time. I'll help Tim. Gus and Cala are with the family. They're also watching with Johnny for anything suspicious on the road in front. C'mon, Tim, Jian and I will help you hunt and gather. We won't touch any of the bodies. They'll have some gear bags around here, I'm sure. Maybe we can find someone else to kill tonight."

Grace bumped her shoulder into Nick and bounced off. "Not funny, Muerto!"

"Not to you, maybe."

Chapter Ten: Treason and Softball

"Vince learned they didn't man all the towers at Atwater," Tim explained to Nick. "He arranged for his brother, Larry, to be on scene at exactly the right time in a stolen car. It's in the Ranch's garage. Talbert and Cloverman overpowered the two guards and killed them. They put on their uniforms, stashed the bodies, and made it through three fences, disabling the lethal one. Their scheme would have worked if not for the girlfriend call."

"I think you and Grace tapping all the family and friends' phones had a lot to do with it. We'll go, and let you sort things through with your boss. The media shouldn't get wind of this before tomorrow morning."

"What did you give the dad?"

"I told him the special operations unit has a fund for special cases. I gave him a couple thousand to stay away from the house until I can call in my people to clean the scene."

"I didn't know you did that. Does Grace know?"

"It's better to keep it to the smallest number as possible. It buys me and the cartoons anonymity. I give them the money and they promise to keep their interview bland, such as reporting a team of unidentified Marshals rescued us. We get enough notoriety as it is."

Tim nodded in agreement. "I saw the bookstore incident with Hardin Travers. I always thought he was Marine Recon. I've seen publicity pictures of him with the uniform on. I know I've heard him say 'once a Marine, always a Marine'."

"The phrase is true... he's not. I was ordered to collect the jacket. He's converting to Islam too. That was a bit hard to swallow, unless he has it in mind to get protected under the Sharia Law pedophilia exemption."

"That's cold, Nick."

"We have people in Islam all their lives trying to escape it, and idiot leftists trying to break into it. It's a mad world, Tim."

"I can't disagree with you there. I'll call next time Grace and I are in the area. We'll stop by for your floor show on the deck."

"We'll be glad to have you. Be more careful out there, Tim. Marshal Chen saved your asses tonight."

"He sure did. That was a great move bringing him aboard the cartoon express."

"Johnny made me recruit him. I shot him before I recruited him."

"No shit?"

"He never lets me hear the end of it either. Any time it rains, he moans his shoulder let him know in advance. See you later, Tim."

Nick joined his crew awaiting him. "I think we'll do our small celebration at the Point tomorrow morning."

"Despite Jean's assertions we're all on the sauce?"

"You don't need to come, Payaso. Johnny, Jian, and I will take care of your portion."

"Very funny. Are you bringing Quinn?"

"I'll make us some omelet sandwiches too, so we don't get accused of being complete lushes. Nice shooting tonight, Dragon. You saved our Marshal buddies."

"They were actually shouting surrender orders to a guy pointing an AK47 at them. I would have shot him the moment I saw the gun barrel rounding the corner."

"Too much riding desks dulls the edge," Nick replied. "I think tonight was a wakeup call for Tim and Grace. They'll either stay out of the field or get back to a training facility with a mockup practice field. Remember, tomorrow... I mean this morning... I'll be walking Deke the long way by the bookstore."

"Since we're on the sauce, a longer walk would be good," Gus said.

"You four work out every day." Cala glanced over at Johnny next to her. "I think Jean was just joking. I don't know how you can stand to do those workouts. Muerto then works with Jean and Sonny. I hope we can see one of Al's softball games. I was never allowed to play sports."

"That gives me an idea, Cala. Would you like to play? They have adult softball leagues around here I'm sure. We have enough people to get a team. I'll talk to Joe at the Monte Café. He can sponsor us, although we'll pay for everything. I bet we can talk Neil and his wife into playing on our team. That would be nine right there. We know a few of the other police on the 'Grove' force too."

"Do you mean it, Muerto. That would be fun, I think. I need to stay in shape during my pregnancy. I hate exercises."

"We'll get equipment and test it out with Jean, Sonny, and Jay. We can test your enthusiasm. If it's not quite what you want to do on a regular team, we can always play some ball on our own."

"That sounds wonderful. I would still like to see Al's game with Cruella Deville as the assistant coach."

"You and me both," Nick replied.

* * *

Since we don't work regular hours, we agreed by vote where and when to practice. The parents picked Allendale Field near where all of us softball team parents lived. The field at Allendale afforded us the opportunity to play at nearly anytime we wished during the day. It was far from the safest place around, but it was when the Monster Squad held practice. Oaktown Cartel owned the Allendale District. Our Godfathers of Oaktown arrived in a limousine to attend all practices and games. To say any practice under Oaktown Cartel protection was a gang no-go zone would be an understatement.

A practice game, scheduled with the Bobcats, coupled both the spring excitement and unusually warm temps in the upper sixties. Lynn and I went out to the pitcher's mound to meet with the volunteer umpires and Bobcat coaches. It was a fun time. The coach for the Bobcats hated the sight of Lynn and I on the field. We won the championship last year in a close run against the Bobcats. To say he harbored a grudge would be an understatement. The umpires, a mixture of seasoned parents who loved the game and late teen guys familiar with the sport, met with us at the mound. Hector Torres and his wife Jill, coached the Bobcats. Their daughter, Felisa, was the Bobcat star.

"I think this year will be the best in a long time and I believe our all-stars will win it all," the umpire, a rotund veteran of many seasons, Manuel Flores said by way of greeting. "It is good to see coaches I recognize and have worked with."

"Let's get something straight." Hector pointed at me. "We want the games called legitimately. Just because this guy beats people in the UFC cage doesn't afford his team special treatment. We will protest any game with his A's where we believe his UFC status caused the Blue to make errors in judgment on calls."

They both avoided our looks of bewilderment. I confess I didn't figure on being handicapped at the beginning of the season because of the UFC. After the initial shock though, Lynn broke off into loud amusement.

"John… and I… aren't playing, Hector," Lynn said finally. "We have never argued calls on the field. We coach the girls to accept every call without malice. That is what we're supposed to do, isn't it, Manny?"

Flores headed the volunteer umpire crew across the league. "Of course, Lynn. You and John have been excellent at teaching sportsmanship. Why would you start the season with such a thing, Hector?"

Hector launched into a Spanish tirade. "We will not be hosed by these gangsters and their minions. This is a girls' softball league. I think they should be banned as coaches."

"John and I speak Spanish, Hector," Lynn replied. "Are you accusing John and I of something in particular?"

Yep. Lynn had learned the intricacies of girls' softball politics. We recognized some of the parent coaches were nuts. Hector hawed and hemmed for a moment.

"You two bully the umpires just by your presence! We know what you bunch do in private life."

"Are you referring to defending our nation, Hector," I asked. "We do that every single day, within work, and beyond it. Do you have an objection to Lynn and me as American Nationalists? Lynn is an American, as I hope all of us are. The umpires call the game by what they see. If they miss a call, we are supposed to give them the benefit of the doubt, and figure it will work out in the end. No umpire is perfect. Are you saying the Blue is working for us?"

Manny did not like that. "I hope that's not what you're saying, Hector. By even a well-founded suspicion of such a thing, I could have you and your wife banned from coaching."

Manny undid Hector. He gulped and retreated. "We...we simply want a fair game called."

Manny didn't press. "Fine. Let's have a good game. This practice game is a great learning tool for all of us. It is the first year it's been tried. Do not undermine it. Play ball!"

We were home team. Al met us halfway after the meeting, on her way to the mound. "Is anything wrong, Dad?"

"Just the usual – adults acting like children. I'm sure the A's and Bobcats will play ball with a much better attitude. Have confidence in your fielders, kid. Don't put any on the base paths that don't earn the trip."

"Absolutely," Al replied.

"Pitch a change-up on the first pitch, Al. The batter will be so far ahead, she could probably swing twice. Keep your change-up in mind every time. Mix it into your pitches constantly to throw off a batter showing tenseness."

"I will, Lynn... thanks." Al practically skipped to the mound.

"I think Al's ready for the season to start."

Lynn smiled. "No doubt about that. We were ambushed on the mound, Cheese. What the hell was all that about?"

"Parents living through their kids. We'll keep in mind our place in this alternate reality – encourage the girls to play ball the best they can and have fun. This isn't the pro-league. Some of the parents, like Hector and Jill, think every game is a war. We're not doing that, Sis."

"Amen to that."

In the dugout, our first and third base coaches approached with big smiles. Lucas and Clint had seen the adults in action already.

"Hector's wound a little tight," Clint stated.

"Watching these parents is the best," Lucas added. "I've missed this stuff so much. How's Manny holding up. I saw his face while Hector spoke."

"Manny handled it well. Hector insulted the entire league. I don't know why he would think that would help during the season. The teen umpires kept tight lipped control on their mouths. I'm not certain what that will mean. I guess that does it for cordiality amongst our brethren coaches. Hector thinks we're a bunch of gangsters, and my UFC status means the umpires will be giving us calls we shouldn't get."

Lucas and Clint enjoyed that scenario immensely.

"Here we go," Lynn said.

Al threw a change-up. Her arm motion was excellent. It looked like she meant to throw a fast ball. The batter swung through it before the ball reached the plate. She then threw a fast ball the batter was so late on, it was nearly in the catcher's glove before the swing. A high offering the batter could not resist struck her out. The A's and coaches cheered. Al continued pitching right over the plate. The batters, now told to take some pitches, ended up in the hole, as the umpire called strikes. Since Manny worked behind the plate, Hector and his wife seethed in their dugout.

"This adult interaction can become quite exciting," Clint observed.

Hector called for the Bobcats to do the pitcher belittlement rhymes. Al laughed at the new chant rhyme and finished striking out the side. Lynn sighed as Jill called time out to meet with Manny at the plate. I smiled as she trudged with head down to the meeting, amusing both sides. Everyone knew this practice game didn't count, but Jill had to protest something every inning. Lynn listened attentively, shrugged at Manny, and began doing dance steps as Jill argued on. Manny lost it, as the crowd began clapping a beat and enjoying the show. Manny simply pointed to the dugout, still unable to speak. Lynn did one of those dancing strolls back to the dugout amidst hoots, hollers, whistles and applause.

"Batter up!"

"Babe... that was the best," Clint stated. "You nearly caused Jill to stroke out. The Bobcats' parents know this practice game means nothing. She's hearing it from them. What did she want anyway?"

"The usual... Al's release point was wrong. She didn't come set. She missed the rubber. Her socks were too low. Her cap was on crooked. The stars are out of alignment. The clouds cast a bad shadow on the field. The batter's box is out of regulation."

We enjoyed Lynn's explanation of Jill's visit while our first batter, Mary, journeyed to the plate. I had already told her Hector and Jill's daughter, Felisa, would throw a fast ball down the center of the plate. Lucas worked our third base coaching position. He only nodded at Mary. She swung level and sent a screamer over the first base bag and into the corner. Mary made third without a throw. Lucas held her there. Our second batter, Callie, walked on four pitches. Felisa received a visit to the mound from her Mom. Jill illustrated everything you avoid doing as a coach. Felisa, a veteran of Jill's belittlement, remained silent with head down. Manny told Jill to get back in the dugout.

Al was at bat next. She hid it perfectly and bunted down the third base line, scoring Mary. Callie made it to third because no one covered the bag when the third baseman fielded the ball. Al ran safely over the bag at first. Jill started out of the dugout, but Manny waved her back in.

"Play ball! Batter up!"

The inning ended with the six-run limit set. I stopped Al for a moment. "Pitch hard, fast, and right down the heart of the plate. We don't want your fielders falling asleep behind you."

"Okay, Dad."

Felisa warmed up at the plate while Al threw her practice pitches. She hit the first pitch a ton, but Callie, our center fielder, caught it at the fence. The next two batters got on first and third with a hit, stolen base, and bobbled bunt. Al's next pitch came in low. The batter topped it back to Al, who spun and nailed the runner at second. Our second baseman, Sherry, easily turned the double play to end the inning. It was my turn as Hector demanded a meeting at home plate between innings.

"Are you going to let her pitch like that?"

"Like what," Manny asked, hands on hips. "You mean over the plate?"

Hector counted them off on his fingers. "Set point, release point, deceptive arm motion, and her-"

"Play ball!" Manny gestured for Hector to go away, dusted the plate, straightened, and yelled, "batter up!"

Despite Hector and Jill, the parents were enjoying a fast paced and exciting game. Jafar joined us in the middle of the inning. "Diane Cameron's in San Francisco."

"Oh my," Lynn replied to his whisper.

"I already texted Muerto."

"Good. Any indication of how long she'll be in the city?"

"I cannot be certain of that." Jafar smiled. "I know who she is meeting with: Tark Ruban, Fuma Sabedin, and Abu El-Tayed."

"Jesus, God in heaven - jackpot." Lynn grabbed Jafar's arm. "Call a meeting. We need all the facts about everything, including missing Senators, the Tark grapevine, and why in the world would they meet so close to our posse."

"I will go to Pain Central now," Jafar said. "I will be ready for all of you when the game ends. Bring me back a pizza, everything but anchovies, including pork sausage."

"You heathen," Lynn accused him. "You got it."

Jafar hurried off, leaving the four of us in stunned silence.

"What should I do, John," little Beth, our right fielder asked. "Can I bunt?"

"Sure. That's a good idea, but you can swing away if you want."

"I want to bunt, and then steal all the bases, including home." Her bright white smile flashed with devilish delight in contrast to her dark features.

"Why, you little minx." Lynn shoulder hugged her. "You go do that. Remember your slides. No head first dives. Got it?"

"Yes, Lynn." Beth jogged to the plate.

"I think these kids developed an edge since last year," Lynn said. "I guess winning a championship will do that."

"Beth made me forget about Tark," I replied, with Clint and Lucas echoing my sentiments. "We need to be in this game, not going on a mission in our minds."

Beth deadened a beauty in front of home plate. She immediately streaked to second on an overthrow by the catcher, sliding in perfectly. Our first batter, Mary, was up next.

"Take the first pitch, Mary."

"Beth and I talked. I'll take two."

Mary's declaration elicited much amusement. Felisa, worried about the speedy Beth at second, threw a high one, almost over her catcher's head. Beth stole third without a throw. Lucas reminded her to slide with hands waving down. Mary and Beth played out the string perfectly. Mary swung wildly at the next pitch, throwing the catcher off slightly, allowing the charging Beth to steal home without a tag. Our two girls high-fived at the plate. Hector and Jill wanted to attack like a couple of pit vipers. The catcher didn't even make a swipe so there wasn't much to argue. We gave Beth rock star status greeting, along with the parents behind us, and of course my entire Monster Squad.

A guy from their side the size of a football field screamed his way around the cage accusing me of everything from poor sportsmanship to selling out to someone... maybe the girls' softball Gods. He threw in racist too, although the girl stealing all the bases is black, so I think that must have been because he ran out of things to yell at me. Dev and Jess intercepted him before he could get close enough to scare the kids. Life as a girls' softball coach can get very exciting in a bad way. Manny stopped the game. I could tell he didn't want any part of getting his head torn off. I motioned for him to stay where he was. I exited the dugout to calm the guy down if I could. Dev and Jess were trying to reason with him. He tried to shove past them. That was not even in the realm of possibility. He stopped attempting the impossible as I approached.

"Calm down, Sir. You're scaring the kids." Then I smelled it. This guy had more than a few good time warmups for the game.

"He's tanked, John," Dev said. "I don't have a spell for that."

Jess and I enjoyed the hell out of that line. "Okay... okay... you must have a daughter playing today, right?"

He glared at me blearily for a moment before pointing at the catcher, who was visibly trying to do anything but watch what was happening. "Thas' my baby there, Harding! You jus' embarrassed the hell out of her!"

"You takin' care of that, partner," Jess told him.

"Jess is right. You've stopped a simple practice game, scared the kids, and most of the adults, all for what?"

"I want you, asshole!"

"No, you don't," Dev retorted. "John could take both Jess and I at the same time. You couldn't take either one of us alone."

Dev grinned at the guy, as he tested his ability to even move while being held by my brothers. Reality began seeping into his buzz. "Tell you what... I have a way for you to return to your seat with dignity before John plucks your throat out in front of everyone, including your daughter. I bet you never heard a Latin spell before, have you?"

"Uh... what does... no. I ain't heard no damn Latin spell."

"Good. I'm going to perform a Latin spell to ease everyone. Once it's over, you raise your hands, say, 'amen, brother', and return to your seat with quiet dignity. Can you do that? It will work great if you can."

Dev had this guy. He was mesmerized. The man wanted an out and Dev offered the only one available. "Yeah... yeah... I can do that."

"Dev! Don't do the rain spell, brother. I want to see the end of the game," Jess told him.

Jess's warning nearly launched Dev and I out of the spell. Dev snorted back amusement while Jess and I lowered our heads.

221

He shot his arms into the air, fists clenched, and delivered the Latin spell for power. In the hushed silence of his delivery, it felt like we ascended into the presence of something beyond understanding. Dev worked the spell with such power, I half expected it to rain too. He finished with climactic, fist pumping completion.

Dev's spell completely captivated this guy. He actually swayed and stepped in place as if he were a cobra being entranced by an Indian snake charmer. At the end, the man shot his fists into the air, hugged Dev, and shouted, "amen, brother."

We watched him walk away with head bowed, but dignity in every step. A few clouds had rolled in, a natural occurrence in April. Jess stared up at the sky with some trepidation. "Damn, brother… you got the power."

The parents, coaches, and both benches erupted in applause. Even Hector and Jill clapped briefly. I grabbed brother Dev by the shoulders. "Jess is right. You got power, brother."

Dev glanced over at his wife, Maria, and his adopted kids. He smiled at their looks of awe. "I wanted them to know I'm not some leg-breaking thug."

"Mission accomplished," I replied with emphasis. I gripped Dev's shoulder again. "I resent that, by the way. We're leg-breaking, rich thugs, rainmaker."

Dev and Jess both enjoyed the hell out of that ending. I retreated to my mundane dugout. In the scheme of things, when you can do what Dev accomplished with words, everything else seemed dull in comparison. I heard Manny shout, 'Play ball!', and shared giggling glances with my young charges, who had no idea what had just happened.

"Now that… was the best!" Lynn stated in a hushed tone.

"Amen to that. I wish we could harness the power of it for our soon to be reckoning with Tark."

Lynn shrugged. "Some things are best left to the darkness."

"They are indeed, Sis."

222

* * *

"Oh, thank the Lord! If not for Samira, I would never have been able to enjoy Dev's spell of banishment," Jafar stated the moment we joined him in the conference room, his pizza in hand. He hugged Samira. "The game was fabulous, but no way does anything eclipse Dev ending that tool's confrontation with the Latin!"

Jafar bumped fists with Dev, and finally hugged his idol. "You prevented a bad scene, my friend. After you did the Latin, the game played on without a snag. Devon Constantine, rainmaker and peacemaker."

"I heard from John you nailed down a triple threat for us," Dev replied while we all sat down around our software infused table with projected screen. "I'm interested in why the senatorial duel disappeared from the headlines. One day after discovery, every news outlet in the country carried it as a terrorist act or unexplained. Muerto must have made one hell of a convincing scene."

Jafar flashed the new headlines on the screen from his table. "They abandoned the terrorist involvement. I know he would say it was skill rather than luck, the fact they evidently shot each other with their own personal weapon made the scene nearly impossible to question. They fired with the correct hand, getting gunpowder residue on clothing and hand. No sign could be found of anyone else having been there. Danders and Barren's feud was well known in the Senate. Tark Ruban's Monterey estate becoming the death scene for two sitting Senators caused havoc within the billionaire's core group. Ruban issued a press release stating Danders and Barren asked if he would provide them with a meeting site to talk over their differences."

"So, it's possible Ruban doesn't have a clue what happened to his men, or why the two idiots battled to the death in his house, huh," Lynn asked.

"Ruban suspects foul play for sure," Jafar answered. "His gathering the last political cards he has with ex-Senator Cameron, Abu El-Tayed, and his go between with the Congressional Houses,

Fuma Sabedin, means he may be getting ready to leave the country. Danders represented his best chance to further El-Tayed's ascension to the Presidency. He needs someone to front the Presidential ticket. I suspect he's settled on Cameron."

"He's probably behind Cameron's new-found wealth on the speech circuit," Casey added. "They're running El-Tayed for Governor of Michigan in the election coming in November. That will give them adequate time to pad his resume. If ever there was a replacement Manchurian Candidate for our last terrorist enabler's eight-year experiment in American destruction, this guy El-Tayed fits the bill - home grown Moslem with terrorist ties and love for the institution of Sharia Law."

"Denny's still in DC working on our Cafrey Isle of Darkness excursion. The right people needed extorting from Moronas's videos. Quillum Stafferson Blinton's widow started making a fuss in the media. Denny shut her up with a video of her flying to the island with Quillum during the same time Moronas filmed Quillum in action with underage girls," I explained.

"Don't write that bitch, Willarie Modham Blinton, off just yet, guys," Lynn said. "She's angling for another run at something... God knows what. I'm surprised Tark doesn't have her sitting in on the meeting. Anyone get a message from Muerto, Jafar?"

"Gus texted me, the cartoons took out three murderers on the loose. Muerto's US Marshal contacts called them in on a hostage rescue/kill mission. They're keeping an eye on the news before joining us on this," Jafar answered. "Muerto gave Cameron a chance to retire alive. He won't be happy knowing she's back in the political mix. Gus thinks they'll be free of the aftermath by tonight."

"We should get his input on this," Lucas said. "We need another scenario like Muerto did on Danders and Barren."

"That damn guy is freaky." Tommy gestured at the headlines concerning the mysterious shootout between Senators Danders and Barren. "He makes the killers, Ruban sent to help with the Salvatores' blackmail attempt, disappear - then creates a perfect scene where two Senators use each other for target practice with their own guns, and blood/alcohol count off the charts. As an admitted Snow White, I'm glad he's on our side. I have a feeling he'll think of some plan involving a grenade."

"Agreed. We need his thinking on this," I added. "Which brings us to another point Lynn mentioned. Why in hell would Ruban schedule meetings with his cohorts so close to us? His grapevine must have alerted him to our adventures here in the Bay Area. We've probably thwarted a few of his plans already that we don't even know about."

"I've heard he travels with a squad of Syrian mercenaries," Clint said. "It's possible he has confidence they can handle us, or he figures even if we learned of his meeting, we wouldn't dare try anything. Add to it the fact Cameron and El-Tayed would want to be as far from their home states as possible, and it makes sense, especially since Cameron knows where Muerto lives. I doubt Tark linked us and Muerto with his Monterey incident."

"How long did Tark get rooms for, Achmed?"

"A week, John, but it's only one room - a huge suite."

Alarm bells went off in my head. I could tell a few of my Monsters thought that bit of information strange. "We need to trace down any other real estate or contact's place where our targets may be actually staying. The hotel room must be a deception. Send the info to Muerto too, Achmed. With all of us working it, we should be able to find where they're hiding. Hack into the hotel cameras and keep watch on that room they rented."

"On it," Jafar acknowledged.

* * *

Rachel leaned into Nick as he fingered the piano keys, singing 'I'll be Seeing You'. Jian brought Joan by for the first time to meet everyone. Four couples danced, including a red-faced Sonny with Jean. Because of Joan's presence, Nick made no mention of the texts he exchanged with Jafar, nor did Gus speak about the ones he sent North. Nick ended the song and closed the cover over the piano keys.

"That's all for tonight, folks. The kids have school tomorrow. I need to discuss some business with Gus and Johnny. It was very nice to meet you, Joan."

Joan shook his hand. "Thank you so much for inviting me. You play and sing beautifully. I play violin. Perhaps we could play together one night."

"I'd like that very much. Do you know 'Ride of the Valkyries'?"

"Oh yes… one of my favorites."

"Ours too. We will play together soon. Goodnight, Jian. We'll see you in the morning."

"I will be here at 7 am, Nick. Thank you for a great evening."

The couple said their goodbyes to the others and left. Nick poured Deke another beer and then walked the kids to their rooms. "Quinn's sleeping through the night so he's good for now. I know you kids want to be in on this. I'll allow one hour on your own to learn anything you can about some real estate or company setting Tark Ruban may have in the North Bay. It may be deceptive in form or mention with his name, or the others."

"Thanks, Dad."

"One hour and no more, Jean."

"If we find anything within the hour, we'll come straight to you."

"Deal."

* * *

"I like Joan," Rachel said. "She looks to be a great match for Jian."

"I vetted her," Johnny said. "I don't know how she'll take to the truth beyond the US Marshal business. I'll let Jian introduce her to that at his own speed if he cares about her."

"That's a big step," Tina agreed. "Finding out about you cartoons was a shocker. Would you have killed me if I didn't want to become part of your 'Addam's Family', Gomez?"

"Nope. I would have made Gus do it."

After the hilarity died down, Tina needed to get another shot in. "Gus would have never killed me, would you, honey?"

"Nope. I would have made Johnny do it."

"I see where this is going." Cala breathes in deeply, seeing Johnny about to respond while smiling at her. "It all flows downhill and Cleaner takes care of business."

"Cala!"

"Don't fret sister of the traveling assassins, you made the cut. Let's get down to Muerto business. What did you get messaged from the North?"

"Achmed learned Tark Ruban planned a meeting in the North with our favorite ex-Senator, Diane Cameron. Also attending are Fuma Sabedin and Abu El-Tayed, the wannabe first Moslem Governor of a state. They want us in the North the moment we get an all clear from Tim and Grace."

"What's wrong with this picture? Don't you think a little break between killing Senators or ex-Senators is in order?"

"Plus a billionaire, a DC Moslem go between, and a Moslem Governor candidate being groomed for the Presidency," Johnny added.

"You know a bit about El-Tayed, huh Johnny," Nick asked.

"He was born in this country, but he is all Sharia Law Mutant otherwise. I have been keeping an eye on Dearbornistan for you, Muerto. If this El-Tayed gets into power as Vice President under the traitor Cameron, he will do great damage. Once taking over as President from Cameron, we will be doomed."

"Cameron as President will not happen, Johnny. I warned Diane what would happen if she crossed paths with me again. I believe the Monster Squad wants input as to how we can erase these threats from America's horizon without being exiled to Monster Island. I have a plan for doing that, but we need to find out the place Tark meets with the people on his string."

Rachel pointed at Nick accusingly. "Did you let those kids solo on this?"

"Would you rather they did it behind our backs? I saw their faces. What I did was allow them an hour to help, instead of forcing them to collaborate against us. Sure, we could pretend Jean is a sweet angel, destined to be a model, psychologist, surgeon, lawyer... or we could accept reality. Jean is a force. She owns Sonny, body and soul. Jean leads without thought, fear, or sometimes... common sense. Sonny anchors her and displays everything a young man should be at his age and beyond. We can't stop this, Rach. Either join me in guiding these two young missiles or we'll have real trouble on the horizon."

"Damn it! How is it a psychopath knows more about raising kids than their own parents?"

"Objective analysis, my love. Let's get to work before the pre-teens make us look like chumps. I'm having a sip either way. Join me at your own comfort zone."

Nick's crew launched onto their networked laptops, using every resource available through Nick's enhanced access. Rachel gestured at Tina. "C'mon, girlfriend. Let's go watch a movie while the assassin tools work their magic."

"Wine will be involved. I'm in for that, especially after learning my fate if I had rejected the Muerto union of killer tools."

"You get used to it," Rachel told her as they left the room.

Thirty minutes later, Jean ran into the room with her laptop. "We got her, Dad! Cameron's ex-husband from long ago owns an estate in the Piedmont hills!"

Gus stood and went to pour another iced shot. "That's it! I'm done with this crap. We have every resource across the world available to us, and a couple of pre-teens make us look like puppies slavering at the adoption window."

Johnny sighed. "Jean's right. I missed the simple step of ex's, and missed everything. Good one, Jean and Sonny."

"I texted it to John as you spoke. They'll dissect the parts. Thank you, Viper and Cracker, for a job well done. Go get some sleep. I will get you two up early. We need to patrol the bookstore."

"We can't sleep now!"

"If you ever want to be a Marine, you'll need to be able to sleep the moment you're given the opportunity. Find a way to block out everything and sleep at a moment notice. It is a superpower you need to master."

"Okay… It's a good thing Sonny and I know you wouldn't pull the Marine card just to send us to bed."

"I want your best performance in school. That requires rest. Goodnight."

Jean hugged Nick, waved at everyone else, and led Sonny out.

"I have satellite coverage over the estate, Muerto. I'm showing heat signatures for a dozen people."

"The Dark Lord will need to confirm it, Johnny," Nick replied. "Jafar texted me a moment ago. He and Samira will go there tomorrow with building inspection credentials, check the area around the estate, and let us know what they find out. They won't get in the house, but they may get a look at the guards or catch a glimpse of our targets."

"What plan did you dream up for this," Gus asked.

"Come with me. I'll show you what I have in mind." Nick led them to his vault inside the downstairs safe-room. He opened the vault, utilizing both fingerprint and iris scan, where weapons and equipment packs were stored.

"Oh shit!" Gus pointed at a vest at the side of the vault. "Is that what I think it is?"

"If you're thinking bomb vest... then yes."

"I cannot believe you would keep such a thing in your house, Muerto," Cala said.

"This vault can withstand the blast."

"Muerto! You plan on putting that on someone and sending them into the same room with our targets and call it terrorism," Johnny said with some amusement.

"It will be terrorism, but not exactly as you describe. We need to get them all. It would be a good thing if we could leave a couple of the Syrian mercenaries alive, but it may not be possible. I have some special syringes to take our targets into a happy place, where I can position them for the surprise explosion. One of their own guys walked into their midst with a bomb vest... the no-good rat. They tried to stop him to no avail."

Nick bowed his head. "No one survived. It was horrible."

"Oh barf! How do you create this crap?"

"Tell the truth, Payaso. This plan will cover all the bases. Johnny and I go in as Amin Jutoh and Ebi Zarin, get the drop on them, give them an injection, set the scene, pull the pin, and yabba dabba du – dead terrorist enablers."

"What about Ruban's money," Cala asked. "We confiscate fortunes. What kind of Robin Hoods are we without confiscation."

Nick grinned. "We could spend a few quality moments with Tark. I'm certain he'll love to transfer our usual fees for exceptional courage and creativity."

"John Harding will shoot you through the head for such a lamebrained plan," Gus muttered.

* * *

Deke growled as they neared the bookstore.

"I knew we should have dropped the kids off first," Nick said.

"Yes," Jean hissed with pumped fist. "It's battle, Cracker."

"What are those people doing," Sonny asked.

"They are preparing to show everyone what imbeciles they are," Cala answered.

Johnny moved in front of the kids, alongside Gus and Nick, while Cala watched their backs, hand on her Glock. "What would you like to do, Nick? How did they know we would be coming this way?"

Nick shrugged. "My bad. I thought about one job too many. This morning, I wrote an opening scene in my new novel, 'Fatima's Fury', did a live conversation with Jared about getting him a new MRI machine for the 'City of Hope', and studied the chances of anyone detecting my new syringe cocktail."

"Your Spiderman/Ninja powers didn't warn you, huh?"

"Nope."

The dozen young thugs in hoodies and facemasks spread in a semi-circle to block their way. Dressed all in black, carrying baseball bats, and containers of stuff Nick could only guess at, the leader pointed at Nick.

"You blaspheme Islam! You kill true believers, and unjustly maim and kill our brothers in the Antifa and BLM movements! We know you, McCarty."

"Believe me, you don't. If you did, you'd strip off the masks and run." Nick held up his cell-phone, Facetiming Neil Dickerson. "I have the Chief of Police watching right now."

"Six more in the rear, Muerto!" Cala drew her weapon as men moved on them from the rear.

"You'll be dead by the time your cop friend gets here!"

Nick brought his phone in a face to face for a moment with Neil. "I'm out of options, Neil. I will need to make a few examples."

"We're ten minutes out, Nick. Do what you need to do."

Nick slipped the phone in his jacket. "Put your bats down and walk away or I start shooting."

"You fire on us and we will own your ass, kafir!"

No one saw the movement. Something flashed in the hazy first light of day, disappearing to the hilt in the leader's groin. He danced at first, hands dropping baseball bat to grip his center, issuing short, ragged yelps in an octave so high, Deke howled with him. He sat finally, rocking and forming a growing coating of blood on his hands. His companions stared at their fallen leader in shock.

"Jean! Sonny! Two shoulder examples in the rear!"

Two knives streaked instantly from behind Cala. She smiled as the two gesturing men in the lead behind them sprouted handles on their shoulders. Both screamed at the same time, collapsing to the ground, grasping their wounded shoulders. Sonny ran forward, plucked the knives out of their targets, wiped the blood on the writhing men, and returned Jean's knife. All the while, a smiling Cala, in a shooter's crouch, aimed at the head of the next nearest one.

"Those are the only warnings we're giving," Nick called out, already aiming his Colt at the man's groin next to his first victim. "Each of us adults has fourteen round magazines. Make a move and we empty our weapons and reload. We are killers. We are expert shots. Take off the masks and kneel."

Cala saw the one in her left peripheral field of vision reach under his hoodie. Jean's knife pinned his hand to his belly, while Sonny's tore into his bicep. Sonny streaked ahead again to retrieve the knives from the now gasping in shock, prone man. He also retrieved the handgun in the man's belt. No one else moved except to get on their knees. They removed their masks, holding them in clasped hands at the back of their heads. Bats and clubs dropped to the sidewalks. Sirens wailed in the distance, growing louder with each passing second. Jean passed hand wipes to Sonny. He cleaned blood residue from the knives and his hands after placing the confiscated weapon near Cala. Jean accepted the used wipes in another clean one, putting them in a pocket of her school pack.

"They did good, Muerto... real good," Cala said.

Three squad cars penned the group in. Officers emerged with Neil the first from his car, motioning for restraint. "Easy... they're down. Call an ambulance and a meat wagon."

He walked over to the Unholy Trio facing the kneeling men with drawn weapons. "Just another school-day walk, huh Nick?"

"Fuck this! Allahu Akbar!" A man behind the fallen one lurched to his feet sideways, reaching under his hoodie.

"Deke! Defend!"

Deke tore the man to the ground by his wrist, dragging him screaming from side to side. Once the man rolled to his stomach, Deke pounced on his back, with wrist still clamped in his jaws, holding the man unmoving with pinned arm.

"Move in! Assist the Marshals in subduing this bunch," Neil ordered.

Within minutes, the men lie restrained on their sides with wrists at their backs. The weapon and ID checks began then in earnest, while more police arrived with ambulance and transport vehicles.

"At ease, Deke." Deke ran over to sit next to Nick, who holstered his Colt and petted him. "There are four stabbings, Neil. We did as little as we could without lethal force, but it was close."

"I'll bet. Who did the knife throwing?"

"I did."

"Where's Jian?"

"Girlfriend."

Neil smiled at Nick and then at the two grim-faced kids, standing in a formal at ease posture. "Best take the minions of Zorro to school, Nick. Stop by the station when you get a chance. I'll phone you if any of this bunch has a federal warrant. Otherwise, we'll book them for assaulting federal agents."

"I lost concentration, my friend," Nick admitted. "I was riding the wave from three other gigs going on in my head. I'm certain they followed us from my house. This might have been a wild gun battle with the kids in the middle of it. I needed to know they're ready when I screw up. They are. It won't happen again, but I know now I can count on them to protect each other if it does. Can I check a few things on the leader's phone? I need to get his identity and learn any connections he has I should know about."

"Go ahead." Neil handed Nick a pair of Nitrile gloves and evidence bag. "Would he be the one with the handle of a knife sticking out of his groin?"

"Yeah. Tell him I want my knife back."

Chapter Eleven: Kill Mission

No one wanted to go near the groin wounded man, bleating on the sidewalk in short shrieks of pain, before the EMTs treated him. Nick had no such qualms. He frisked the man with professional ease, finding his iPhone in a wallet type protective case sealed inside the inner Velcro pocket of his hoodie jacket. Nick bagged his other belongings, including knife and .32 caliber ACP. One glance inside the wallet case and Nick called Jian. He answered on the first ring. Nick grinned as a female voice asked Jian what was wrong.

"White-eyed devil! Why are you calling me?"

"I just texted an address. Get in your Dragon-breath-mobile and get here. I have a transport for you. Calla will go with you. See if Joan can give you a few plastic garbage bags."

"Moving now." Jian disconnected.

Nick waved off the EMTs approaching. "See to the other wounded. I will transport this one."

They glanced at Neil who gestured his approval for Nick's redirection. "What's wrong, Nick?"

"Big trouble in River City. Jian is on his way with a car. He'll be transporting him to a federal facility for care."

Neil understood what that meant. He nodded and set about the task of rapidly clearing the prisoners around Nick and the wounded man.

"Cala!"

Cala hurried to Nick's side. "Yes, Muerto?"

"I need you to go with Jian and this ass-clown to our special facility for treatment. He is an important federal witness as of right now."

"Of course. I will take care of him."

Nick then stuck the man with a syringe loaded with the drug cocktail he planned to use in what he now understood to be a top priority. Despite the pain, the man passed out immediately. "Leave the knife in, but soak the wounded area with peroxide, and stuff towels around it. I will join you and Jian as soon as I can."

"Of course," Cala replied.

Jian arrived five minutes later. Neil guided his Toyota Rav 4 next to Nick, Cala, and the wounded man. Jian opened the back of his Toyota, where he had already lined the interior with black plastic bags. He and Nick loaded the wounded man, with his grotesque groin protrusion, onto the black bag covering.

"Do you have a towel or something, Dragon?"

Jian hurried to the front glove compartment. He brought around a yellow cotton polishing towel, handing it to Nick, who stuffed it around the knife handle. He then jammed the man's hands around it and shut the Toyota hatch. Lastly, he handed the man's personal belongings and weapons in the evidence bag to Cala.

"I will be along, shortly." Without waiting for acknowledgement, Nick rejoined his group, while Jian and Cala sped away from the scene.

Neil met him there. "If anyone asks?"

"Transferred into federal custody and flown to Washington DC. I will bring the documents into your office later."

"Good enough. Would you all like a ride to school?"

"No. We'll be fine. Thank you. I will tell you what I can later."

"Understood. See you then." Neil moved back as the Unholy Trio, Marshal Deke, and the minions of Zorro continued down the sidewalk.

"How are you going to explain this to Mom?" Jean knew Nick had a long ago decided on course of action in revealing violent situations to Rachel. He told her everything.

"I have no idea. The old crap about 'honesty is the best policy' sounds nice, but has many drawbacks in this instance. I know you and Sonny will give me a chance to get around to it."

"We will, Dad. Mom sometimes reads me like I'm a little kid. I'm working on improving my withholding evidence under interrogation though."

That statement garnered some amusement. Nick put his arm around Jean. "Don't bother. I should have it handled by the time you get home from school. If not, I'll let you know. You'll be continuing to stay at our house, Sonny. Do you have enough clothes there?"

"Yes, Sir. Is something wrong at my folks' house?"

"I'm not sure yet. We have an unexpected complication from their previous adventure. It could be a thread from something of mine though. I'll be investigating that venue within the next couple hours. Call your folks now. Tell them their past may be haunting them. Today would be a good day for your dad to go into his San Francisco office. Your mom can go with him and do some shopping with the money I transferred to them."

"Right away," Sonny acknowledged. He called his parents on speaker for Nick's hearing. Phil Salvatore answered.

"Are you okay, Sonny?"

"I'm fine, Dad. Nick says you and mom better go to San Francisco right away."

"What has he done now?"

Sonny's mouth tightened. "Saved your lives many times over. It has to do with something from yours and mom's recent screw-up he's investigating."

"Oh, good Lord… does he think Tark Ruban is involved?"

"No more talk on an open line, Phil," Nick ordered. "Take Clarice with you to the passport office. Pack a bag. Stay somewhere nice with a lot of lights and keep your eyes open. I'll let you know when to return. Your actual job is the last place anyone would look for you. Get moving! We'll take care of Sonny."

"Please do what Nick says, Dad."

"We will. After... after this gets over with... come home with us."

"I will, Dad. Go on now. Take care of Mom. Goodbye."

"What did you find, Muerto," Gus asked as they resumed their walk.

"The guy in the front has a security ID from Tark Ruban Enterprises. Bringing the ID with him on this faceoff plot may be the dumbest move ever. It could also mean he planned to formally go to the Salvatore's home directly after waylaying us on the streets. We'll find out soon enough. He may prove to be an asset making everything easier in the North."

Gus smacked palm to forehead. "You're thinking of putting him in the vest."

"Astute observation, Payaso."

"I thought maybe you were coming to your senses about the plan."

"It may not be a perfect plan, but this new ingredient could improve my chances of selling it to the Dark Lord."

"I hope not. I can envision so many things going wrong, it freezes my mind."

"Negative vibes are not helpful, Payaso," Johnny said. "Muerto needs our enthusiastic support for this ridiculously dangerous plot."

"Kabong! I thought you approved of the plan completely," Nick replied, listening to Jean and Sonny's suppressed humor.

"From the moment you inserted the infamous pairing of Amin Jutoh and Ebi Zarin, my enthusiasm faded. Those two characters should be retired completely after their last adventure together."

"We succeeded on mission with only slight problems. Remember, it wasn't us ringing the alarm bells. Our passports held through inspection. They didn't want to take the chance we were playing them. We know Tark's number. I'll have Denny make our new terrorist friend, Amir Mohammed Kostler, make a call to Tark telling him he has two killer operatives in the area. Tark will ask him how he knows his location. Kostler can laugh and say he knows Tark's every move. If Tark accepts Kostler's line, he'll want two more top notch hired guns. If he doesn't, I may need to wing it."

"You can wing a line in the high school play. This, you can't wing, Muerto. Think it through after you talk with the guy at Johnny's place."

"Agreed."

"One good thing… you guys won't all be getting blitzed down at the 'Point' this morning," Jean said, jetting ahead with Sonny close behind.

"What's that old Rodney Dangerfield line… 'now I know why tigers eat their young'?"

* * *

"Hajar Kassis," Nick slapped the man's face with subtle wake up slaps.

Kassis groaned as if coming out of a deep sleep. "Stop! Why… are you slapping me?"

Reality seeped into Hajar's consciousness, along with pain so intense he screamed until hoarse. Strapped to a gurney, Hajar found while gasping in distress he could move his head enough to see the handle of a knife still protruding from his groin area with a bloody towel around it. He found his screaming voice once again before he began to beg in Arabic.

239

"Please! I...I need a doctor! The pain... Allah be merciful! Help me!"

"Doctor Muerto is here, my friend, ready to help. I need a couple of things from you first. I saw your security ID from Tark Ruban Enterprises. Did he personally send you here?"

"You! You are no doctor! Take me to the hospital! Oh... pain... give me something for the pain!"

"Not yet." Nick moved to Hajar's middle with his hand hovering over the knife handle. "Let Doctor Muerto adjust this nasty knife slightly."

Kassis screamed when Nick touched the knife handle. "Wait... wait! Yes... Mr. Ruban sent me along with... some others from his San Francisco office. He wanted you involved in a police matter. Mr. Ruban knew your address and all... about you, McCarty!"

Jian, Cala, and Nick all enjoyed a brief moment of amusement. "Sending you means he knows nothing about me. Did you have a secondary plan after this police involvement ploy?"

"The... Salvatores... your friends... he... please! The pain... I cannot think!"

"Here," Nick said. "Let me adjust the knife a bit more."

"No! Wait! Ruban wanted to know... what happened to the two Senators. He knew men were with Senators Danders and Barren. They have disappeared. He believed the Salvatores... would know what happened to them all."

"Does Tark know Amir Mohammed Kostler?"

"Yes. They meet regularly. Amir... wanted the hellish City of Hope destroyed. He needed Ruban's help."

"I will give you something for the pain, so you may speak freely with me," Nick said. "Do not disappoint me."

"I will tell you anything you want to know! Make... make the pain stop!"

Nick injected him with a morphine derivative, mixed with sodium pentothal and oxycodone. He only gave him a dosage to relieve enough of the pain for Hajar's communicative skills to improve.

"Tell me what you think these people like Tark, Amir, and the Senators want besides their usual criminal enterprises."

"I…I…" Kassis thought hard. He wanted to please this man. "Chaos first… then order through Sharia within the caliphate of world domination. Soon, they will have enough of the Antifa and BLM gangsters to cause the people in America… to demand anything that will stop the violence. With our people in key positions, we… can establish Sharia, immediately putting down and controlling the thug factions."

"You have thought long about this, have you not, Hajar," Nick asked, continuing in Arabic.

"I have. All true believers wonder at why our people are invited into countries where the citizens want nothing to do with us. They know… we never assimilate. It is an incredible plan. I see… our numbers growing into dominance. We soon will be in control of all nations."

"If we continue as we have so far, I believe you are right," Nick admitted.

He administered a full dose of morphine, taking away all feeling. Nick then injected a local anesthetic to numb Hajar's groin region before removing the knife. After stripping Hajar from the waist down, while applying pressure on the wound with a fresh peroxide soaked towel, Nick did some minor repairs with a liquid surgical sealant.

"We will be on a time limit to use Hajar," Nick said. "I'll contact John. We'll hook our suicide bomber to an IV until we can fly him North for his date with destiny. This will be a tough sell to Kabong and Payaso. I don't think they care much for my daring plan."

"If the two teams are to avoid connection with the deaths of these very public people, your plan may be a gamble, but it is the only one I can think of to keep from being tied in with the killings," Jian said.

"I agree with Dragon. My husband knows it will be the only solution," Cala added.

"This places a new ingredient in the mix which can eliminate a little of the danger. We'll stow away Hajar with an IV and I will start a conference call with the Dark Lord on a secure line. All of our talking it out won't mean anything if John's crew can shoot it full of holes."

                         * * *

I listened with the Monsters at Pain Central to details of Nick's new plan for hitting Ruban and company. It amazed me how Muerto creates intricate plots to wipe out a bunch of people, and yet finds ways to avoid being linked with the deed. We'd probably all laugh at his past plots, along with this one, if he hadn't made the ones in the past work. I leaned forward after glancing around at the smiling faces of my cohorts waiting for my official reaction.

"Let me blurt this out briefly so we're all on the same page. We get Denny to have Amir Mohammed Kostler call Ruban, letting him know two of his operatives, Muerto and Kabong, using their Amin Jutoh and Ebi Zarin identities, helped Hajar Kassis escape police custody. Kostler asks Ruban if he would like Kassis brought to him by his two agents. Hajar Kassis, according to Kostler, has learned information he must deliver to Ruban in person. The reason Jutoh and Zarin were in a position to help Kassis is because Kostler hired them to kill the infamous Nick McCarty. That's the key to the gamble, right?"

"Exactly," Nick answered. "If Ruban believes he and Kostler want the same man dead, Kostler could get Ruban to use Jutoh and Zarin to get the Salvators. Hajar carried a .32 caliber ACP. That will be the tricky part. I will need to down the Syrian guards before they know what hit them with the ACP once we're inside. That can be Hajar's doing before he exploded his bomb vest. Johnny gets the drop on Ruban and his guests easily. We give them my sleepy-time syringe treatment, set the scene, and blow Hajar to kingdom come along with the others."

"That's a lot of guys to kill with a .32," Casey said.

"Did you just insult me, Case?"

After some amusement, I turned to our conferenced call participant. "What do you think about the viability of getting Kostler to sell this gambit to Ruban?"

"He will say anything to stay away from Dr. Deville. The plan will work if Ruban wants Kostler's two supposed hired guns to bring Hajar to him. I like all aspects of it. If the ploy works, very bad people die without our being caught in the mix. As Nick said, it's a good gamble. Nick and Johnny will be in the most danger. Being able to shoot any of the Syrian bodyguards with Hajar's ACP takes some pressure off." Denny paused for a moment. "This needs done. If it goes wrong, move in, kill them all, and make the bodies disappear."

"If Muerto and Kabong believe in the plan despite the possible danger, I vote we back them, and correct any errors old school," Lynn said.

Lynn's vote drew affirmation from everyone.

"Okay... we're in, Nick," I told him. "I imagine you need to get your potential suicide bomber North as soon as possible."

"I'd like to fly him there today. I can't predict there won't be problems from his wound. We'll leave this afternoon."

"See you then."

* * *

"I told you John would love the plan," Nick said

"John didn't say he loved this plan," Gus retorted. "I don't think he realized you were already at our hangar at the airport, or that we loaded Hajar into the helicopter before the call."

"I didn't want to worry him with minutiae. Ready, Cala? Off we go into the wild blue yonder!" Nick skipped toward the helicopter.

"Coming, Muerto." Cala smiled at Gus, Johnny, and Jian. "Has Muerto gone over the edge."

"No," Gus answered. "He gets this way when on a kill mission."

"Payaso is right," Johnny agreed. "Remember when he was in Chicago blowing the gangs into another dimension? He acted like he was a kid going to Disneyland."

"Yes. I am told Muerto smiled when he shot me," Jian added.

"He smiled when he tortured me," Johnny admitted. "It is not personal... just business."

* * *

"I must say this is perfect."

"I told you I had this, Kabong." Nick, dressed in black slacks, t-shirt, black Giants baseball cap, darkened skin, and sporting four days of beard, pushed a wheel chair with Hajar slumped in it, along the sidewalk to Diane Cameron's ex-husband's estate entrance. "The bomb vest is hidden under the wheelchair seat. Your MP5 fit perfectly in the seat's rear storage area. Here come the Syrians."

Two tall men in dark suits approached them from the door. One pointed at Hajar. "What happened to Kassis?"

"He was wounded in the protest," Nick answered in Arabic. He handed the man their passports. "Amir told me I should show these to you."

The Syrian looked over the Saudi passports carefully before nodding his acceptance and handing them back. "Thank you. Will Kassis be able to speak?"

"Yes. He is merely sedated because of the pain," Johnny answered. "We will bring Hajar out of it so he may tell Mr. Ruban what he refuses to tell anyone else since we rescued him."

"Mr. Ruban wants what the Salvatores stole and them tortured to death."

"We have been ordered by Amir to complete any mission Mr. Ruban wants done," Nick said, "including the man Amir wants dead - Nick McCarty."

"Follow us."

Johnny took over the wheelchair. Nick stepped in front of him, following the Syrian guards closely. As Nick crossed the threshold, he saw the other four Syrians sitting at a table near the entrance to a huge living room with domed, ornate ceiling. Without pause, Nick executed the two guards in front of him with hollow point rounds for the .32 caliber ACP. Before the other four could react, Nick was amongst them firing from point blank range into heads and faces. Completing his rapid fire assault with extra kill shots, he followed Johnny at a dead run into the living room where screams from Diane Cameron and Fuma Sabedin mixed with shocked demands from the men.

"On the floor, face down or I open fire," Johnny shouted, MP5 aimed at Tark Ruban's groin. "Do it quickly or I begin shooting pieces off you."

"McCarty!"

Nick waved comically at Diane Cameron. "Hi there, Diane, you traitorous bitch. You and your pals better hit the floor. Tell them. You know me."

"He will torture us without hesitation! McCarty is a murderous demon! Do as he says!"

"Yes, do as he commands! I will clear this up once we are safe," Tark told the others while getting on the floor face down.

Abu El-Tayed followed Ruban's lead as did Cameron and Sabedin. Nick administered the syringes to render the prisoners unconscious, except for Ruban. Nick restrained each one. Johnny and Nick then lifted Tark Ruban into a chair. Nick fired an arc from his stun-gun nightstick next to Ruban's groin. Ruban yelped, trying to throw himself backwards. Johnny held him steady.

"We're in with all down," Nick said. "Are you on, Achmed?"

"Yes, Muerto. Loud and clear."

"Okay, Tark… here's the deal. Give me all your account numbers for a funds transfer, and I won't barbecue your balls off. Want a demo?"

Silence.

Nick gave him five seconds of hell with Tark screaming until he passed out. Johnny slapped him awake, sobbing and crying. "Give me the account numbers or a device I can find them on."

"Please… the pain… oh God… the-"

Nick gave him another five seconds. When Ruban became coherent enough to speak, he rattled off three account numbers.

"The numbers are good, Muerto," Jafar told him. "This was a very profitable mission if you can keep us out of it."

"Working on it." Nick injected Ruban rendering him unconscious.

Johnny and Nick seated Ruban, Cameron, and Fuma Sabedin on the couch. They positioned Abu El-Tayed in a chair near the couch. Nick adjusted their poses for the blast to hit them with the most force. They wheeled Hajar into the room. Nick and Johnny hurriedly put the bomb vest on him before positioning Hajar sitting on the floor amidst the soon to be deceased. They copied as much electronic data as they could from both the computers and the smart phones before Nick set the timer for five minutes.

"We're coming out Cala. Lucky I thought to fire this .32 in Hajar's hand, huh Kabong?" Nick wiped clean the .32 caliber ACP and placed it in Hajar's hand.

"Hurry, my love," Johnny added. "Muerto set the timer for five minutes. He is acting out for Gus and Jian. Please save me."

"Parking in front now, husband."

Nick and Johnny rolled the wheelchair out to the van where Jian and Gus stashed it inside. Cala drove away an instant later. She drove toward Pain Central as did the Monster Squad's action van, waiting for the outcome of the plan. The huge explosion rocked the street beneath them as they rode along. By prior agreement, the two teams conferenced only for a short time before Jafar drove Nick's crew to the Monster Squad hangar.

"That was a very short mission, Muerto," Jafar said. "The Monsters did not even get an opportunity to participate. We will be subjected to the ire of Cruella Deville because she was unable to kill something."

"She made sure Amir Mohammed Kostler performed perfectly. Is it true Denny placed a monitor with Lynn watching Amir while he made the phone call to Ruban?"

"Oh yes. He needed to throw down three shots of Beam before his voice stopped shaking. Lynn kept staring at him through the entire call. Kostler took Ruban through every facet of your planned help in killing the Salvatores, Muerto himself, and getting the blackmail material. Add in the supposedly vital information Hajar obtained and Ruban was so happy, he wanted to send a car to retrieve all of you. Kostler convinced him not to with nearly flawless patience."

"I bet old Diane Cameron nearly fainted dead away at the thought of having me killed."

"I noticed you didn't have much fun with Diane before blowing her to pieces," Jafar replied. "What do you bunch have planned next."

"I'll let you know. I plan to have Jared call you about a new MRI machine for his hospital. Since we made a fortune from Ruban, I'd like whatever one he wants shipped right away. From the City of Hope's Facebook page, Jared has made major improvements in medical care until the hospital complex can be built. He's attracting paying patients from countries all around them. They return to their countries with stories highlighting the improving lifestyle in the City of Hope. With Kahn's vetting of refugees getting more precise daily, the population welcomes vetted refugees abandoning Islam with less suspicion."

"You sound as if you will be visiting soon, Muerto."

"Not until we knock out all the people providing fortunes to end it. I'll be interested in what you learn from the data we pulled off the phones and computers."

"I will get it to you right away," Jafar said. "Maybe we'll have a down time for a while."

"My wife would like that, but she knows I don't do well in down times. Singing and playing the piano, coupled with my writing, has been taming me somewhat."

Jafar stopped the van near the hangar. He shook hands with his passengers. "We have girls' softball to help Monster attitudes, Lynn especially."

"We'll fly down for a visit around a scheduled softball game. I'll entertain at my house afterward. Send me a schedule."

"I will, Muerto." Jafar drove away.

"Did this mission calm you down, Muerto?"

"It went so smooth, I may need something else, maybe a fishing trip or book signing."

"The only one around us that will take you is the one you did the short writing class in," Gus said. "Maybe we should stick to small celebrations at the 'Point'."

"I agree with Payaso," Johnny said. "We used up enough Karma on the mission today, we'll be lucky to get home in one piece. Five minutes? Really?"

"It was perfect timing, Kabong. Haven't you ever seen those Mission Impossible movies? Our gig today was like one of those."

"All I know is you nearly made us all into suicide bombers."

After they boarded, Nick did the 'Mission Impossible' theme song with such fist-pumping flair, his companions joined in as Cala lifted off.

* * *

Jean and Sonny met Nick at the door with Deke leaping as if on a pogo-stick. Rachel held Quinn, who laughed and waved.

"Wow… great welcome. Uh oh… I don't see smiles on you youngsters' faces. What cataclysmic event happened while I've been away." Nick knelt to commune with his beer buddy.

"We figured you would want a full report on the news reports since your elimination of those treasonous imbeciles," Jean replied.

Rachel blocked Nick's hug attempt. "I don't think so! You let Deke slime you and then want a hug and kiss from me? Wash up, Muerto. We'll see you up on the deck with veggie plate and iced Beam. The kids will not be swayed from their report, so hurry."

"Well… okay… but Deke slimes you and Quinn, and I never refuse hugs and kisses."

"That's different." Rachel spun and headed upstairs with a giggling Jean following. Sonny smiled at Nick before climbing after them.

"Deke… my old friend… this is the double standard of life," Nick instructed, while hugging the dog. "You can slime

249

everyone, but apparently the aftermath has limitations. C'mon, I'll go wash first and we'll join them on the deck."

Seated comfortably at their conference table, everyone picked at the veggie tray, including Quinn, who loved carrots and ranch dip on his still teething gums. Nick, with Deke draining his beer bowl near him, sipped from his iced Beam with the satisfaction a nearly psychopathic killer can feel within contrasting scenes. His planned disposal of enemies, without anything in the deed tracing to his actions, provoked a general feeling of wellbeing.

"Okay... I'm focused on the report, Viper. Go ahead."

"A suicide bomber murdered six Syrian mercenary guards in the employ of Tark Ruban, billionaire financier," Jean recited in category form. "After incapacitating Ruban's guests, the man, a security employee of Ruban's, detonated a bomb vest in the midst of Ruban, Diane Cameron, Fuma Sabedin, and Abu El-Tayed. The media is trying to pin it on right-wing extremists, but the suicide bomber's background is eating them alive. There were no survivors."

"Horrible... simply horrible... what is this country coming to, when a few patriots visit justice where none expected it. The headlines should read 'communists and Islamic terrorist sympathizers' die at the hands of American patriots." Nick finished his never to be repeated soliloquy with fist pumping fervor. "Yes! America's defenders triumph once again without being caught by upside down justice. So... what's the frowns for?"

"Although informed of the details, the Momster rebelled in exponential form at your ordering violent action from children after you left on mission," Jean answered in monologue form.

Nick traded glaring stares from Rachel, with the Terminator dead gaze of death. Rachel had never been able to not shudder inwardly when being subjected to it. She believed beyond anything in the world, Nick would not harm her in any way. Yet the violent element in his stares of dark promise, both frightened and enticed her, as they had done since his first revelation of what he did in reality.

"These kids exist in our reality, Rach. This isn't a sitcom on CBS, where the characters perform in politically correct form. It's not a new 'Addam's Family' movie either, where people die or are eliminated according to comic form. We were in the midst of a deadly assault. The kids reacted as they had trained - without hesitation, and without mercy – on my order. Their accuracy ended a surely killing outcome."

"I'm here on the other side of the trench, Muerto. Neil may not be able to prevent them from being thrown into the juvy system for that kind of exploit."

Nick sipped his Beam. "Did you just insult me, Rachel?"

"How many would die, Muerto. I realize no force on earth could take and keep these kids from you. I thought we were in the avoidance category of situations like that."

"I figured we were in the trust Muerto category of training during real life events. Cala protected them at all moments. She's a killer I have no qualms about. Cala would have drilled every one of the bad guys in the head. She shoots expert. There's no denying it was fortunate I recruited her before she was honor-killed or drawn into Islamic darkness. Jean and Sonny are blooded now in combat with weapons. Many police officers retire without a single incident, although that statistic has probably changed in this new day of chaos."

Rachel took a deep breath rather than spew nonsense. "I get it. I don't like it."

"At times, you will be forced to accept it though, babe. You wanted complete honesty in knowing details of this life I live in darkness. I don't want you outside the loop either. I need you with me in all things. Sometimes, I feel guilty about starting again in this – not so anymore. The leaders of the world's nations sell out their citizens for 'One World Order' on a daily basis. The dependence on us shadowy killers to battle in the darkness increases moment to moment. We welcome the opportunity because some of us, me included, were born to kill. That I regained the ability to feel all other things in life I owe to you, Jean, Quinn, Deke, Sonny, and my entire crew."

251

"The kids choose their path as they age," Nick went on. "I've lost them to a darker path. We tried steering them into meaningful other careers. We can only guide them now. Their own common sense has pushed them into not being victims. For whatever reason, the two of them became protectors. They train daily with passion. How many video game, text messaging, lost souls their age, spend their entire lives staring at a small screen, making fantasy moves while the world passes them by?"

"Jean and Sonny do their homework, defend the weak at school, and train constantly. I've never dreamed of commitment like that," Rachel admitted. "I relish it, yet I keep wondering if they'll miss being just kids."

"We are kids, but kids with superpowers," Jean replied. "Anyone seeing me and Cracker on the playground, or anywhere else with schoolkids, knows we won't walk away. We've earned respect as dad taught us, through helping and protecting those kids who can't or won't do it for themselves. He explained we will deal with the same thing as Marines. We will protect America and her citizens. Sonny and I have teachers who hate America. We know we'll be protecting them too, even when they hate us."

Rachel reached over to grip her daughter's hand. "That is a career with passion and dedication. I've already seen you and Sonny have it. Don't hold it against me when I find it impossible to understand."

"We rule the school, Mom. No girl, or many boys, even think of harassing me. The roughest other boys in the school turn away when Cracker passes them. The boys who have trouble on the playground or anywhere else come to us. I want to do this always! It's exciting and right... all at the same time. Like dad said... we're blooded in combat reality now." Jean smiled, a faraway look in her eyes. "You should have seen when that one guy reached for his gun. My blade pinned his wrist to his stomach. Cracker's throw split his bicep."

"Oh... my... God... this is too much. I liked the general, fact filled explanation from before." Rachel shifted Quinn to his swing. Quinn yelped in appreciation, trying before the swing could be started to force motion. Rachel turned it on and Quinn was in heaven. "Mama needs a drink. I didn't know you had more confrontations, Sonny."

"I get tested, Ma," Sonny replied, repeating the tag for Rachel he was permitted to use. "I'm always on guard. Like Nick taught us, situations become crap piles when the victim gives up. When forced, I beat down the leader of the pack, who wanted me to join their group, the trouble disappeared."

Everything settled down after Sonny's explanation.

Jean waited with impatience for Sonny to explain the rest of his confrontation. When he didn't, Jean did. "The mutant is nearly six feet tall, from one of those Somali refugee bunches we infected ourselves with. Sonny leg whipped him perfectly. The big dork started crying when he hit his head on the hall floor. Sonny faced off with the kid's gang then. I kicked the next one moving toward Sonny in the nuts. Sonny smashed the one behind him in the throat. Done deal. We owned the school."

Nick grinned. "You two never said a word to your adult overseers. Any idea why such a thing was bad?"

"Unintended consequences, Sir," Sonny answered. "Their families could have come after us and our homes. I... I did something on my own to prevent that, Sir."

Nick perked up. "And that would be?"

"I snuck into the kid's family house, rearranged all their furniture, and drew magic marker devil's horns on Jamaal. He never moved." Sonny grinned. "I nearly gave him a Muerto haircut."

Nick noticed the look of adoration on Jean's face, momentarily in plain sight. She hid it quickly, but stared at Sonny in an entirely different way. "You and Jean have skills. Your solution to the bullying incident was dangerous, but I'm sure well thought out. You did understand they could have killed you without threat of prosecution, right?"

Sonny nodded. "If caught, I would have given them your phone number, and told them to call you, and they would receive a hundred thousand dollars."

Nick could not breathe or talk for many moments, leaving all but he and Sonny knowing why. After long moments waiting for Nick to speak, he finally nodded. "You knew I would arrive with death."

Sonny nodded with solemn acceptance of his decision to employ Nick as his Archangel of death. "I knew you would come. I knew you wouldn't pay for my freedom. I knew you would come with your crew and kill everyone. It was selfish and self-absorbing crap on my part, but I knew I needed to make a statement they would understand. I should have brought it to you instead, Sir. That, I regret."

Sonny paused with hand gesturing for more time while he thought through his next offering. "I nearly killed him... but I didn't. I wanted to so much... it scared the crap out of me. I pass him in the school and he looks away." Sonny again paused to Nick's understanding. "If he didn't look away... I'd race over to plant him in the hallway!"

"Keep the anger inside. Plot every move, anticipating every option he has, and every option you have," Nick advised. "Always be wary of known enemies. The list grows with age, Sonny. I'm glad you're in touch with reality. We can't act out what common sense and logic dictate. I know what you fear. You are not them."

Sonny straightened, startled at Nick's observation.

"You have a moral code inside, just like Jean. You two can't be me, but you certainly can't be anything like your parents, Sonny. You need to put that fear to rest."

"It's hard to do when they keep committing felonies. Do you think paying them that money will lure them into doing the right things?"

"Hard to say," Nick admitted. "Reporting to me anything they find makes more sense than getting tortured and killed by billionaire traitors and political gangsters. Anything else earth-shaking to discuss?"

"Have you heard the rumor school teachers help organize Antifa riots?"

"It's not a rumor, Jean," Nick answered. "The Monster Squad has one of the militant leaders, a middle school Berkeley teacher named Corvette Telarca, under surveillance."

"A couple of our public school teachers are planning a protest outside Fisherman's Wharf. Sonny and I overheard them talking about it in the sixth grade classroom when no one was around."

"Why were you two around?"

"We have them under surveillance for what they've done and said in school," Jean answered. "They tried to get the principal to ban raising the flag. We need to be extra careful when watching them. They know about you and leave any area they see me and Sonny in."

"What's this proposed riot/protest about?"

"Antifa wants the statue of Santa Rosalia, patron saint of Italian fishermen removed because the cross she holds offends Muslims."

"What?! Okay... that's it. I'm getting my gun and set things right."

Nick chuckled at how animated Rachel became at the news. "They can't do it, Rach."

"I bet that's what the people said when the idiot sheep removed all the confederate generals' statues. Now, they're working on having our national memorials torn apart. Get your sniper rifle loaded. You have work to do tomorrow."

Amusement prevailed for a few moments.

"Good one, Rach. Tomorrow's Wednesday. How do the school teachers get to riot on a school day?"

"Tomorrow is a teacher's day," Sonny answered. "It's listed as professional improvement day. We want to be part of the counter protest."

"Gee... how many bad things could come of that? The crew and I wanted a nice Irish morning at the 'Point'."

"You can skip a day getting blitzed at the 'Point', Dad. This is important. We need to stop these gangsters. They're the new Fascists they shout so much about being against. They want chaos to control everything."

"Someone has to stand against them," Rachel said. "Otherwise... sure as hell... we'll be watching them yank Santa Rosalia onto the ground. I'm going with Deke and Quinn."

"You do know this may end in a riot, right?"

"I don't care," Rachel retorted. "Call the cartoons. We're countering the Antifa gangsters' protest."

"Yeah, Mom! We'll show them they can't tear our country apart."

"They carry urine, baseball bats, and pepper spray," Nick pointed out. "If this protest breaks into a riot, there will be danger."

"Text for a sober meeting at the 'Point', Jean. Tell all the cartoons to be there, along with Tina. We need to organize. We'll use the cover of being on a nice family day at Fisherman's Wharf. Did you learn what time the protest takes place?"

"Noon, Ma," Sonny answered.

"I just texted everyone," Jean said.

"I'm firmly against this. My cartoons will see the fallacy of this action and end it before this goofiness begins," Nick replied.

"Play 'Ride of the Valkyries'," Rachel ordered. "Maybe it will get you to step up."

"Why don't I play and sing 'Hard Headed Woman' instead?"

"Or 'Coward of the County'?"

"Or 'Lucretia Mac Evil'," Nick fired back.

"The cartoons and Tina will meet you at the 'Point'. Gus wrote 'define sober'," Jean said.

"No more than two Irish," Rachel replied.

A moment later, Jean received the answer. "He'll be there."

Instead of all the suggestions for songs, Nick sang 'The Gambler', putting particular emphasis on the lyrical lines, 'know when to hold 'em... know when to fold 'em... know when to walk away... know when to run.' Jean made him sing 'God Bless the USA'. A truce was offered and granted at that time by the amused Rachel.

Chapter Twelve: Mob Rule Schooled

"Let me get this straight, girlfriend." Tina glanced around in confusion at Otter's Point beach. "You want to take the baby and kids into the middle of a riot? Did you fall on your head?"

"We can't let these goons tear down Santa Rosalia," Rachel stated.

"So? Order the cartoons to intercede," Tina argued. "If a riot breaks out, Gomez can shoot them all in the head."

"Ah... no... I can't do that. I'm supposed to be staying low key until my adjustments in the North quiet down on the news. Rachel's already decided she's going. That means I'm going, but it's not mandatory for anyone else. She's right on this, but it will be dangerous."

"Deal me in," Gus said.

Everyone else then affirmed they were going. Nick explained from where they should make their approach after he patrolled the area for snipers. "I will do my checks before they get all their people together. I know a few buildings from which a vantage point of the Fisherman's Wharf front can be used. If there's a sniper, no one approaches the site until I handle the shooter."

"We've helped out the Monterey Blue before. If we do get mixed into this mess, how will the police react?"

"I don't have anyone I can contact like Neil. I know there are more than a few police officers who know us in a good way, but we can't count on them if they are ordered to stand down like they were in the other riots."

"What about calling Grace and Tim," Johnny suggested. "Maybe they could give us cover to monitor the Antifa protest through the DOJ. They are considering labeling the gangsters as a terrorist organization. That would give us a lot of leeway on site."

Nick dug into his bag and retrieved his phone. "Good input, Johnny."

"Nick?"

"Yep… it's me again, Grace. We received word from a confidential informant Antifa plans to protest/riot at Fisherman's Wharf to tear down the statue of Santa Rosalia with the cross in her hands because she offends Muslims."

"I love that statue! What can I do?"

"Can you get us official DOJ orders to monitor and prevent a riot. They do not have permission to stage a protest. I already checked. I got stonewalled about what the mayor plans to do about it. I'm guessing this will be another stand down incident, where the Blue get told to watch the riot from the perimeter."

"I'll get on it right now. Keep your phone handy. Why don't you get your sniper rifle and blow a couple heads off? The rest of the little guttersnipes will run like hell."

"Have you been talking to Rachel?"

"No. Did she suggest the same thing?"

"Same idea. Okay… get back to me when you have something."

"Don't let them tear Santa Rosalia down, Muerto."

"I won't, but that prevention may require my sniper rifle."

"When has that ever stopped you."

"Stop at all cost… got it."

"What do you know about an incident up North of you, where a suicide bomber took out a political conference meeting? After that mysterious shootout between two sitting Senators, we're really taking heat here."

259

"I only know what's on the news. You can't do much about two Senators who hate each other getting into a shootout. Was alcohol involved?"

"Yeah, it was. None of us in the office cared much about 'Little Bull' and 'Crazy Benny' anyhow. The hypocrites both owned private firearms too. A terrorist event like the suicide bombing, coincidentally happening at the same time damning evidence about the ones killed came to light, caused an uproar you cannot believe. The evidence is rock solid though: terrorist affiliations, money laundering, foundation fund fraud, and selling Top Secret documents to the highest bidder. We're trying to trace the person who released the evidence data to no avail."

"It seems like things are changing under the new administration. Call me when you can."

"Will do." Grace disconnected.

"Grace will work on the cover for us. She wants the statue tear down stopped, officially or unofficially. I guess she's a fan of Santa Rosalia."

"Seriously, if we're doing this… and I'm almost afraid to mention it… but do you have a plan, Muerto?"

"I always have a plan, Payaso. This time, it will be so convoluted, and yet ultimately incredible, they may build a statue in my honor."

Gus snorted in derision. "Oh crap, Kabong… that means he's winging it."

Johnny nodded solemnly, while finishing off his second Irish coffee. "Indeed, Payaso, I believe you are right. I noted he has had no Irish coffee treats, despite our deserving a celebration for the end of Tark."

Nick shrugged. "I've stupidly permitted this venture to become reality. I have my wife, baby son, daughter, future son-in-law, Cousin Itt, and my entire team attending a guaranteed riot. Naturally, I'm winging it. When you consider the fact Saint Rosalia won't give a crap whether we save her statue or not, it all becomes a convergence of the weird. Before anyone says it... yes... I know this action thwarts the Sharia Law Mutants. Sometimes... I really miss the simple solution of a well-placed hand grenade."

"Good... cowboy up, Muerto," Rachel piled on. "This needs to be done. Start plotting your usual Muerto madness."

"Sometimes, I miss the days when I duct taped you into the bed."

* * *

Nick allowed Jean and Sonny to lead casually with Deke heeling to Jean. He and Rachel followed with Rachel pushing their newly created Kevlar covered stroller. The bubbling, happy Quinn bounced around inside, giggling and throwing dog treats over Deke's shoulder. Each time, Deke would sense the treat and snag it out of the air, provoking a Quinn laugh fest and hand clap. Nick's crew followed in strolling fashion, Jian's Joan being a last-minute addition.

Nick scanned the area around Fisherman's Wharf in Monterey with his small highly accurate range finders. He saw the glint of sunlight reflection on what he could only assume was a rifle scope. Nick kept focused, watching for movement of the glint. "Slow down a bit. I... oh shit... okay, we're mission enabled. We have a sniper. Take over, Payaso. Use Deke to stall. We're loud and clear on network, right?"

"Yes, Muerto, you are loud and clear," Johnny intoned, working his network connections through the satellite laptop in his backpack.

Nick squeezed Rachel's hand for a moment before fading away into a different direction. He maneuvered calmly away, circling the parking lot to the approach he had decided on. "The sniper's on the Harbor House building. I'm on my way by roundabout approach to it. Stop at the railing with the marina view of the boats. Take in the sun, sea, and act like tourists."

"Understood," Gus said.

Nick steeled himself for the next part. No way did the sniper get atop the Harbor House without a bad entry. The closed sign indicated plainly there was no one working the place. Nick entered quietly, knowing the sniper had not reactivated the alarms. The lock was a simple lock-pic done in seconds. He threaded noiselessly through the building to the upper access, his mouth tightening as he passed the dead bodies along the way. He stopped for a moment.

"I may take a few moments with the sniper. Do not react."

"Understood," Gus acknowledged. "He killed the store workers... didn't he?"

"Yes," Nick whispered.

* * *

The sniper scanned the area where the Antifa group formed to protest, smiling at the amount of money his involvement meant. The jolting agony of Nick's stun-gun vaporized all thought from the sniper's mind in a split second. Nick hesitated, trying to legitimize torturing the bastard. He grunted in frustration.

"Just kill him, Muerto," Gus reasoned. "Anything else will be messy and unexplainable."

"I know... but nothing will be explainable in this scene." Nick choked the killer out, covering his nose and mouth with gloved hands. He took the man's cell-phone with him as he eased away from the twitching body. "He has a silenced Glock, which I imagine he killed the three people in the store with. I'll be down as soon as I can."

"Understood. We're letting Deke smell everything while we take touristy pictures of our group," Gus said. "The Antifa bunch arrived. It looks like the security people have stand down orders. They have people with Isis, Antifa, and BLM signs. They do have coolers with God knows what in them, along with baseball bats. There's no question the security people are observers only. This should have been stopped immediately the moment a horde of masked freaks appeared."

"We have official orders, thanks to Grace and Tim. Our main purpose remains saving Santa Rosalia." Nick joined them at the large open walkway, where across from them, what looked like possibly three dozen masked thugs donned more thug paraphernalia. In a semicircle between the entrance to Fisherman's Wharf and the thug gangs, stood a dozen police officers in riot gear watching them readying to riot. "It's too late for preventing the swarm from forming. I'll take a copy of our orders to the police detachment. I plan to make sure if this turns into a riot, they won't be standing there with thumbs up their asses watching the carnage. Let's get the gear on, IDs in reach."

"We better get over there," Johnny said. "It looks like a few of the tourists don't approve of the enemy flags flying. I see a couple of wheelchairs in the citizen mix."

"I need to take Deke with me. Rachel locked and loaded before we left, as I believe Tina did. You kids watch their backs and all around."

"On it," Jean acknowledged.

"Any masked freak running at me gets capped," Tina added.

"Don't worry about us," Rachel said. "We're on your network. If we need help, we'll call for it. I'm worried if they get repulsed here, they'll go straight for the statue."

"We'll make sure that does not happen. Cala has our backs. I don't want you in the front, Reaper." Nick did a final check on Jian's gear, while Johnny and Gus checked Cala and each other.

Wearing US Marshal vests, complete with stun-gun nightsticks, firearms, and mace, they spread out and walked toward the police line in front of the Antifa gang. The mob made catcalls at the Marshals while pumping their signs up and down. Nick reached the helmeted line of police, looking for someone in charge. He didn't recognize any of them with helmets on. They all wore nametags, but he picked an officer with sergeant's stripes.

"Are you in charge of this detail, Sergeant?"

"You mean this cluster-fuck... yeah... I'm in charge. Join us. We're going to watch these badass Snowflakes riot and probably rip the place apart while we watch. Did the mayor call the Marshal's Service in to witness the destruction too?"

"New orders, Sergeant. I'm US Marshal Nick McCarty. I received orders directly from the Department of Justice to stop property destruction, and protect the Santa Rosalia statue, along with all innocent civilians not associated with Antifa."

Nick showed him his ID while handing the Sergeant a copy of the DOJ warrant. "We can use backup and we have federal control over all actions relating to this illegal protest."

"You got it! Can I keep this copy of the orders to show that pussy we have for a mayor? Otherwise, the idiot will raise holy hell because we're doing our jobs."

"That is your copy. My detail will front this. As a warning, we will be taking them down hard. These Antifa idiots are nothing more than terrorists."

"Agreed. We'll back your play. Good luck."

"Spread your detail around and use any means necessary to get the runners unmasked and on their knees. We have a database we've been adding to for these terrorists."

"Understood."

Nick led his crew over to confront what looked like the leaders. "Smash every phone within reach if something starts. Uh oh... look at that old-timer with the flag on his wheelchair. Cala! Watch our backs."

The wheelchair man and companions around him, holding United States flags, faced off with the Antifa group. When the lead thug tried to snatch the flag, the old guy expertly blocked him by moving the wheelchair from side to side. The frustrated thug instead pulled the old man's water bottle out and doused him with the contents a split second before Nick side-kicked his knee, collapsing it, and sending the thug to the cement screaming.

Nick never hesitated. He punched, kicked, chopped and tore off hoodies and masks with his reinforced gloves on. Deke shadowed him with trained patience, scaring off any lunge from the sides with rips and tears. Stunned off guard, the thugs retreated, trying to bring other weapons to bear, only to be then assaulted with stun-gun nightsticks. Gus, Jian, and Johnny formed the wedge with Nick at the front. They left sobbing and screaming bodies with each step. One tried swinging at Nick's head with a baseball bat. Nick took it away from him with a violent twist. He struck his attacker with a hard poke in the groin, sending yet another screaming to the cement.

Three tried to bring out pepper spray cans from the coolers. Nick's team, aware of the tactic, reacted to the ploy instantly. Night-sticks smashed with fracturing velocity anyone who tried to open coolers or reach under or into hoodies. The wedge expanded outward without mercy or hesitation, leaving the able Cala and enthusiastic police to tear off masks, while positioning the surrendering thugs to their knees. It took only moments for the terrified parents' cellar dwellers to cry and beg while kneeling with hands locked behind heads. The BLM and Isis backing gangsters had no choice but to join them, although many were beaten to their knees.

"I'm US Marshal McCarty. Your group will be detained under the Department of Justice and the Department of Homeland Security Agency's direction, to be unmasked, photographed, and fingerprinted. This is not an option. You have assembled illegally, without written permission or assembly insurance, for the sole purpose of rioting and destroying property. Any of you previously in our databases of known BLM, Antifa, and Muslim terrorists will be detained indefinitely. The rest of you will receive the maximum penalty in fines and charges. Your names will be added to the terrorist databases. Prison awaits any repeaters. You all will be restrained. Anyone resisting will be dealt with violently. Keep your hands locked behind your heads until manipulated into restraints."

The next hour acted as the backdrop to many repeaters from riots already quelled by Nick's crew or John Harding's Monster Squad. They reacted in typical terms of attempting to resist their serious arrests. Johnny and Cala interacted to make sure anything they did to resist ended in a stun-gunning zap. It only took a few examples for the thug crew to understand there would be no appeals except in court. The only surprise to the mix came when a bearded man raced at Nick from the crowd of onlookers, knife in hand.

"Deke! Protect!"

Deke ripped the attacker to the cement, dragging him back and forth until the man released the knife. With honed fury, Deke tore the man's wrist as an added portent of death, before settling with fangs at his throat. The man screamed out insults for being taken down by an unclean beast. He sobbed out victimhood and called the attack blasphemous while the onlooking crowd yelled for Deke to rip his throat out. Nick went over and hugged Deke.

"Good dog! I see extra treats for you. We'll need to wash away the slime from this one first though. I'll make it up to you."

"You… you set this attack dog on me! It is unclean! This is blasphemy!"

For the first time ever in public, Nick nearly bludgeoned the man to death. Instead he slowly straightened away from the man. Deke retreated with him. Gus, observant of his partner's murderous nature, moved in to restrain the man, while Johnny photographed and fingerprinted him. Only moments later, Johnny ran over to where Nick talked with the EMTs as they loaded his first active wheelchair aggressor.

"You stirred the hornet's nest now, Muerto," Johnny said, pulling Nick away. "This is Lon Seorgelas!"

"The traitor from Texas, fighting for Isis?"

"One and the same. He never received permission to return. It would be highly interesting to find out how he managed to reenter America after becoming a top Isis leader."

Nick stared at the young treasonous traitor, his terminator persona rising in a flood of consciousness. "Stay with him, Johnny. He is ours to take. We're good otherwise, so take him with you to our special place. Take Reaper with you. We'll finish here and get rides by some other venue."

"Would you like me to prep him, Muerto?"

"Yes... very much so. I would like all his information easily so I can attend to his demise. We have only a few legitimate questions before I end the interrogation with a cleaning."

"Understood."

* * *

Johnny yanked the outrage expressing Lon Seorgelas to his feet. "You are under federal arrest for treason. You joined Isis to fight against America and her allies. There will be no plea bargains for you, traitor!"

Johnny hustled him away, gesturing for Cala to come along. They took Nick's Ford with prisoner, not bothering with a blindfold. Seorgelas would never return anywhere.

"Where are you taking me? I...I was viciously attacked by a dog. I need a hospital! I am a United States citizen! You have no right to arrest me!"

Johnny snorted in disgust as he drove toward the Carmel Valley. "I cannot stand the sound of this guy's voice, my love. Make him quit bleating like a sheered sheep."

Cala stun-gunned the horrified Seorgelas into coma like compliance, sparing no moment until he literally vibrated in the Ford. "Did Muerto say to prep him?"

"Yes," Johnny answered from his driving. "We need some answers. We don't know one way or another if they will be helpful. Lon will answer them anyway."

"I will tell you nothing!"

Johnny sighed, remembering Muerto's interrogation technique, one on one, for guys who thought they would tell him nothing. He extracted his iPad from the bag near him. Cala road in the rear passenger seat with 9mm Glock pointed at Lon's head. He passed it to Cala, who cued the Muerto deep-cleaning, intestinal video stream to play for Lon. He threw up five minutes into the video. Cala held the bag she was ready with, and then explained to him how he could avoid many things from the video if he cooperated. Johnny noticed Seorgelas looked unconvinced, even with Cala prepping the recalcitrant Lon for interrogation with video aids. Seorgelas, despite the stun-gun and video lesson, still believed he was being tricked. Cala and her prisoner exchanged eyeball glares.

Cala decided to intensify her first approach when she hushed Lon with the stun-gun at Johnny's request. "I think I know a way to shed Lon's reluctance. I need to do what Lynn and Muerto do first: stick to the basics."

"Yes. If he is alive for Muerto to talk with, that will be sufficient. We are ten minutes from home."

Cala stun-gunned Lon in brutal cycles, finally convincing the man in the aftermath, he would indeed plead to tell them things. Lon became light years more helpful. "I… I snuck into the country from Mexico. I had my old passport. They could not have cared less."

"They didn't detain you for further action," Johnny asked. "They would have traded you off if the authorities had recognized you. We are lucky you stupidly fell into our hands. Did you have anything to do with this Antifa riot?"

"I…I helped organize it. How did your… Marshals learn of it? The police would have done nothing to stop us. The mayor sent word they would not interfere. He tried to bargain with us, hoping to avoid a confrontation. We naturally agreed."

"Why in the world would you rush us with a knife? You obviously hid in the background after we confronted the thugs."

"I have been out of the news. I was thought to be an Isis leader. I became a joke overseas until Tark Ruban sent an emissary asking if I would like to serve him in the United States. Now, I have heard one of the brethren did a suicide bombing, killing Ruban and a host of others. The Antifa mob decided to do the protest anyway, hoping to distract attention while others toppled the Santa Rosalia statue. When the Marshals confronted us before I could lead some of our group to the statue... I lost it... and attacked. I should have brought a gun, but we were told not to. Ruban left word I was to stay out of jail. He is gone now anyway."

Cala called Nick without direction from Johnny. "They are planning to topple the statue while people are distracted at the Wharf, Muerto."

"Thanks, Reaper. Heading there now. Did he have anything else of interest?"

"No. He missed his fifteen minutes of fame being a traitorous scumbag, so he took an offer from Tark Ruban to cause chaos here in the USA."

"Good work. Tell the traitor what really happened to his buddy, Tark. I'll be over when I can. You saved me. Rachel would have made me put it back in place or remake it myself if there was a single flaw."

"Understood, Muerto." Cala turned to Seorgelas. "I have permission to explain what happened to Tark Ruban and his associates. We blew them to hell, and set up one of Tark's employees as the suicide bomber."

Seorgelas began sobbing openly.

"I think Lon understands his future is limited," Johnny said.

Cala smiled. "I believe Muerto wanted him to know about Tark for just that reason. Let's get over there now, my love. I feel a new YouTube classic forming."

"Yes... oh my God... I will finally be rid of the leaf eating giraffe competition."

* * *

Before Nick could leave with his remaining family and friends, the veteran in the wheel chair with VFW flop hat in place, called out to him as he pushed Quinn in the baby carrier. Nick

269

transferred control of Quinn's carriage to Rachel and went over to shake hands with the man.

"What you Marshals did was incredible. No one has the balls to face down these punks. They spit on the flag, on the military, and on their nation. How did we ever get to this?"

"I don't know, Sir, but we plan to correct it one body slam at a time. Thank you for your service and facing down the goon squad, Sir."

Nick left him laughing.

"Oh God, Nick," Rachel said as Nick rejoined her and took over pushing Quinn again. "Can't you run ahead and make sure Santa Rosalia is okay?"

"Bless your little statue loving heart. No… I'm not leaving anyone behind. I'll speed my feet a bit if you promise not to whine about the pace."

"I'll give you a pace!" Rachel batted at Nick's head but he was already outdistancing her.

   * * *

Six furtive figures in black masks approached the statue of Santa Rosalia. They brought heavy duty rope and a camera man. Nick watched with Deke next to him in a sitting position, all senses perked toward the invaders. Nick saw Deke struggle to remain silent, but a nearly inaudible growl from deep within the dog's soul seeped outward into the light breeze. Smiling, Nick observed as the group hushed each other, trying to detect where the ominous sound originated. He stepped around the statue into the lighting, dressed completely in black, including Muerto mask and cape. Deke trailed after him slightly to his right.

"What the fuck do you think you are, asshole," one of the Antifa thugs asked, straightening from his cringing stance cowering at Nick's appearance.

"I am El Muerto. I heard a bunch of little Snowflake freaks thought they could bring down Santa Rosalia. I have come to make sure that never happens." Nick's device altered voice halted the group. "Go away, and never return, or I will avenge Santa Rosalia by gutting each and every one of you."

"Take your fuckin' puppy dog and get the hell out of here before we beat the shit out of you." The leader puffed out, thinking Nick was alone and bluffing. "We'll spray the shit out of you and your dog."

"No... you won't."

The leader jutted forward, pulling what looked to be a larger bear spray can of juice. The shot from the darkness pierced his wrist. He screamed in a most unlike thug way, dancing around while gripping his hand, bleating curses and nonsensical threats of retribution he would never be able to make come true.

"Did you think I came alone, punk? I brought my crew, the Unholy Trio, Dark Dragon, and Reaper with me."

"You... you shot me!"

Payaso, Dark Dragon, and the resplendent in red, Reaper, encircled the thugs. They carried stun-gun nightsticks, each of them firing an arc periodically.

"I didn't shoot you. Viper did. She's only ten. We've decided since your ilk train your spawn to kill us, we needed an example showing you we are just as committed. Viper? Let Cracker take a shot. Same target – knee."

"Wait! No... don't-"

The small caliber .22 caliber slug passed through the leader's left knee. Screams and writhing on the cement kept interaction at the minimum for a time.

"Cracker's only ten too. See... we can train our young just like you train yours," Nick advised. "Let's complete this lesson."

Nick attacked without warning or hesitation. He used his nightstick in concert with his cohorts to reduce the half dozen thugs to pleading piles of surrendering nothingness. Reaper ripped off every mask with a flourish. They were all Middle Eastern young males. Gus took photos while Jian gathered digital fingerprints. Gus noticed Nick's face as they worked. Once past a turning point, Gus knew nothing would stop Nick. Gus edged into the space between the captives and Nick.

"Use your imagination to leave these punks for the authorities, all wrapped for incarceration. C'mon, brother, you included the kids on this op. Don't let it end in extermination."

Nick hesitated before gripping his partner's arm. "Thank you. Reality and beyond are messing with my mind. This op will make a great video for Kabong. I'm good, brother. They grovel now… but turn into murderous obscenities of nature the moment we turn our backs."

Jian rushed over to physically block Nick's return to the prisoners. "You will spoil this exceptional YouTube video with the Unholy Trio, Dark Dragon, and Reaper."

Nick took a deep breath, watching Johnny pleading silently with Reaper keeping the broken thugs in hand. "I hope my decision doesn't lead to more innocent deaths on my head because we didn't fix these imbeciles permanently. I'll lead."

Nick swaggered on camera, kicking and bludgeoning the downed captives. They cried like babies, begging for mercy, blaming everything from their childhood to global warming for their actions. Nick zapped them all with quick shunts of pain.

"Shut up! I am El Muerto, with my avenging crew of the Unholy Trio – Payaso!"

Gus moved with nightstick clubbing in stretching type mode to stand near the captives with jolting feints, eliciting more screams.

"And El Kabong… the terrible!"

Johnny dashed into the captives with flailing strikes employing a razor sharp blade, further enhancing the cries of horror. To make sure no one viewing the video thought it was a game, he cut with slicing expertise, producing scars never to be erased. The video, blanketed with screams, halted production for a moment.

"Dark Dragon!"

Jian slithered amongst the captives with physical full power chops and strikes, ending in perfect small jolts of agony, his audible soundings enhancing his attacks.

"Reaper!

Cala strolled in red, luxurious perfection amidst the captives with killer eyes, Nick did not notice until it was nearly too late. Cala moved. Nick raced to catch her wrist after realizing she would cut all of the captives' throats.

"Reaper! Stand down!"

Cala exchanged glances with Nick. "Maybe… until the next time." Cala flashed the knife to each late-night participant's throat before backing off.

"I think that concludes the physical threat here. As you idiots can see, we will act on behalf of our nation. There are no take-backs at this level. If we discover anything out of the ordinary you have not told us, we will hunt your asses down. Believe me, you don't want that. Look on this statue of Santa Rosalia as sacred. We have your names and fingerprints. Guard this gentle lady with your lives. Whatever happens to her will happen to you. I think it's time for the wrap-up, Muerto."

"I think you're right, Reaper," Nick replied. He took out a sap, tapping the leather wrapped billy-club against his side. "This conclusion to the evening involves pain. Pain teaches us a lot. It can teach young imbeciles and terrorists that in America, you idiots will find final pain if you ever cross paths with us again. This little beauty is a sap. It's an oldy but a goody."

Nick then went to work on their captives. He cut no corners, nor did he leave any part on the captives unbruised, making fractures with the rib strikes. After only seconds, it became obvious Nick was an expert with the leather wrapped tool of violence. His crew struggled mightily to keep the six in place for their dose of learning. Nick proceeded through them with expertise. At the end, as he walked away, Gus grasped his arm.

"Sorry, Payaso… it was a mission enabling moment."

"Indeed - it was. You handled it to perfection."

"This Unholy Trio cartoon adventure will finally bury that giraffe eating a leaf, haunting Kabong on YouTube. With all the police and interest at Fisherman's Wharf, the mutants were right – the distraction worked perfectly."

"How do you want to end it?"

"We'll restrain these guys ankles and wrists behind them and together in a nice hogtied bundle. With the rope wound around the base of Santa Rosalia and then through the hogtied opening in each guy, they'll present a nice picture of good Antifa goons."

Gus chuckled. "Kabong will love that ending."

Fifteen minutes later, Cala set their camera on tripod to take the final section of video with all of them in it, posing with the six roped and hogtied Antifa thugs. Nick urged Johnny and Cala to complete the scene with their own speeches for the wrap-up.

"Lon's not going anywhere. Let's go to Crabby Jim's at the Wharf and get something to eat. Although they won't like it, I want the references to the kids edited out of the video."

"Absolutely, Muerto," Cala acknowledged. "I hope Rachel understands. The Sharia Law Mutants train their kids to kill. Our kids, like Jean and Sonny, with the passion and commitment to defend the nation, must be trained for the possibility of civil war in the streets."

"They should be in the Ford by now. Rachel's been on our network during the whole thing. Have you been listening, Rach?"

"I'm here. We're staying well back from the crime scene and quiet. Cala's right, but it doesn't make a mom any more accepting of her role as an accomplice to making ten-year-old kids into soldiers. Strip off the masks and walk to your left."

* * *

Seated at a large table near one of the firepits at Crabby Jim's restaurant, Nick noted how quiet his young snipers stayed during the meal. "Are you two okay?"

"We're more than okay, Dad," Jean whispered fiercely. "We don't want to screw up the trust you've shown in us by shooting our mouths off."

"Jean's right, Sir," Sonny agreed. "You allowed us to do what we've been training to do. We didn't want to miss when on target. We also don't want to act like a couple kids. Jean and I are more than that."

"You sure are," Nick agreed. "Did you call your folks and tell them it's probably safe for them to come home?"

"They're staying one more day before coming home." Sonny hesitated. "They wanted a guarantee it will be safe."

Everyone laughed except for Rachel.

"Easy, babe. I know what you're thinking," Nick said.

"No, you don't. If you did, I'd be in restraints already. Sonny? Please don't talk about your parents when Ma is around, okay?"

"It won't happen again, Ma."

"On a lighter note, Jafar sent us the schedule for Al's softball games. The Dark Lord coaches with assistants Cruella Deville and The Man from Nowhere. There's a game this Saturday. I say let's go visit our new home away from home, see the softball game, and I'll entertain later."

"Great change of subject, Muerto," Rachel said. "I'm in. You did good tonight, Joan. Didn't she, Tina."

"Yep. She knows the score," Tina said. "No matter where you go or what you do after tonight always remember the golden rule."

"What happens in Gomez's Addam's Family, stays in Gomez's Addam's Family," Joan replied. "I am in. Can I go with you all on Saturday?"

"You're officially invited," Nick stated. "You will need to obtain final permission from Dark Dragon."

"Then it is a yes," Joan replied with a pat of assurance on Jian's hand.

"In that case then, you are welcome to accompany 'Whipped Dragon'."

Chapter Thirteen: Black Death

A huge guy took a seat behind the batting cage, with a six man entourage, glancing over at me and smiling. Jess joined me in the dugout. "That's 'Black Death', John. Tommy's been telling me he wanted to meet you, but ruled out the Warehouse, because he says it's a cop bar. His name is Tolo Whitt. Tolo's from Jamaica. He's running over the UFC heavyweight division. He's impressive as hell. Tolo's manager ain't here though. Dev's with Maria and the kids at a school meeting. Don't do anything that requires the Latin, brother."

I grinned in appreciation of Jess's reference. "I hear you. Go on and enjoy the game. Lucas is really into it today. Explain everything about Tolo to him or he'll be in the dugout next. I need to concentrate on the game."

"You right about that. Tight game, brother. The girls are tense as hell. Want to do some 'Hammer' with me?"

Oh my... that one got me. Just my loud appreciation of Jess's suggestion elicited giggles from the girls. I pushed Jess toward the dugout opening. "Maybe later. Tell Nick that one."

Jess smiled. "Will do. Brother entertaining later. Did you decide yet on his house or the piano bar?"

"Not yet. It's still under discussion."

"I voted for the bar," Lynn said. "That Mojo Lounge sounds like a great place for Jess and Nick to do 'Hammer' together."

"We'll work it out, DL," Clint said. "The Giants have their ace reliever in. Go give our batter a pep talk. Jenny looks about ready to pop a vein."

Remembering where the hell I was, I called time and hurried out to the on-deck circle with little Jenny, our shortstop.

This little girl could play shortstop... and I mean turn double plays, stop line drives... anything. Jenny believed she could stop anything on defense. On offense, she hated touching a bat. Lynn and I worked with her constantly to ease up and swing from a stance she felt comfortable with. Her batting average was zero for the season. That fact was not helping. I needed to call in the big guns.

"Hey, Jen, I called Dev. He had a school meeting, but right now, he's doing a hit spell in Latin for you. He found an old text relating to success and bent it into a hit spell. I wanted you to know Dev's bringing the Latin for you."

The change was incredible, making me feel guilty as hell for the lie. I had a backup plan in case Jenny didn't get a hit, involving another lie that Dev didn't complete the spell due to the rings of Pluto not being aligned. Jenny pumped her fist, staring up into the sky for a moment before meeting my probably guilty gaze.

"I got this, John. I got the Latin now! God bless, Dev!"

Off she went to the plate, all business, and ready for war. I returned to the dugout, enduring the accusing stares of my assistants. Clint smiled.

Clint grasped my arm with comical seriousness. "What have you done, DL?"

"Last half of the last inning, DL. What have you done, Cheese? I detect a ripple in the force," Lynn added. "We're tied five to five. Did you tell Jen not to swing and see if she can get on base with a walk? The other girls will get a chance to see some of the reliever's pitches that way."

"Not exactly." I went for the whole tamale. I needed Jen to believe. She needed a charm, like an old sweaty lucky sock or something. I'd talk to Dev later. I'd also need to iron out an extenuating circumstances explanation, so if this worked, the other girls wouldn't be expecting miracles.

Lynn grabbed my ear, shaking it and my head. "Cheese?"

"Watch and learn from the Dark Lord, oh ye of little faith."

The Giants' reliever nodded at her catcher with a big smile. It was plain they both had filed away the memory of Jenny's three strike outs so far at the plate. The pitch streaked across the plate at super speed, and exited the ballpark with bat propelled multiplication over the right field fence, the first actual homerun I had witnessed in our league since we joined. Our stunned silence turned into loud jubilance as Jenny ran the bases with a solemn, measured stride, drinking in the cheers from her dugout and stands. She did, however, slap hands with Casey, coaching third, before putting one flap down while styling on the last part of her homerun journey. We all met her there. It was softball girls gone wild for a few moments. Lynn and Clint, of course, tried to stare me down into immediate capitulation to the facts. I waved them off happily.

"Dev brought the Latin for me!" Jenny leaped onto home plate, fists pumping and feet dancing. The girls engulfed her for a victory dance as the Giants walked off in forlorn defeat. It's a lesson lacking in today's politically correct montage of madness. Kids need to learn both victory and defeat before later life, not during it.

"You dog!" Lynn poked me repeatedly with finger in chest as we backed away from the celebrating girls. "You told Jen that Dev did a hit spell for her? Oh my… that is just so wrong on so many levels. You're grounded. I'm sending you to the penalty box."

"Excuse me? Is this the same Lynn who cut Himura's throat while he bowed?"

At the mention of Yakuza, Ryuu Himura's death,rem while bowing before his knife fight with Lynn, she had to snort back a quick reply as my adlib drew major amusement. "Okay… good one. You do understand every girl on the team will be demanding a Dev Latin spell before batting or fielding, right?"

"I'll handle it. Dev will know what to do." In the glow of triumph's aftermath, I called the Latin King. He listened patiently before losing all control. It took ten full minutes to get him down off the plateau of having regaled Maria on what I had done, followed by howling yips of enjoyment at my predicament. My eavesdropping assistants joined him.

"I...I don't know what to say, brother. You've made my entire weekend. Maria and I will be enjoying this Dark Lord tidbit for months to come. We're coming tonight, no matter where Nick's entertaining. I'll try and think of something before then."

"Dev! We're going to get pizza right after the final handshakes. I need you. When you walk in, get ready for girls on their knees praying to the Devon Constantine Latin God."

Another long moment of amusement passed before Dev could speak. "We'll be there. Jenny actually hit a homerun over the right field fence at the mere mention of the Latin, huh? Yep. I need to be there for pizza with you all. See you in a bit."

"Thanks, brother."

My cohorts appreciated the Dev solution with forlorn headshakes and pats on the shoulder. I shrugged. "Dev will think of something. I better have a word with Jen."

"We'll go with you," Clint said. "I don't want to miss a moment of this dugout miracle."

I felt a little relieved as I hugged Jenny near her jubilant teammates. "Remember, Jen. Not just a spell hit that pitch out of the park. That was you, kid. You swung the bat. You powered it over the fence. The Latin may have nudged you slightly, but no one, but you, hit the ball out of the park."

Jenny shrugged. "I know. Doesn't it feel wonderful to believe in magic, John?"

"Yep. Sometimes, it does. Remember something else the Latin didn't do for you – the way you played shortstop looked like all-star team material to me. You robbed the Giants of at least two runs with your glove. That is like hitting two homeruns."

Jenny's face brightened even more. "Yeah... I need to tell my dad that one. He's worked with me on defense constantly with mom blasting grounders at me."

"Now you're reaching into reality, girl - practice, dedication, and your folks."

Jenny hugged me around the neck again. "Will Dev be at the pizza place?"

"I just talked to him. The Latin King will be there."

"That's great! Thanks, John!"

"It's your day, Jen. Enjoy the moment in the sun. Those moments come few and far between."

The ten-year-old shrugged. "Yeah... I've noticed."

I watched her enjoying the sun's rays, quietly soaking it in myself. Al joined me. "Hey Al, great game."

"I'm hearing you put the mojo on Jenny. I got a single, a strike out, and two foul popups... and you didn't think to give me, your daughter, the mojo?"

Al nailed me right to the core. I looked at her expectant face of childhood betrayal without a clue. Her lip tremor was the first glimpse she punked me. One glance at the perpetrator of the deed waiting ten feet away with full on humor bending her at the waist, and I knew I had found the instigator. Al danced around and pirouetted at my expense before hugging me tightly.

"Mom got you. I'm just glad you found a way to give Jen a lift. That was awesome. We're going to have a great night, Dad."

"Yeah, we will. It's too bad we're not going to Nick's place for entertainment. It appears the party will be going to a bar nearby for adults only."

"That's okay. Jean, Sonny, and I will be trading stories and skills. Amara will be watching all us kids in Lynn and Clint's bunker with Tonto, Naji, and Deke guarding. With all the babies playing around together, this will be a party for us. Everyone wants a Guardians of the Galaxy fest too. Can I take our Blu-Ray discs to play?"

"Sure. Hearing you describe a 'Guardians' viewing night makes me wish I could stay there with you."

Al giggled. "All the adults feel that way. Uh oh, Dad. Here comes a big dark giant. Do you want me to kick his ass?"

"Watch…watch your mouth, young lady," I replied, while trying not to lose all sense of adult dignity over that ace. "Go commune with your teammates. We'll adjourn for pizza soon."

"Okay, Dad." Al gripped my arm. "I love you."

Good Lord, Al caught me off guard with that one. I sucked it in like the poser I am at intimate times. "I love you too, kid. Never forget that."

"I won't." She ran off with the big dark giant bearing down on me. I gave Lora the fickle finger of fate gesture, a silent warning of payback soon to be visited upon her. She looked around before making an inappropriate sexually explicit gesture before following Al.

I turned to face the giant. It appeared he planned to run me over. I didn't move. He stopped inches from me. We were not eyeball to eyeball.

"John Harding?"

I waved a hand, while continuing to look at his neck. "Down here."

I heard muffled laughter from my cohorts, gathering for the unexpected meeting. I saw Nick with Lucas in my peripheral vision, joining Clint, Casey, Jafar and Lynn. I knew Tommy and Jess were close by too, not that it mattered.

"I am Tolo Whitt, the 'Black Death'."

"Congratulations. You must be very proud."

"It is not wise to disrespect me, little man."

I stayed where I was, grinning at his neck. "I heard you say you're Tolo Whitt, after you charged into my airspace. Big whoop. This is a kids' softball game. Pick somewhere else to meet. We'll

282

be at the Mojo Lounge tonight in Fremont. I'll discuss whatever you want with my manager present. For now. Get out of my face."

Tolo tensed. I began picking spots to cripple him. Then I heard it. It wasn't Latin, but it was just as effective. Strains of the Bobby Bloom song 'Montego Bay' pierced the violent reverie between me and 'Black Death'. He backed away, looking around. The sight and sound stunned Tolo and his entourage. Nick and Jess did a calypso dance rhythm in perfect sync to Nick's handclapping energetic rendition of the song with gathering kids and parents. In seconds, we had a dance off. Giants players and parents mixed to add their handclapping beat.

Nick had them all without any music other than his voice and the handclapping beat. The moment he finished 'Montego Bay', he launched into 'The Banana Boat Song' in a duo with Jess. Oh my... Nick owned the park. Nick and Jess doing the Day-O lyrics with swaying calypso beat enticed the entire crowd into joining in. Tolo didn't know what to do. Even his entourage was getting into the beat. Nick and Jess ended with a flourish. The applause, cheers, and whistles went on for a long moment. Jafar joined me with his iPad out, finishing the video.

"I played the whole thing live for Dev. He was going nuts. He told me this is the last game he ever misses."

"Thanks for thinking of doing it. I bet he got-"

"We are not finished," Tolo told me. "I will meet you at this Mojo Lounge at 7 pm."

"I'll be there. Bring your manager, in case we do discuss business, instead of cheap threats."

Tolo wanted a piece, but had enough sense to walk away. The crowd dispersed slowly as the next scheduled game would be starting in another fifteen minutes. My A's and Giants shook hands, as did the parents and other onlookers. Nick's music put the entire game in second place. We joined the rhythm duo amidst our happy group of kids and adults.

"You guys were incredible. I don't think anything else could have gotten Tolo's neck out of my face. I have a meeting with him at Mojo Lounge at 7 pm. Let's all meet there a bit earlier at 6 pm. I'll call ahead for reservations and warn them we have a large crew."

"I'll take care of that, John," Jafar said. "I'll get the limos to take our crew in style too. Since all the kids will be at Clint's house, why don't we meet there?"

"Good input," I agreed. "Thanks for doing it for me. Lora always claims I mess things up when I make reservations. For now, we have kids awaiting pizza. Dev will be joining us to bail me out of my small fabrication. It won't be as entertaining as Nick and Jess doing the postgame show, but I'll bet it will be good."

* * *

After a rousing welcome from everyone, Dev did a remarkable talk about individual preparedness and confidence. After skirting the entire issue of his spell supposedly giving Jenny the power to hit a homerun, Dev reminded everyone about practice building belief and assuredness in play. The Latin King was golden. At the table with the Monsters, Monster dependents and friends, he drained a beer before engaging with us.

"We need to run Dev for mayor and dump that liberal snowflake woman running the Blue into the ground," Jess stated.

"Now wait a minute." Dev gestured for calmness as the Monsters all cast their votes in favor of Mayor Devon Constantine. "Apparently, only a few of you know my checkered past. DL and I ended up in the tank a couple nights together. I love what I'm doing and I will never be a politician. Jess has a good idea though. We need to run a decent candidate. We should run Jess's Mom. Flo would make a terrific mayor."

"Oh man, Dev, I think you nailed it," Lucas said. "Flo would be perfect. She keeps up on everything political, runs her neighborhood watch, and everyone respects her. I think you should take the idea to her right away, Jess. She'll have the money backing and all the campaign workers she needs."

Jess nodded in agreement. "I'll go over her house right after we get through here."

"We can use my office for a campaign headquarters," I volunteered. "We'll make this happen. Oakland hasn't had a decent mayor in decades. Dev can write her speeches."

"No... he can't," Dev replied. "I had to beg Maria to help me with my speech just now."

"My mom can speak to any subject in a heartbeat," Jess added. "If I convince her to run, we won't need to worry about giving her something to say. We may need Nick to fly here once in a while and entertain at a rally though."

"Count on it," Nick agreed. "If I do 'Hammer' with you and Dev at a rally, your mom will be crowned mayor."

"That's what I'm talkin' about," Jess said. "We need to work that tonight. DL... don't be rippin' no throats or hearts at the bar, brother."

"No way do I spoil this show tonight. If Jess convinces Flo to run, we should start that ball rolling tonight. Achmed? Can you hunt down a poster place and get something going?"

"Sure. If Jess can send me a good photo of Flo, with a few of her hard-edged lines, I can get some made for tonight, along with flyers."

"You the best," Jess replied. "I'll take a great picture of her today, along with some lines for the poster. She'll love it."

"It's settled then. We start the Florence Brown campaign for mayor tonight," I said. "Now, since it's only us Monsters over here, I want to hear about the Muerto saving of Santa Rosalia. Great video."

"I was ordered to stop the destruction of Monterey's Santa Rosalia statue. In reality, I was told if I didn't stop it, I'd be sleeping alone for a long time," Nick replied.

"I... well... okay, maybe I did say that," Rachel admitted to much amusement. She leaned forward with a whispered addition. "Muerto used Jean and Sonny twice in combat mode, once with knives, and once with a rifle."

Nick gestured at the softball players and friends table. "See… they're just normal kids when around kids. The mutants train theirs to kill us. At some point, our kids will need to meet them in combat for our nation. I think maybe we need to move on that fact soon. Sonny and Jean can handle anything."

Rachel jiggled the sleeping Quinn in her arms. "They're planning on training Quinn from the time he can walk."

Lynn enjoyed that word picture the most. "Oh my… Quinn and Clint Jr. will be in very similar programs."

* * *

Jafar joined us at our section, covering nearly a third of the Mojo Lounge. "The owner stopped by personally. He called in a couple extra people and he'll only allow so many into the place tonight, depending on space. 'The joint is yours', his words. He gave the people tagged to play tonight a break. I did my research. Seven grand made his mouth water, especially since we're allowing others in to fill the place."

"Excellently done, little brother. Any other parameters to meet?"

"The owner thinks Nick may need to go play a bit to test out the tuning."

"I'll go do 'Ride of the Valkyries' and follow it with 'Brandy' for the test phase."

"Do Brandy first before anyone gets here," Lucas instructed, taking Sarah's hand. "C'mon, honey, let's dance to this one."

"I do like that song," Sarah admitted, allowing Lucas to pull her towards the dance floor. They were not alone.

Nick played a long prelude with all the right notes before launching into the song, listening intently for any note out of tune. His singing rendition slowed the regular version of 'Brandy', allowing a sweet, toned down dancing interlude for Lucas, without ruining the song in the slightest. His powerful, fist pumping 'Ride of the Valkyries' mesmerized his audience. He extended the intense chorus, bonding with the house piano. By the time it ended, no one in the restaurant bar looked anywhere else but at Nick.

Nick spotted the arrival of Tolo Whitt with entourage, swinging right into 'The Banana Boat' song. Jess and his wife, Rochelle, carried the calypso beat with Dev and Maria joining them. The others began crowding the dance floor, following the original couples' dance patterns. Alexi and Marla moved to a two-table meeting venue near the wall. When John gestured Tolo and his entourage to the table, Marla made a swift exit. Tommy sat near Alexi. I brought a Bud brother with me for refreshment. Nick took a break after he finished the song, promising to begin again once the fight discussion ended.

"Anyone else like something to drink?"

"No. Let us begin," Tolo ordered. "This is my manager, Pierre Carone."

I held out my hand to him. "I'm John Harding. My managers are Alexi Fiialkov and Tommy Sands."

I smiled and pulled my hand back when it was ignored. "Okay… that's enough of the niceties. If you can't be polite, get the hell to the point, and then get the hell out of the bar."

Tolo pointed at me. "You are very lucky we are in the bar."

"Do not provoke this man," Alexi warned. "You have posers with you. John has brothers and sisters here, so dangerous, men who know them get down on their knees with palms in the air when they pass on the street. Say what it is you want. Let us conduct business quickly and painlessly."

"The Rattler has publicly said he will not fight you because you saved his life," Carone stated. "Carl Logan will be in rehab for another two months because of that cheap shot you did to him, Harding. Darius, the so-called Destroyer, won't even discuss anything to do with you. That puts 'Black Death' next in line for the UFC title. We will accept a fifty/fifty split in a title match at the MGM Grand."

Tommy began laughing with Alexi chortling along with him. Tommy gestured at Pierre. "You...you're a funny man. Come back with UFC permission for the fight to take place, along with the MGM Grand agreement to host it. Then, make it a sixty-five/thirty-five split, and we'll consider the offer."

"This is an outrage!" Tolo disliked Tommy's style. I thought it was right on the mark. "You will fight me for the title. Did my visit to your little girls' softball game teach you nothing? I can-"

Lynn's knife was at Tolo's throat, accompanied by various weapons held point blank against his cohorts' heads by my Monsters. Blood trickled down as Tolo gulped. "Did I just hear you threaten my little Al? You didn't come here to sign for a fight, Betty. You came to die. I'll let John explain the rules to you this once while I lower your blood pressure at the neck for a moment."

I hate threats. I'd rather rip this moron's throat out. "Okay... when I stop talking, you and your sheep stand quietly, leave the bar, and never look back. Any other negotiations will be done in a formal setting with the UFC. Never be seen in Oakland again. Never speak a sentence with my family attached in words. If you do, I will maim and kill everyone you have ever known. Don't bother acknowledging. I don't care if you understand or not. You're on our list. From now on, I will know where you are every second of your existence. Get the fuck out of my sight!"

Lynn whispered to Tolo. "Stay silent and do what you've been told, Betty. Anything else, and your body pieces will be floating in the Bay by morning."

Lynn moved her knife away, smiling as Tolo gripped his throat in a gasping lurch to his feet. He fled the bar with his manager and nitwit minions following. "What the hell was that about, Cheese? I thought he was playacting in the park."

Jafar stepped over closer to us with laptop in hand. "Tolo has been a member of the Jamaican Posse since he was old enough to walk."

"I thought he wanted a match. Maybe he thought some Jamaican Posse talk would get me to deal the way he outlined. Hell… Tommy and I were simply negotiating."

"DL's right," Tommy added. "To get back into the MGM arena, we would have taken a sixty/forty deal."

"I will investigate this further for us, John," Alexi said. "We should learn if Tolo has acted on threats before. His manager seemed more of a puppet."

"Thanks, Alexi. You're right Pierre said very little. When Tolo started shooting his mouth off, Pierre kept his shut. It's possible he's bludgeoned his way into the other UFC matches the same way."

"I will get in touch with his past opponents and learn what his contract deals have been like," Alexi agreed. "I'm glad Nick took a break during this talk. I have been looking forward to an evening dancing with Marla."

"I'll update Nick. I think he's been as anxious to entertain after our softball field dance-off as the rest of us are to hear him. I'm glad they have a karaoke machine here too. I want to see him, Jess, and Dev do 'Hammer'."

Nick stood as I approached. "I saw your negotiations went sour quickly."

"Tolo Whitt made threats we normally deal with in the boat on the Bay while feeding the sharks. He's from Kingston, Jamaica, and a member of the Jamaican Posse."

"We had some dealings in Kingston, didn't we, Payaso?"

Gus joined us. "My brother Phil got taken there along with his future wife, Julie, and her brother. I sailed us into a spot Nick knew about. He went ashore, blew the shit out of the Jamaican Posse and brought Phil, Julie, and Damian to the Kingston pier, a little the worse for wear, but alive. He sure confiscated a nice payday that time."

Jess invaded as we thought over the new piece of information about Muerto and Payaso. "Nick! Dev has the karaoke set for 'U Can't Touch This'. You get between me and Dev like the light in the forest."

Nick cracked up at Jess's 'light in the forest' description. "Okay... let's go do some 'Hammer'."

With the sound and beat backing him, Nick did 'U Can't Touch This' slightly in front and center of Jess and Dev. These three danced in sync as if they spent the day practicing. The hand clapping accompaniment from their audience provided a backdrop like no other. Nick voicing MC Hammer while doing Hammer's hand movements was incredible. The moment the song ended, the applause cut short as Dev had programmed Montego Bay to start immediately after with its driving beat.

Our three entertainers switched to the calypso rhythm and beat instantly. Nick could mimic Bobby Bloom's voice nearly to perfection. The applause rocked the house. The three celebrated their performance before Jess escorted Nick behind the piano. Then it was on. The Piano-Man took only short breaks for the rest of the night. I think Nick sealed the deal for Jian and Joan. By the time the entertainment ended, those two needed to get a room. Although it was only 10 pm, I could tell Nick was done. He played 'I'll Be Seeing You' to end the evening to thunderous applause.

He received rock star status in our section. Muerto was indeed the most mysterious anomaly ever. I shook his hand. Lora and I had danced through every set. The guys took turns dancing with Rachel while Nick played and sang. She knew all kinds of dance steps. Rachel taught us to do line dancing to the country tunes Nick played. When Nick did Michael Jackson's 'Thriller', Rachel knew all the moves, much to Nick's surprise. She had everyone who could fit on the dance floor doing the moves.

"You need to retire from the Muerto business and go into entertainment, Nick."

"No can do, Dark Lord. Payaso can tell you, I don't do well without the Muerto business. It would be like you ditching the cage fights."

"Yep... you got me there. Can you stay another week?"

"I wish. We need to get the kids back home, not to mention Phil and Clarice will be returning from San Francisco. I believe I've taken care of all the loose ends from his extortion plot, but I can't be sure just yet. What do you plan to do about 'Black Death'?"

"Alexi's investigating his background. I'll know more tomorrow. What will you do for the rest of the evening, Muerto?"

"Turn on some music and dance with my wife. I didn't know she could dance. I also plan to sip a few in between. Singing is thirsty work. Update me about Tolo when Alexi finishes checking him out."

"Will do, brother."

* * *

Nick copiloted for Cala with everyone relaxing in the back of their UH-60M helicopter. Gus moved near him. "I've been watching you since last night. Something bothered you about the Jamaican Posse angle. You keep looking for texts or missed calls on your phone."

"When I brought Phil and Julie out of Kingston, I investigated the Jamaican Posse to learn what I needed to do. I ran across a pair of brothers in the bar where they held the kids. They acted as enforcers due to their size. Their last names were Whitt. The smaller brother's name was Deon. I never learned the larger brother's name. It was dark in the bar. I thought Tolo looked familiar."

"What's the angle?"

"I thought I killed them with a hand grenade."

"Are you thinking of correcting the error, Muerto," Cala asked.

"It wasn't an error, Reaper. I had hostage rescue duty. I was masked. Tolo didn't know me. I'm curious what Alexi Fiialkov learns."

"If you sail down to Jamaica, you'll need the cartoons."

"Let's not jump to conclusions, Payaso, but yeah, I would need the cartoons along. Cala and Jian will need to stay for protection duty. Plus, if something went wrong in a place like that, we'd need to get bailed out. Money buys anything on the island."

"Agreed."

An hour later as they tied down the UH-60M inside their hangar, John Harding called. Nick listened while his crew waited. "I think you're right DL. That guy is bad business. At least he's back in Kingston. Thanks for the update. See you soon."

"Is anything wrong, Dad?"

"Not really," Nick answered. "Alexi Fiialkov learned Tolo Whitt coerced his opponents in the UFC matches to fight him on his terms. He's already under investigation by the UFC. They suspended him two weeks ago. Tolo thought to get back in the arena at the MGM on John's back. He figured they wouldn't turn the money down. Alexi sent formal notice to the UFC that John won't be fighting Tolo. That's it. Let's go home and settle into a nice rut going to school, writing, playing songs, and-"

"Getting smashed down at the 'Point'," Jean inserted.

"Yep... I see an electronics free zone in your future, cupcake."

* * *

Nick, Gus, Johnny, and Jian sat in their usual spots at the 'Point', sipping the Irish coffees Nick brought. They watched with amusement as Deke ran the empty beach chasing gulls and sniffing everything in sight. Johnny entertained shortly before with the stale bread he brought down with him. Standing amidst a swirling torrent of birds, Johnny tossed crumb bits into the air, enjoying the birds' hovering catches. Nick's phone rang.

"Thom? How's the new Governor of our Isle of Hope?"

"Not so good, Muerto. I can protect the Isle. Until a couple weeks ago, this has been like 'Fantasy Island'. We're helping kids from all over the islands. I may even need to hit you and the Monsters for another building."

"You got it, my friend. What kind of problem are you having. We've dealt with every kind of plumbing, housing, sewage, and desalinization problem I can think of at our experimental city in the Western Sahara."

"We tune into their Facebook page every day. It's incredible. That new doctor, Jared Kostler, is doing God's work there. This problem I have involves the Russian Mafia connection located in Frenchman's Cay in the British Virgin Islands. A mafia boss named Gleb Sokolov expanded operations to create a protection racket on the ferry boat lines connecting us with the main island. We've been making do with flying the helicopter transport, but Sokolov stated he will shoot it down the next time it's in the air."

During Thom McGaffey's explanation, Nick moved to a tensely straight position on his chair, the terminator shadow flowing over his features. "You've called at a good time. Keep your phone with you. I'll call once I get a plan in motion."

"I'm sorry to dump this on you. I didn't want Chuck and Sal to find out about this. I knew they'd want to fly over with an army. I know you're taking contracts again. I hate to ask for a freebie, but I need your quiet type of assistance."

"Understood. Don't give it a thought. I'll be calling you soon." Nick disconnected. He turned to his friends who witnessed the dark curtain plunge over their small window of quiet times. "Gus, I need for sure. Johnny would be most welcome. Jian, I need you here with Cala in protection mode. This will be tricky. We don't have time for long range planning. I'll call Paul. We need military flights all the way to the Virgin Island's King Airport. From there we take the equipment to the ferry docks. A guy named Sokolov is creating an inland pirate franchise, selling protection to the ferry businesses between the main island and our new Isle of Hope, including threats to shoot down our helicopter transport."

"Let's get back to your place and find out what we can," Gus said, beginning to collect his gear. "I figured if you had one more week of luxury, I'd need to hire you myself to kill someone."

"That's just hurtful, Payaso."

* * *

"This is a small window of anonymity, Muerto," Gus said, after giving Nick the range findings on a nearly fifteen-hundred-yard shot. "We can't stay in this nest all morning. You do have a time frame in mind, don't you?"

"Johnny's ready and online, right, Kabong?"

"I move the moment you say, Muerto. I know this was the ideal spot for the shot into the dock area, but Payaso's right about a time frame."

"Fifteen more minutes," Nick said, honing into the exact pier location of the boat Gleb Sokolov would be boarding to go on a terror mission to keep the ferry lines in his protection ring. Through extensive research, Nick and his crew plotted every movement of the Russian Mafia boss. He trusted underlings only so much. His operation in the British Virgin Islands was crumbling. Gleb needed to make this new venture work.

A limousine arrived at the pier.

"Confirmed," Gus said.

The driver hurried to open the rear door. Gleb Sokolov exited the vehicle for his last few seconds of life. A fifty-caliber reaper drone slug entered his head, smashing him into the limousine door frame and onto the pier approach. Nick then executed everything in the limousine and switched to a magazine of incendiary rounds to blow the limousine upside down, firing at the fuel tank. He loaded another magazine.

"Muerto! Not the boat..." Gus's voice trailed off as Nick blasted Sokolov's boat from stem to stern until reaching the full fuel tanks. The explosion destroyed the dock, the ship, and the pier finger out into the water. "Good Lord! You could have destroyed the entire Marina."

"Let's discuss that after we get the hell out of here, Payaso." Nick packed away equipment at breakneck speed. He smiled after a moment. "I bet we won't need a distraction getting away from here."

"Small doubt about that," Gus agreed, glancing at the flames in the distance. "You've been paying a lot of attention to Tolo Whitt on the internet lately. I haven't mentioned it until now, when I saw the complete terminator picture evolve in real time."

"John Harding needs some space. The 'Black Death' will at some unfortunate time create a problem because of his expulsion from the UFC. We know he's in Kingston right now."

Johnny began chuckling. "Oh… Muerto… you dog. You have been eyeballing a double mission ever since we arrived. What exactly is it that you have planned?"

"I'm wondering if Diego's mates, Jed and Leo, would like to cruise in the night to Kingston so I may relieve the world and John Harding of a dangerous speed bump on his road."

"In… without comment," Gus declared.

"I am in without hesitation. Leo is your man. This whole gig will be put into pulp fiction literature, right Muerto?"

"Absolutely."

* * *

Tolo Whitt awoke in a sweat. His mouth was dry, heartbeat racing, accompanied by a shiver rocking over his body. A black-masked shadow appeared over him, waving for a moment. Tolo tried to reach the black fiend's arm. His hand weakly fell to his side.

"Hi, I'm El Muerto. You tried to hurt and extort a very good friend of mine. I'm here with you for the end. I injected you with a death no one will ever find, because here in the islands, you jackals do many things never questioned by the authorities."

Blind panic formed in Tolo's face, tears streaming down his cheeks as the tightening in his heart blasted all other thought away. Nick drew near, grasping Tolo's hand. "I love a good ending, you worthless piece of shit. Relax and enjoy your descent into hell. If I ever get there with you, it would be wise to seek a different level."

* * *

"Oh my, Kabong, Muerto didn't do the guards," Gus said as he increased speed away from the port. "He's turned into Muerto the merciful. Good Lord, God almighty, I'm glad to see you here, speeding away from a port soon to be under a microscope of crap."

"It's all good, Payaso. The Unholy Trio did damage without anyone knowing. We'll need to hope Kabong's last adventure can keep the giraffe eating a leaf at bay."

Johnny gripped Nick's shoulders. "It is an honor to serve with you, Muerto."

"Ditto that," Gus called over his shoulder.

Nick smiled. "I wonder if Jean will mind our celebrations in the days to come at the Otter's Point beach gathering."

"She's on our tail, Muerto," Gus called out. "Get ready for it, brother."

"Oh yeah." Nick leaned against the boat's side with a smile. He began singing 'Montego Bay', keeping the beat with his hand on the boat's hull. Gus and Johnny joined in a moment later.

* * *

"Oh my God! You lushes are so out of control!"

Nick leaned back in his chair, sipping the whiskey mixed coffee elixir with extreme pleasure. "Thank you, Daughter of Darkness. I hope your iPad and iPhone are still in vogue when you're allowed to use them again."

Jean giggled. "Oh sure, shoot the messenger."

The End

Future Story: Nick & Jean Bonus Story VI

After being elected Mayor, Rachel gave in to Nick's suggestion to hire a manager, two servers, a cook, and a busboy for the Monte Café. The slight alteration in their lives did not affect anything other than giving Rachel time to spare. The Monte Café still acted as the McCarty crew's meeting place, doubling for impromptu city discussions. Any time Rachel conducted city business, Benny and Sammy the werewolf tried to be on hand at their rear corner table. This morning's business incorporated a new chaperone. Nick took over for Benny with Sammy at his feet. He busily wrote in his thirty-sixth series novel, featuring the assassin Diego the laptop keyboard his workplace.

The Monte, unusually crowded with regulars and tourists on a Monday morning, kept the two servers and manager busily making work for the busboy and cook. Rachel spoke with two of the city council members at a table across from Nick. The noise of a busy restaurant on a Monday morning encouraged more people walking by on the sidewalk to read the outside posted menu and stop in. Nick glanced away from his monitor as Sammy let out a short growl. Astur Jama, the impeached former mayor, entered the Monte with two Somali bodyguards in suits and sunglasses. She wore a pale blue abaya with matching hijab. They approached Rachel's table. Jama pointed at Sammy.

"That creature should not be in here."

"Sammy's always welcome here. You're not. State your business and then get out of my restaurant."

Jama's lips tightened. Her bodyguards moved closer to Rachel's table, only to stop as Sammy the werewolf let out a rumbling lowkey growl. "I have heard rumors you plan to run for Governor. I will run against you and win. I want the ongoing harassment of the Somali community to stop."

"We closed your two mosques because you and your cohorts used them to stockpile weapons. Your Somali Mafia gang thugs like these two here with you will continue to be arrested any time they congregate. The Somali community who have assimilated and rejected Islam's death cult are happily living normal lives, protected by our US Marshal contingent and police department."

"How dare you blaspheme Islam!"

"Oh... I dare much more than that. I will not be changing any policies. We're having great success deporting all supposed refugees who commit crimes to their country of origin. Many, who lived in fear of being killed by your thugs because they left Islam, chose the 'City of Hope' in the Western Sahara. They're a huge success with the city spreading rapidly in the formerly barren area. They have industry, tourist resorts, entertainment, and best of all: lots of jobs to be had. Maybe you should get rid of the slave costume, renounce the death cult, and go get a real job."

"Did...did you just call me a slave?"

"Open your ears, Jama," Rachel retorted. "I said slave costume. Of course, it stands to reason, if you wear slave apparel, you must have a yearning for it."

The bodyguard on Jama's left reached for Rachel. Sammy ripped him to the floor, silencing all the chatter and restaurant noise. Sammy rested across his captive, jaws at the man's throat. The other bodyguard had Nick's Colt .45 barrel at his head.

"No one touches Mama in her own place, idiots. You have your answer, Jama. Get the hell out of my sight."

"On your way out, keep your fingers locked behind your heads," Nick instructed. "Failure to do so will get you shot in the head."

Nick patted his leg. Sammy leaped to his side. The bodyguards did as they were told, following the furious Jama out the door. Nick gestured calmly at the silent crowd. "Sorry about that, folks. We have a few city problems still to be sorted out. Please enjoy your meals. Put on some music, Senta."

"Okay, Nick." Senta Rapone, the Monte Café manager, switched on the jukebox. Soon the sounds returned of a busy restaurant.

Nick sat next to Rachel, taking her hand, while facing the two uneasy councilmembers, Irene Castle and Thomas Sperry. "Jama's upset because we now have Homeland Security working with ICE agents to deport known criminal refugees. They have her under investigation for harboring fugitives and being tied into the mosques used as armories. My US Marshal Special Unit continues to work with Chief Dickerson to end the Somali Mafia threads here."

"It's just that... we're taking heat all around the country for cracking down on the refugees. We're being labeled racist Nazis," Irene said.

"Look, Irene," Rachel replied, "if you can't take the heat, then resign. I need a city council that wants the laws of our land enforced. Before we began enforcing the law, people weren't safe walking anywhere in the city. The tourist trade is thriving once again. Did you read what Sharia Law is, like I asked you to?"

"Yes... it's horrible, but I don't want Pacific Grove to be turned into a police state."

The other councilmember, Thomas Sperry, waved her off. "You're nuts, Irene. Labeling law enforcement as a police state is ridiculous. Who cares what we're called. Rachel answers every charge like that in the news and on TV, calmly pointing out the facts. She makes the real racists look like idiots. Thanks to her, we have the city back."

Irene nodded with a sigh. "You're right. I need to think more about my neighbors than what some liberal idiot in New York spouts off about. Is it true you're doing hourly sweeps, Marshal?"

"It is," Nick replied. "We allow no congregations of thugs anywhere in the city or outskirts. The inspections of the mosques we did initially, showed just what Islam portends for the rest of us. They not only stock piled small arms. They had grenades and rocket launchers. With the sweeps, we've stopped gang intrusions from other thugs besides the Somalis."

"That 'City of Hope' you mentioned impresses everyone who sees their growth and opportunities," Irene observed. "What do they demand before allowing new people to relocate there?"

"They demand only the rejection of Islam and that the new arrival works. Dr. Jared Kostler formed a medical institution there on the cutting edge of health care in the region. My friend, Khan Eshieh, has proven to be a leader of incredible talent. He and his wife visit Rachel and I often. We try to get to the City of Hope at least once a year. They've taken in over three hundred of our Somalis who wanted to be completely free of Islam and out of danger from the Sharia Law Mutants."

"Do they really kill each other if they leave Islam?"

"They do worse than just kill, Irene. Those rumors and stories of mutilations, burnings, and beheadings of former Muslims that get by the liberal media are true. They throw acid in the faces of their women who dress wrong or do not obey. They honor kill their own children. One of my US Marshals, Cala Groves, barely escaped an honor killing."

"I...I know Cala."

"She can tell you all about her murderous male family members."

"Jama is dangerous," Rachel stated. "She's the smooth talking false face of Islam they trot out to deceive. She prances around in her pretty slave costume, while the other women locked in the death cult receive female genital mutilation, beatings, and burkas with eye holes. Thank you both for joining me this morning. I will learn what can be done about repairing the curve of Lighthouse Avenue."

"Thanks, Mayor." Thomas shook their hands. "I'm glad we have you here, Nick."

"I love the 'Grove'. I'm not going anywhere. Stay strong, you two. There will always be invaders, especially since we keep tiptoeing around the Sharia Law Mutants. Be safe out there and call us if you see anything we need to deal with."

"Will do," Thomas replied guiding Irene out.

Nick glanced down at Sammy, who sat listening attentively to everything with his head slightly cocked in concentration. "You are a very good boy, Sammy the werewolf. I know it took restraint not to rip that mutant's throat out."

Sammy head bumped Nick's knee.

"Yes. I know we need to go for a walk. C'mon, babe, we'll walk Sammy down to the 'Point'. Gus has already texted me three times wondering when we'd get done and meet them all. I think he has some order of business. Cala texted and said the T-Rex told her she was driving, and to bring Bushmills, beer for Sammy, and wine. Jean and Sonny took their kids to Santa Cruz Beach Boardwalk for the day."

"Lovely." Rachel bent to hug Sammy. "You have to be Deke reincarnated."

"It does seem so at times," Nick added. "I'll text the crew and tell them we're on foot, so don't hurry."

The owners of Monte Café exchanged greetings and well wishes with their customers.

"That was quite a meeting back there with Sammy the werewolf presiding," their manager, Senta Rapone remarked on their way out.

"Sammy does have a nice touch when presiding over politics," Nick agreed.

* * *

As they walked down the hill on Forest Avenue toward Ocean View Blvd, Nick heard an engine roar behind them. He picked Rachel up and ran around the corner of Pepper's Mexicali Café, crouching at the corner of the building and parking lot, with Sammy gearing for assault next to him. The car, a Mercedes Benz, slowed to a crawl as it passed the café. Nick shot the driver through the head, adding two shots into the gunman with a submachine gun pointing through the back window, trying to target them. The driver slumped over the steering wheel jerking it left into the parking lot, over the curb, and into the garbage bin there.

Nick ran at the vehicle, firing into the next head popping into view from the passenger front. At the rear window of the vehicle, Nick smiled at the screaming Astur Jama with blood and brain material covering her.

"No!" Astur screamed, holding her hands in a shielding gesture. "You... you cannot just execute me!"

Nick backed away from the window a few feet and fired two slugs into Jama's face. "Yeah... I can."

Rachel moved next to him, peering with interest into the car. "Gee... you really do have a way with politicians, Muerto. That's one governor's office rival down. I'll call Neil. You call the cartoons and tell them to put the meeting on hold for the moment."

Nick called Gus while listening with amusement to Rachel's act of breathlessness and fright as she spoke to Chief Dickerson. "Hi Gus. Put a hold on the meeting. Rachel and I had a run in with Jama."

"Are you two okay?"

"Yep... I'll take pictures for our meeting at the 'Point'."

Gus chuckled. "No survivors, huh?"

"Just Rachel, Sammy the werewolf, and El Muerto."

"Those are the only ones I give a shit about. Text me when you're ready. I'll call everyone else. Are you still going to walk down to the 'Point'?"

"Did you just insult me, Gus?" Nick grinned as Gus disconnected with a laugh.

* * *

Chief Dickerson smiled at the distressed Rachel, shaking his head. "You can drop the act, Mayor. No one, but me, you and

303

Muerto are in public view. Jama lost her mind coming after you two. Even if she had succeeded in some dimension in her head, what did she think would happen while dealing with your crew?"

Rachel sighed, peering through the doorway of the Tessuti Zoo's doll shop across the street, Neil had guided them to. She glared at the media trying to break the police lines around the Mercedes. "Who knows? The vultures arrived in full force. I was pretty good though, huh?"

"Excellent," Neil answered. "Nick could use some work on his compassionate features."

"Sorry... my happiness features warred with the compassionate side and all I had left was professional courtesy."

Neil glanced at the owner, nervously watching the spectacle. "I'm not really enthused with having you two here. Go on your way. I imagine you were walking to the 'Point'. If I have any follow-up questions, I'll drive down to Otters Point and discuss anything further with you there."

Nick gripped Neil's hand with bowed head. "God bless you, my friend. We will take our leave of you for now, but we will always be at your beck and call."

Neil pushed Nick away, whispering. "Get going, you pirate. I know you executed Jama. Nicely done."

"Chief Dickerson! I'm ashamed of you thinking such evil thoughts of the Mayor and her US Marshal husband."

Sammy head butted Neil as an exclamation point. Neil knelt and hugged Sammy. "You are just the cutest dog ever... bloody killer... but very cute. Get your human cohorts on the road, Sammy."

As Sammy led the way to the bottom of the hill where Forest Avenue intersects with Ocean View Blvd, Rachel took a deep breath, watching the waves crash against the rocky coastline. "Neil was right. What in the hell could Jama have been thinking? Like he said, even if she succeeded, Jama would need to deal with our crew."

"I have pictures and digital fingerprints of the guys with her in the car. We'll run them once we get to Otters Point. Two of the guys accompanied her to the Monte. The guy trying to blast us from the rear window wasn't one of them. His identity may give us a clue. Maybe Jama found herself in the middle of killers who had no intention of backing off."

"I guess we'll just enjoy the fact of a world without Jama."

"Yep," Nick agreed, "and Neil let me keep my Colt."

"We're quite a pair, Muerto. Do you really think I can win the governor's office?"

"If you can stand the heat of a race where every time we sneezed, the media will give it an anal exam, not to mention our past, then yeah, I believe you would win. If you let 'Trailer Trash Momma' loose, it could be the most entertaining campaign in California history."

"I'm willing. We need something else in our lives besides you shooting everyone in the head."

"That's very hurtful. I shot Jama in the face and you didn't even blink. You even made a sarcastic, callous comment about it."

"I was grieving on the inside," Rachel replied.

"Yeah… I'll bet."

* * *

Nick passed around his phone as Johnny worked the facial recognition software and fingerprint database. "I know these are bad to look at for you, Tina, but I need to know if you've seen any of Jama's companions stalking around us."

"Nope." Tina handed Nick his phone. "Did Jama have any last words?"

"She said, 'you can't just execute me'," Rachel answered. "Nick said, 'yeah… I can', and shot her in the face. He was deeply moved by her appeal though."

Rachel's statement drew loud amusement.

"Uh oh," Johnny said. "The gunman in the back was that warlord's brother you killed, Conrad Laquab. The gunman with Jama was Jacob Laquab. He probably made her stay in the car. Jacob must have suspected you from the beginning when Conrad disappeared. I'm checking on how many Laquabs might pop out of the woodwork. I alerted the kids."

"Thanks, Johnny. Poor Jama got caught in her syndicate of gangsters for the last time. We'll go on alert for the next few days and increase the deportations when the Somalis protest because their gunmen got killed."

"They'll be out in force," Rachel agreed. "Any without papers, we ship immediately. I'm going on offense. Nobody better try making me defend combating assassins. Right after I leave here, I'm calling a press conference."

"I have something else I need help on," Gus said. "My brother Phil contacted me for the first time since our Boston visit long ago. He feared a backlash if someone found out we are related because of what we do. I can't say I blame him. He and Julie had little Katie to worry about. Katie used to Facetime me a couple times a month. When we were involved in a few well publicized missions, the contact with Katie stopped."

Gus paused to gather his thoughts. "They battled constantly after she turned sixteen. Phil thought things returned to normal when she was accepted at Boston College. Unlike many of the goofy kids today, Katie worked for her BS Degree in Biochemistry. She graduated at the top of her class. Accepted into the virus engineering research project, Katie worked toward her Masters Degree. She did so well, she received a research grant."

"Gus… if you're giving us reason to know Katie can be trusted, we're convinced," Nick said. "What's happened?"

"She went down to Cancun to celebrate with three friends. Despite Phil and Julie begging her not to go into any foreign country for the celebration, Katie ignored them and their story of being taken in Jamaica. Apparently, they rented a villa on the beach. The second night they were there, they disappeared. The good part is that their research group have chips implanted. Katie has one."

"Aren't they only good for short distances?"

"Maybe in the old days, Dragon. The tech is much more powerful today. The consulate reported they read a signal on Katie out at sea, a couple of miles offshore. They don't have anything powerful enough to pinpoint her location. Phil said they have received no ransom demands. Rumors of pleasure ships, kidnapping women into sex slavery, have become epidemic."

"Jay's settled in here," Nick said. "With Dragon and Reaper on the home front and Jay in reserve, they can also depend on Neil and the PGPD. We'll take the Marauders with us. It's time for us to call in a few favors. We parked the Lucky Lady II, ready for action at the American Yacht Harbor in St. Thomas. Thom still governs the Isle of Hope. He knows we need the Lady kept in combat shape with all the tools. We'll sail her into the approximate position once I get Paul to lend us CIA assets to intensify tracking of her signal."

"If we're doing all that, let's go right now and sweep the town," Johnny said. "Maybe we can smack down the instigators who'll hit the streets the moment they hear the news."

"We'll do it while I work on Paul," Nick said. "I'll call in Quinn and Jay. I don't want to interrupt Jean and Sonny's day with the kids in Santa Cruz. We'll take the werewolf too in the reinforced van."

"Thanks for this, guys."

"After all these years together, Gus?" Johnny shook his head. "No questions and no hesitation. Cancun and the surrounding sea may not ever be the same."

"If Katie's okay when we get there, she'll be okay when we leave, brother," Nick added. "Let's get Trashy in a safe spot with Tina and go tear the streets apart."

"I will drive," Cala said.

"I'll arrange the press conference for when Jean and Sonny get back." Rachel kissed Nick. "So much for a nice walk, huh?"

"It looks like we'll need to put off the walks for a while."

* * *

"They killin' us in the streets!" The leader of the dozen other masked men with clubs in their hands, walked the last block of Lighthouse Avenue before the two-sided string of shops and restaurants started. Beyond that point, the hotel district continued to the ocean. "We will have justice for Jama!"

Quinn and Jay detached themselves from the first building on the commercial part of town with Sammy the werewolf treading next to them. The two men held their IDs to be seen, although it didn't appear the group would care. "That's far enough. We allow no congregations of masked men. Take off the masks and get on your knees with hands locked behind heads. You are all under arrest."

A ripple of laughter, accompanied by gang gestures greeted Quinn's order, a moment before the leader reached under his hoodie. Sammy tore him to the pavement, ripping until the man stopped struggling. Quinn signaled the werewolf to hold. "That was not a request. We will use deadly force. We have a sniper. Do not try to run. Kneel and live."

A huge Somali youth tore off his mask from the center of the pack and strode toward Quinn. "Big fuckin' man, with attack dogs and snipers! Good thing! I bust you to pieces otherwise."

Quinn smiled. Jay glanced over at his partner. "Oh man, brother, don't do it. You'll make a mess. Your dad will be pissed. Sammy gets wild at the smell of blood."

"Quinn... I am your father," Nick whispered over the network in Darth Vader voice. "Jay's right. You snatch his throat, Sammy will snatch one too."

"What you smilin' at, kafir?" The big guy walked into Quinn's airspace.

"I was smiling because I wanted to snatch your throat out." Instead, Quinn blocked the knee to his groin, turning slightly. The uppercut with his left as he pivoted with a full power shot, lifted the Somali, breaking his jaw, and dropping him unconscious to the pavement. "A mentor of mine, John Harding, took on six of you gangbangers at once, with bats in their hands. Want another 'pick six' special offer?"

"Son," Nick whispered between clenched teeth as his spotter and companions, Gus, Jian, and Johnny fled his side on the rooftop to get down at street level. They were over a block away. "That's not funny! You knew I had the older cartoons with me!"

The eleven still standing, wavered at the completely relaxed Quinn, flexing only his fists. Their leader, on the ground under Sammy, hissed at them. "Do it! Bust this asshole!"

Jay drew on them. "Pick more than six and I empty my magazine into your heads! Try me!"

Jay's warning made them mill around uneasily, with him hoping backup arrived in physical form soon. He knew Nick would kill them all without hesitation. Six moved forward, bats in hand, primping and thumping them into their hands. Quinn shot forward, smashing the one in the lead with an overhand right, leaving him standing with his opponent's bat, and the thug rolling around weakly on the ground.

Quinn used the bat to poke, smash, parry, and completely overwhelm the five remaining. In seconds, they lay strewn in a tight circle of anguish with broken faces, smashed ribs, and ambulatory groin shots. Quinn spun the bat in his hands, already a master in multiple martial arts forms. "The rest of you can get on your knees or use your bats."

"Fuck the bats." The thug reached and Nick put a .50 caliber round through his head, pitching him into a bloody, heap six feet from where he was standing.

His companions dropped to the pavement, hands locked behind heads, staring at the pulped head of their companion. One of the ones Quinn had smashed in the ribs regained breath and regaled Quinn with sobbing complaints. "You used the... bat. We were the ones... with bats."

Quinn chuckled as he restrained the ones at his feet. "Oh my, I'm sorry. Is there something you don't understand about stick fighting? At some point, you get hit with sticks, Betty."

Gus, Jian, and Johnny arrived seconds later to restrain the rest, remove masks, and take pictures, digital fingerprints, and DNA samples from their prisoners. Neil arrived with three squad cars, a meat wagon, and the coroner's van. He surveyed the scene with recognition of violence seen before with a McCarty name attached to it.

"Only one dead," Neil joked, thought about it, and looked beyond the scene. "He's still out there on a rooftop with me in his sights... isn't he?"

"Uh... that would be affirmative, Uncle Neil," Quinn said. "He says hi, and eat a piece of fruit once in a while."

Chief Dickerson glanced off guard at his slightly bulging waistline. He shot up his middle finger in three different directions. "Not funny, Muerto, I have a glandular disorder, you prick."

"Dad says, 'portions porky', his words."

Neil sighed. He looked up at the sky, then back down at the bodies being attended to, while his officers bagged weapons, IDs, and digital fingerprints. "Did you break apart these six thugs? I can tell Sammy the werewolf took down the mangled arm one."

"It was a misunderstanding, Uncle Neil. They thought we'd just let them walk away from the scene. I needed to convince them that was not going to happen in a less deadly way. The victim drew on me and the werewolf was already busy. I bet a bunch of these idiots will be on the ICE train back where the hell they came from."

"That would be my take too. They were on their way to riot in broad daylight. I thought we had this stuff handled. In one day, the leader of the thugs and three of her minions try to assassinate the mayor and a federal agent, followed by an attempted riot in the center of our business district."

"Ben told me the school is much better. The worst trouble makers there have been deported with their families back to Somalia. Oh, how they howled when we helped the ICE agents ship them. Up until then, they looted and pillaged at every opportunity. The moment we made them pay for their despicable behavior, out came the poor terrified and oppressed Muslims. Oh barf!"

After some amusement, Neil patted Quinn's shoulder. "You've already done the database work. We'll take it from here. Tell Nick I received his text about a mission on the horizon. We'll help keep watch here until he gets back. I think, no matter what, Rachel needs to wear armor and the hell with concealing her weapon. She should have a quick draw holster on her hip."

"Dad agrees. He says thanks and we'll be patrolling the rest of the day. Dad says take an hour for a jog by the beach."

Neil repeated his one finger salute in all directions.

* * *

"Permission to come aboard, Sir?"

Nick shook hands with his old friend, and Governor of the Isle of Hope refuge. "Come aboard, pilgrim. You know the cartoons. This is my daughter Jean, son Quinn, and son-in-law Sonny. They are all Marines and US Marshals."

"Great to meet you all finally." Thom McGaffey hugged Gus and Johnny, after shaking hands with the young agents. "God… it's good to see you two pirates. I'm still following the adventures of Jed and Leo in Nick's pulp fiction. Is he still basing your fictional lives on real life events?"

"Most of it, Thom," Gus replied. "Muerto's working on a Diego adventure now where Diego takes a contract to eliminate the top Somali warlords, imported as refugees into a Minnesota town. He, of course, brings his trusted partners on mission, along with the infamous Fatima."

"Outstanding! I was afraid after the last Fatima episode, where she blackmailed a Senator on the take, Diego might finally shoot her between the eyes."

"Fatima makes my dad laugh while writing," Jean said. "He'll never get rid of her."

"The Lucky Lady looks great," Johnny switched subjects. "She's locked and loaded for sure. We'll need everything you have in reserve, depending on how badly this latest Muerto plan goes into the tank."

"How dare you befoul the name of El Muerto with your petty grumblings, Kabong! Do not force El Muerto to again reduce you to Unholy Trio mascot."

"Oh no… not that. He's talking in third person, Payaso. Batten down the hatches."

"Already done. Thanks for your great work on the Lady, Thom," Gus said. "I hope we'll be back in less than a few days."

"Thanks to the adjustment you guys made years ago, no one has tried to take over the ferry line. They do an excellent job for a reasonable price. Have a good voyage. I pray I'll see you soon."

"El Muerto guarantees it!" Nick held on to the second deck boat railing with fist up as Thom left the boat. "El Muerto… away!"

Quinn and Sonny helped with ropes and plank for leaving the pier. Sonny signaled Gus in the pilot house. The Lucky Lady eased out of port with Nick still hanging on the side.

"Dad! Really!"

"Oh, calm down, Daughter of Darkness," Nick admonished. "El Muerto must ready himself for the mission ahead."

"You just killed five people. I think you're ready."

Nick dropped down next to her. "This will be different. We have no idea except numbers of heat signatures. Thanks to Katie and her girlfriend's chip, we detected the boat, identified it, and learned who owns it. They could have a dozen girls working the boat. We hope to save all of them."

"Sorry... I just wanted to get you down off the railing."

Nick grinned. "El Muerto will not forget this disrespect."

"I hope not. I hate repeating myself."

Gus moved on their target craft, a yacht much larger than the Sea Wolf or Lucky Lady. He stopped dead in the water, dark and silent. They were nearly a mile away, but could see and hear the party going on into the early morning hours. Gus anchored the Lady for the time being. Jean, Sonny, and Quinn, dressed in full combat gear, readied their raft, propelled by an electric trolling motor. They would be circling the boat after Nick reached their target from the water. His approach would be an underwater one, pulling along a submersible pontoon with his gear.

"How the hell will you find the girls, scattered everywhere, and get them into one place where you can protect them, Dad?"

Nick made final checks on his advanced tech scuba gear, with full breathable face mask, instead of dive mask and breathing regulator. "We've gone over this before, Viper. I won't know for sure until I get aboard. They're partying. I need to investigate how many non-partiers there are before boarding. They will either need to be dealt with or bypassed with Gus and Johnny watching every inch of the ship from the Lady. Johnny will be on the M107. If he sees I've been made, he'll fire bursts into their pilot house until you three board and support. We'll be on the network. Once I get the girls safe, no prisoners, no mercy - if we can snare someone to ask about this mess without endangering the hostages, then we'll do it."

Nick gripped Jean's arm. "Follow orders, Marine! Ask Gus. We did this before when I executed those guys who wanted to kill you and your mom."

"Yeah... but you were young then."

"Why you…" Johnny blocked Nick from going after his very amused daughter. "See what you need to contend with when your kids get older. Disrespect is right around the bend, brother, waiting to pork you when you least expect it."

Nick's retort stopped Johnny in his tracks, enjoying the moment, knowing Nick was probably right. Johnny grabbed Nick's shoulders with a smile. "Are you ready for this? I have heard the story many times of you acing those billionaires trying to kill Rachel and Jean. You are a little longer in the tooth than back then. That is a mile kick in midnight black waters."

Nick shrugged. "I have a light at the end of the tunnel. I'll go now while the ship's beaming light and making noise. Hell, if it wasn't for needing to stay underwater during the final approach, I wouldn't even need the expensive stuff I have for pinpointing their location."

Nick clutched Johnny's hand. "Don't worry about me. Worry about the bastards that have Katie. I brought the Marines because they need seasoning on an op like this. I will slit every throat between me and Katie. I will kill everything on that boat within reach after I have the girls in a safe place. My weak spot is on deck. You and Gus will watch that as always. Weapons free if Muerto attracts attention."

"Understood, brother. I have watched you do amazing things over the years. I pray you can do one more for Katie."

The Terminator flitted into position across Nick's countenance, the dead eyed gaze of deathly promise Johnny recognized immediately. "If Katie is fine when I board, Katie will be fine when I leave that boat. As we both know, innocents may die during this op, brother. We have only one dog in this hunt."

Johnny nodded. "You know there's something beyond this we will need to take care of."

"The Procurer of this travesty will die at our hands if I can keep anything alive while this rescue goes on, or if the prick is on board, we'll confirm identities. After seeing this yacht, even from afar, I can imagine a rich asshole setting himself into a position to entertain other deviants. I need to find a likely suspect aboard and I'm thinking I will find him in the master stateroom. Gus knows. You know. I live for this. Like Cruella Deville always says, 'it is what it is'. I want Katie safe and I want to do an intestinal cleaning of the one who put her on that boat."

"After this op, there will be many days with the Irish at Otter's Point, my friend."

"Absolutely."

Nick eased into the water, found the correct buoyancy for his submersible to stay at a few feet underwater. He then opened the snorkel side of his enclosed mask, making sure the air passages cleared. While paddling with smooth strokes toward the target, Nick watched his GPS coordinates inside the mask with pinpoint readout. Once certain his gear worked correctly, he checked communications.

"Muerto on the move. Check in, control and network."

"Loud and clear," Gus said. "We have clear sighting on all decks of the ship, including jacuzzi. Partying without letup. Girls are made up of regulars and ones unused to what they are doing. I count five girls and twelve males. Seven of the males are dressed in crew type outfits."

Nick tensed, reading between the lines. "You see Katie! That is a good thing, brother."

"Understood," Gus said with willpower. "Marauders?"

"Viper, Kong, and Cracker on line," Jean stated tersely. "Sorry about before, Dad... mission enabled."

"Stay tight and honed-in on every word. Forget about anything else besides Katie," Nick replied tersely. "I will tell you when to approach at slow silent speed. Circle until then. Check armor, gear, and every detail while sighting in on the yacht. When the order is given, assault the boat in Marine fashion. Do not pay attention to anything else other than good people alive and bad guys all dead."

"Understood," Jean acknowledged.

Nick arrived in view of the boat, only fifty yards away. He floated with range finders in hand, examining every person visible and every deck with those persons partying. "In range. Close recon. I see Katie."

The silence on the network painted the picture better than anything from the assault force.

"We wait!" Nick established buoyancy and circled the yacht. "They party on all three decks. We have their sleeping schematics. Gus and Johnny will update us as needed. Relax, check gear, and picture oblivion for this travesty. We'd be waiting blindly with no information in other circumstances. This isn't one of them. Do not hesitate!"

"Understood!" That came from Sonny, Jean, and Quinn.

The lights stayed, but the partying retreated into the cabins. Johnny called out excitedly, "we have views. I locked onto their couple forms. Sending my info to your helmets. This boat even has an under craft launching platform."

"Damn... that's good stuff, Kabong." Nick drifted slowly around after tying off his pontoon at the fantail mooring and diver ramp. "Gee... this is really nice. They have dual stairways for accessing the deck. I'll be low enough to strip out of my gear, even if someone does walk around unexpectedly on deck. Lucas would kill me if he saw this boat and knew what we planned to do to it. This yacht must be in the fifteen-million-dollar range, even used.

He marked staff positioning at each moment. Nick liked the security aspect. The security people tagged with enforcing the boat's rules drifted amongst the dancing and partying couples with disdain while throwing down any drink coming their way. He could tell they had measured the guests, found them wanting, and decided they could party along with them. All they thought needed was a professional attitude to business. Then he felt the bump.

Submerging, Nick saw the huge shadow of a shark against the light cast by the ship's entertainment lights. The big bad of the undersea creatures had found him. In all his years diving, on mission and off, he had never been confronted by a shark of any kind. They had moved around him, far on the outskirts. None had ever decided he was a happy meal. Nick pulled his razor-sharp knife from the sheath at his ankle. He waited for the second hoped for bump, praying he did not miss his adversary's stalking before the first visit. Watching the blackness approach, blotting out other light, tensed every nerve and muscle in Nick's body.

Instead of revving into attack mode with jaws ready to tear its prey apart, the ultimate eating machine in the universe bumped by Nick. He latched onto the fin, plunging his ten-inch blade repeatedly into the shark's head without letup until it lost movement and life. Nick drifted free, watching the killer sink with other creatures' shadows hitting it from all directions. Nick moved position to the other side of the ship, brushing any shark residue from his knife and person. The psychopath called out from the depths of his being in triumphant celebration. Nick took a deep breath as he surfaced. *Calm down, Betty, you ain't shit. We got lucky.*

"What happened, Dad? We heard you sucking wind," Jean commented.

"I had to kill Jaws."

"Damn… you better have had your cam on."

"Gus and Johnny are on point to watch my back. They don't have time to play with video cam recordings. Mission talk only from now on."

"Rah!"

Nick drifted, trying for line of sight with each part of the boat visible. "I'm not seeing anything, Payaso. How's your view?"

"Good from our position. There's a guy in the pilot house, but he's the only one I see. The Marines are circling now at a distance. They may have a better view."

"We see the guy in the pilot house," Quinn said. "We've circled once with good view of the outer decks. No guards are walking the decks."

"Let me know when you've completed three circles," Nick replied.

"Will do."

Nick drifted to the rear entry platform on the fantail. He lifted his equipment pontoon onto the deck with silent expertise. He began stripping off his gear, placing it next to his pontoon, carefully letting the water drip off before placing all outer gear on deck. It took time to get out of the dry-suit in the water, but he wanted no splash noises around the now silent ship. Wrapping his weight belt around the dry-suit, Nick buckled it in place and let the bundle sink. He climbed aboard in his bathing suit.

"Hold, Dad," Jean warned. "There's a guy leading a woman from the main deck staterooms to the jacuzzi on the second deck. He has refreshments, so he'll be there a while. The girl is very young, but not Katie."

"Understood. Watch him while I get ready."

"Holding position."

Nick opened the pontoon, donning the black drawstring bottoms and pullover top. After putting on black socks and deck shoes, he fastened the shark killing knife to his ankle. Nick slipped into a tightfitting harness holding his Colt .45 caliber handgun with silencer. He then strapped a treasured personal weapon, an old MP5, around on his back. He placed the small packet of syringes in a pouch next to his .45 and MP5 magazines.

"We can hear the sound of music and jacuzzi gushing noises even from our position. I don't think you'll need to be super silent, Dad," Jean said.

Nick heard the ocean waves lapping against the boat. He picked out the whirlpool sounds of the jacuzzi. The music did not carry to him over the jacuzzi workings. "On the move."

He climbed the steps, noting his deck shoes made no noise. Nick remained crouched at the top of the stairs leading to the main deck, watching the entrance to the staterooms. Seeing no movement either between rooms or toward the deck, Nick hurried to the steps taking him to the jacuzzi deck.

"They're warming up to do the wild thing," Sonny stated. "We see you. Climb the inner staircase. Their backs will be toward you. Stick them both, Nick. We don't know if the girl is there willingly or not."

"Thanks, Chief." Nick climbed to the jacuzzi level and used the syringes on the couple. They had only enough time to bat at the slight sting before passing out.

Nick picked the girl up and laid her down on the deck. He dragged the man out as quietly as possible after turning the music up slightly. He retrieved his phone from its pocket on his weapon harness. Nick took pictures of the man and woman, after which he did their digital fingerprints. They were sent automatically to Johnny.

"Got them. Working IDs now. The hatch from the jacuzzi deck goes straight into the pilot house."

Nick turned and opened the hatch leading inside the elaborate pilot house. The crewmember turned. Nick shot him in the head. "I'm leaving everyone up on this level alone. I'll make the master stateroom my headquarters for gathering girls. Hopefully, I'll find Katie first. Moving on the staterooms now. The crew's quarters are down below. It's time to take and protect the main deck, Marines. Be ready to move on the staterooms in assault form if my quiet approach gets noisy."

"Rah!"

"I'm still picking up great heat signatures," Johnny said. "Very little movement inside."

"Thanks, Johnny."

Nick moved down to the stateroom entry hatch. Although quiet, the silencer still produced a muffled sound. If he could avoid using it, Nick planned to make no sound with his kills. He opened the first stateroom door with miniscule movement of the handle to the unlocked position, easing it open far enough to slip inside the opulent quarters. Seeing the two figures lying in passed out sleeping positions, Nick moved to the bed, identified the girl as not being Katie, and used a syringe on her. He climbed on the man's chest, knee into his solar plexus. Clamping off the mouth, Nick drove the dive knife to the hilt up through the chin into the man's brain. Death shuddered in vibrating waves under him. Nick waited patiently until all movement ceased before jerking his blade free.

The stateroom across the way proved to be a slight dilemma as the door was locked. He left it and moved to the next stateroom. The door opened easily and noiselessly. Nick moved to the bed, finding Katie in a drugged state, unmoving but breathing normally. Nick went around and used the syringe on the man. He would need to pay for his sins against a brother closer than blood. Another locked door greeted him across the way. Knowing where Katie was, Nick put his shoulder against it and broke the door free. Inside he shot the rising man through the head. The girl barely moved except to groan.

Outside the remaining locked room, Nick glanced at the main deck beyond, seeing his Marines watching him with weapons at the ready. "Go do the crew. I have Katie safe. No survivors."

"Rah!"

Nick broke through the last stateroom door. The couple did not move. He shot the man in the head while he lay snoring. Nick recognized the young woman as Katie's friend. He picked her up in his arms and walked her to the master stateroom's bed. He repeated his transport with each of the girls as combat sounded below deck. After retrieving the girl from the jacuzzi area and the one he had used a syringe on first, Nick attempted to waken Katie with a wet cloth. He could only get her coherent for a moment.

"I...I know you," Katie stammered out. "My... Uncle Gus... is your friend."

"He is my brother. He can hear your voice right now, honey." Nick lifted her in his arms with the sheet around her body. "You will be with him soon."

Katie hugged Nick. "Thank you."

"Believe me, honey, finding you alive is the greatest thing I can think of at the moment, except for hearing from three Marines who shoot their mouths off when they shouldn't, and then clam up without a sound when they should."

"Holy crap… we were giving you a moment," Jean barked in his ear. "Crew dead. Quinn got nicked over his ear, proving your cement head was passed down intact."

"Gee… thanks, Sis."

"On our way to you, Sir," Sonny added.

"Move in, Gus," Nick said. "Park the Lady anywhere you want."

"Steaming to you as we speak, brother."

Minutes later, Jean helped Katie groggily get dressed in the master stateroom. Nick bandaged Quinn's head while Sonny transported the rescued girls to the fantail where Johnny transferred them aboard the Lady. Jean accompanied Katie, holding on to her tightly, easing her down the stairs to Sonny. He helped her cross to where Gus waited for his niece. She cried out his name before breaking down into tears as he held her.

"Shush, baby… it's all okay now. You'll be speaking with your folks in minutes. My brother Johnny and the Marines will take you to a quiet place on my boat to talk with your parents in real time."

"Aren't you coming, Uncle Gus?"

"Soon, baby. Your Uncle Gus needs to assist his brother Nick in a few final duties before we can leave. Go with Jean."

"C'mon, Katie," Jean said, putting an arm around her. "We have you all set inside our wheel house."

Johnny patted Gus's arm. "I will drive the Lady away from the screams, brother. We will return when you and Muerto are finished."

"We may be a while, Johnny."

Johnny shrugged. "Such is life… and justice."

* * *

Only hours later, after first collecting all money, electronics, and answers, did Nick settle Avril Stuart into his last painful journey into eternity. The man who defiled Katie, passed during the period, in a manner only to be surpassed by Dante's classic image of hell. The two old friends worked in icy concentration, finally satisfied the billionaire owner of the yacht, Avril II, had been the one taking and holding young women in bondage. He left no trail because he had them killed when they no longer interested him.

"I believe we have enough money added to our accounts to give Katie an entire wing at the college to continue research," Nick said. "Nothing but time and dedication will erase this, brother. Katie will make it happen. I hate to mention this, but we need to decide about the boat. We know enough people to make the Avril II part of our fleet, or ship her to Monster Island."

Gus gripped the railing where he and Nick talked. "Let's blow it to pieces. You and I can get her running away from any chance finding by ships or planes. Johnny will follow us out in the Lady. We can let the kids have some fun. It may be a slight healing process."

"Your will, my hand, brother. It sounds good to me. I'll go see about the engines. They fired off more than a few shots down below."

Gus gripped Nick's arm before he could walk away. "Screw it. Let's sink her with all the bodies locked in where they are. We need to get Katie back to the states. I think we rode the vengeance trail far enough."

Nick smiled. "I can do that."

Everyone aboard the Lucky Lady watched the final bubbling disappearance of Avril II beneath the waves, as the sun dawned over the scene in hues of yellow and orange majesty.

"We want to see the video of you killing Jaws," Jean said. "How big was he?"

Nick shrugged. "It was dark and I forgot my tape measure."

Johnny began playing with his tablet the moment Jean mentioned the shark interlude. After a few moments, he gulped while taking a deep breath and muttering. He reversed the video to the beginning of the confrontation as the shark approached, clearly visible with the low light, high definition cam. Johnny held the tablet for his friends to see. The enormous head brushed against Nick. The shaky mounting and clutch of the fin followed. They watched the closeup of Nick's knife pounding down, slowed by water resistance, plunging into the shark's head without pause until the wild thrashing Nick had not noticed while killing it, ceased. The shark fell away into the depths, its huge body streaming a blood trail.

"Holy shit!" Jean took the tablet and replayed the scene. "What would you have done if it came at you, mouth full of teeth, chomping like Pac-man on steroids?"

"Said hi to Deke for you."

* * *

The identities and disappearances of the five men of prominence caused a ripple throughout the world. As the Unholy Trio reunited at Otter's Point nearly a week later with Reaper, Dark Dragon, and their entire crew with children, the white caps smashed against the rocks in spectacular form. Although quite chilly that early morning, no one minded as Sammy the werewolf chased gulls and kids around the beach. The adults celebrated in quiet satisfaction with Irish coffees and snacks.

"In one mission, you pirates got rid of two potential governor rivals, and one future Presidential competitor," Rachel remarked. "Not to mention a billionaire backer of all things deviant and liberal. We've been waiting to hear how Katie's doing, Gus."

"She's fine. My brother, Phil, and sister-in-law Julie, have been hounding the shit out of me trying to learn what happened.

Katie refuses to discuss it with them. The money we gave the four women survivors hushed them for eternity. It's a process."

"Muerto has returned with an easy aura about him I find quite appealing," Rachel replied. "I believe his more violent tendencies are at an end."

Nick grinned. "Doin' right ain't got no end."

The End… for now.

Thank you for purchasing and reading **Cold Blooded VIII: Rule of Nightmare**. If you enjoyed the novel, please take a moment and leave a review. Your consideration would be much appreciated. Please visit my Amazon Author's Page if you would like to preview any of my other novels. Thanks again for your support.

Bernard Lee DeLeo

Author's Face Book Page -
https://www.facebook.com/groups/BernardLeeDeLeo/

BERNARD LEE DELEO - AUTHOR'S PAGE -
http://www.amazon.com/Bernard-Lee-DeLeo/e/B005UNXZ04/ref=ntt_athr_dp_pel_pop_1

AMAZON AUTHOR'S PAGE (UK) -
http://www.amazon.co.uk/-/e/B005UNXZ04

Made in the USA
Middletown, DE
27 September 2017